Shakespeare's Second Historical Tetralogy
Some Christian Features

LOCUST HILL LITERARY STUDIES
No. 35

Shakespeare's Second Historical Tetralogy

Some Christian Features

Edited by
Beatrice Batson

LOCUST HILL PRESS
West Cornwall, CT

© 2004 Beatrice Batson
All rights reserved

Library of Congress Cataloging-in-Publication Data

Shakespeare's second historical tetralogy : some Christian features /
edited by Beatrice Batson.
     p.   cm. -- (Locust Hill literary studies ; no. 35)
     Includes bibliographical references and index.
     ISBN 0-9722289-4-2 (lib. bdg. : alk. paper)
     1. Shakespeare, William, 1564-1616--Histories. 2. Richard II,
King of England, 1367-1400--In literature. 3. Henry IV, King of
England, 1367-1413--In literature. 4. Henry V, King of England,
1387-1422--In literature. 5. Great Britain--History--1066-1687--
Historiography. 6. Historical drama, English--History and
criticism. 7. Christian drama, English--History and criticism.
8. Shakespeare, William, 1564-1616--Religion. 9. Christianity and
literature--Great Britain. 10. Literature and history--Great Britain.
11. Kings and rulers in literature. 12. Middle Ages in literature.
13. Religion in literature. I. Batson, E. Beatrice. II. Series.

PR2982.S497 2004
822.3'3--dc22

2003066045

Printed on acid-free, 250-year-life paper
Manufactured in the United States of America

Acknowledgments

The staff of the Shakespeare Special Collection of Wheaton College expresses sincere thanks to all who gave us their papers for publication in this volume. As Editor of the essays, I wish to express personal thanks to David Malone, Head of Special Collections, for his constant encouragement, to Keith Call, for his invaluable help as editorial assistant, and to other members of the staff who helped in any way to bring this volume to its present status. Special thanks to Tom Bechtle of Locust Hill Press for his splendid guidance and extraordinary understanding throughout each stage of shaping the various essays in this book.

Contents

Beatrice Batson • Introduction • *ix*

Contributors • *xxvii*

Clifford Davidson • The Coventry Mysteries and Shakespeare's
Histories • *3*

David George • Sons Without Fathers: Shakespeare's Second
Tetralogy • *27*

John Rumrich • Dear Expedience: The Imagery of Shakespeare's
Henry IV Tetralogy • *57*

Joseph Candido • The Chronicles of Emptiness: Loss, Disappointment, and Failure in Shakespeare's Second
Tetralogy • *83*

Charles R. Forker • Spilling Royal Blood: Denial, Guilt and
Expiation in Shakespeare's Second Historical Tetralogy • *107*

John W. Velz • England as Eden in *Richard II*: The Implications
for the Second Tetralogy • *129*

Paul White • Shakespeare and Religious Polemic: Revisiting
1 Henry IV and the Oldcastle Controversy • *147*

Ellen Summers • "Judge, My Masters": Playing Hal's
Audience • *165*

Index • *179*

Introduction

Beatrice Batson

Study of the Christian dimension of Shakespeare's dramas seems to command the interest of numerous outstanding scholars. In the minds of some critics, this is a phenomenon that was completely in disfavor as recently as a decade ago. I am persuaded, however, that perceiving a Christian dimension in the dramatist's writings or practicing a Christian approach to his works is by no means new, albeit even a glance at the published works of the last few years definitely indicates a renewed interest in the subject. At the same time, there is a long and reputable history of ways in which the Christian tradition intersects the language of Shakespeare. Careful study reveals the accuracy of this fact even though A.C. Bradley, a scholar probably known to every reader of Shakespeare, stated that Shakespeare wrote his dramas "without regard to anyone's beliefs."

It must be remembered that the era in which Shakespeare wrote his plays embodied a pervasive belief in a personal God who created and sustained his creation. Therefore, to the Elizabethan mind, this created world was unquestionably the instrument of God, and the entire creation bore the stamp of God upon it. Each human being was also of significance because all men and women were created in the image of God, and all could know the Creator's guidance in their individual lives. Shakespeare reveals in numerous dramas that the Scriptures provide insight into and an understanding of good and evil in a fallen world. As a result, no human being was without that essential guidance. What is clear, then, is that God the Creator not only gave significance to the world but also provided direction for a moral and spiritual life.

By the eighteenth century, readers and critics began to point to Christian insights in Shakespearean drama, but scattered references did not remain the pattern for the Christian scholar. In the *x*   *Introduction*

nineteenth century, for example, with the English translation of Hermann Ulrici's *Shakespeare's Dramatic Art* (1846), which emphasized a Christian reading of a number of plays, other scholars began to focus on the Christian dimension of the dramatic writings. Among thinkers of renown were Charles Wordsworth's *Shakespeare's Knowledge and Use of the Bible*, and toward the end of the century there appeared Henry S. Bowden's *The Religion of Shakespeare* (1899). Wordsworth studied biblical allusions and religious concepts, grounded in the Bible. What Bowden basically did was to reveal evidence in Shakespeare's works of his sympathetic attitude toward the "old faith," or the Catholic faith—a subject commanding the attention of present-day scholars. Both writers offered compelling reasons for studying the Christian dimension of Shakespeare.

By the twentieth century, a larger body of scholarly thinking on Christian features of Shakespeare's writings began to appear. In America, author William Burgess published *The Bible in Shakespeare* in which he held that Shakespeare the dramatist believed the orthodox views of the Christian religion that were current in his day. To come to this conclusion, Burgess perceived Shakespeare's language to be literally saturated with a Christian dimension through a careful study of parallel passages in Scripture, allusions, and paraphrase.

Later, in the 1930s, scholars appropriated additional and varied critical approaches. Lily B. Campbell's *Shakespeare's Tragic Heroes* (1930), with its focus on the study of characters as well as the history of ideas, was an influential and scholarly work. To this day, her book is highly regarded by teachers and scholars. In his *Allegory and Mysticism* (1931), Sir Israel Gollancz considered *The Merchant of Venice* to be a Christian allegory, but in this decade there was special emphasis not on allegory but on the symbolism of Shakespeare's language. It was undoubtedly G. Wilson Knight, author of several books including *The Wheel of Fire*, who became the leader of this approach. Of particular interest to Knight was what he thought to be similarities between Shakespeare's dramas and the parables of Jesus.

During the 1930s and into the 1940s, scholars frequently looked to the medieval period, especially to the Prayer Book and the stories of the era. *The Medieval Heritage of Elizabethan Tragedy* by Willard Farnham made an excellent contribution. Richard Noble's *Shakespeare's Biblical Knowledge and the Use of the Book of Common Prayer* (1935) demonstrated clear understanding of Shakespeare's

Beatrice Batson xi

Christian dimension. What Noble emphasized was a strong belief that Shakespeare more than any other playwright of his era assimilated the language of the Prayer Book and the Geneva Bible.

During the 1940s, interest continued in a Christian approach to Shakespeare's drama. Some mention should be made of E.M.W. Tillyard's *Elizabethan World Picture* (1943) and *Shakespeare's History Plays* (1944), but his focus was primarily on Providential order in history. S.R. Bethell also published in the 1940s but, unlike Tillyard, showed little obvious interest in the historical approach. Following somewhat in the tradition of G. Wilson Knight, he published in 1947 *The Winter's Tale: A Study.* To ferret out the symbolic meanings embodied in the plays was of primary importance to Bethell. It would be unwise to neglect to mention two other books by Bethell: *Shakespeare and the Popular Dramatic Tradition* (1944) and *Literary Criticism and the English Tradition* (1948). All of his writings demonstrated interest in the relation between Christianity and Shakespeare's dramas. In 1946, John Henry de Groot contributed a work that revived interest in Shakespeare and his Catholic connections. That work, *The Shakespeares and the 'Old Faith,'* did not limit study to the probability of Shakespeare's Catholic faith, but posited the belief that training in his home that exposed him to iconography as well as to the teachings of the Catholic faith should be considered by scholars.

In the 1950s there were two influential books that argued that the dramatist considered religion to be extremely significant, especially the Catholic faith. H. Mutschmann and K. Wentersdorf published *Shakespeare and Catholicism* (1952), in which they concluded that the Catholic faith not only influenced him as an artist, but in religion. In fact, they held that he was a Catholic throughout life. Perhaps few critics were more impressed with the position of Mutschmann and Wentersdorf than M.D.H. Parker. In her book, *The Slave of Life* (1955), a summary of their viewpoint filled an entire section. Her work also included additional sections on the influence of two Christian giants, Augustine and Aquinas, on Shakespeare.

By the 1960s, several additional writers, using various approaches, began to make an impact on teachers and scholars. With the tools of typology and analogy, for example, J.A. Bryant in *Hippolyta's View: Some Christian Aspects of Shakespeare's Plays* (1961) sought to interpret the dramas as Christian poetry. To a large extent, R.G. Hunter's *Comedy of Forgiveness* (1965) also appropriated typology. In 1969, the Christian scholar Roy Battenhouse, who had

xii Introduction

published widely for many years, published his influential book, *Shakespearean Tragedy, Its Art and Its Christian Premises*. He cogently argued that Scriptural premises undergirded the dramatist's writings and that there was a theory of tragedy implicit in the language and structure of the tragedies. In his thinking, the intellectual basis of the art of the tragedies was Aristotle; Augustine's and Aquinas' Christian concepts gave depth to the Aristotelian principles. The dramatic embodiment of Aristotelian principles combined with the Christian thinking of Augustine and Aquinas resulted in tragic drama called "Christian Tragedy."

In 1973, Peter Milward, a prolific author and Catholic scholar, published *Shakespeare's Religious Background*. In his usual objective and fair manner, Milward studied the dramas in relation to the prevailing religious currents of the Elizabethan era. After careful thought and study, he discovered traces of the Catholic faith, features of Protestant reform, instances of Puritanism and spreading religious indifference. His conclusion was clear and direct: a study of the dramas as a whole will result in an understanding of Shakespeare's moral and theological position. This is only one of Milward's more than 300 books, with the majority on some phase of Shakespeare's Christian dimension.

The decade of the 1980s was not without outstanding scholarship on Shakespeare and the Christian tradition, but mention will be made of Chris Hassel's *Faith and Folly* (1980). This work focuses on six romantic comedies; his primary concern is on the influences of liturgical, Pauline and Erasmian paradoxes on Shakespeare's comic vision and form. Hassel's work is by no means limited to this book; he has published numerous essays and books—all on the Christian dimension.

In 1994, approximately one year before his death, Roy Battenhouse published an excellent book entitled *Shakespeare's Christian Dimension, an Anthology of Commentary*. In addition to 92 abridgments of commentary on 26 plays, the work contains a supplementary bibliography of more than 250 items, all on the Christian dimension, with each item intended as a significant guide to deeper exploration of his selected subject. To paraphrase his purpose as he discusses it in his book, he states briefly: (a) to provide samplings of the tremendous impact of Shakespeare's Christian heritage on the shaping of dramas, (b) to offer teachers and students the option of alternatives to the various modern critical approaches, (c) to offer a foundation for critical debate. This book has been widely read by those who choose not to write or teach from a

Beatrice Batson xiii

Christian perspective but certainly by hundreds who appreciate what the study of the Christian dimension of Shakespeare's works entails.

The subject of religion and its impact on Shakespeare's writings still commands the interest of outstanding scholars. It is doubtful that any era has claimed the attention of so many excellent scholars as the present time. One has only to observe the enormous volumes by Naseeb Shaheen, especially on the numerous references to the Bible in the various genres. But the naming of scholars could be very extensive: one thinks of Michael Alexander, David Beauregard, John Cox, David Daniell, Clifford Davidson, Huston Diehl, Michael Edwards, Charles Forker, Donna Hamilton, Chris Hassel, Maurice Hunt, Judith Lopez, Kristen Poole, Grace Tiffany, John Velz, Robert Watson, Paul White, and scores of additional reputable scholars who unabashedly declare their interest in religion and Shakespeare.

The focus of this volume is on Shakespeare's Second Historical Tetralogy and the Christian tradition. The eight essays included were delivered in preliminary form as lectures at the Shakespeare Institute held at Wheaton College in 2001. The institutes are primarily held for teachers of Shakespeare at the undergraduate level, and these teachers, not always research scholars, constitute the largest segment of the audience. Almost all of the speakers, however, are well-known research scholars.

Writers of this volume share a similar critical outlook, but approaches differ. What is also apparent is that even though some essays concentrate on the same play or speeches or characters, their arguments and perceptions vary. Each essay depicts fresh ways of uncovering new findings in the tetralogy, and each makes a unique contribution to the first book devoted entirely to the Christian dimension of Shakespeare's Second Historical Tetralogy. I recognize that bits and pieces have been written on Christianity and the second tetralogy, but never has there been an entire volume devoted to the subject from a Christian perspective.

In the arrangement of the essays, Clifford Davidson's chapter, which establishes possible relationships with the Coventry Plays and with the tetralogy's medieval roots, appears first. Following Davidson's essay is David George's, which stretches across the entire tetralogy and provides considerable information on the historical background. John Rumrich's essay, with its emphasis on imagery, especially "walking" imagery, also includes all of the historical dramas of the tetralogy. Joseph Candido touches the entire *xiv*   *Introduction*

tetralogy with his countering of the many critics who give a Machiavellian "adder" to goad every intention in each play of the tetralogy. From a different perspective, Charles Forker and John Velz focus primarily on *Richard II*, while Paul White gives particular emphasis to Sir John Oldcastle. Ellen Summers' essay constitutes the final chapter, one that shows the significance of only a few words in a Shakespearean drama.

In his study, Clifford Davidson ponders possible connections between Shakespeare's second tetralogy and the civic plays that he probably saw (or could have seen) in the streets of Coventry, not impossibly, he says, at the location where Richard II broke off the contest between Bolingbroke and Mowbray. Recognizing that the view of the monarchy was "inconsistent" and "complex," Davidson treats quite extensively the subjects of kingship and history. In fact, the actors of the mystery plays were preoccupied with the same subjects and problems as resonated in the tetralogy. The writer cites the threat by Henry V to the people of Harfleur as very similar to statements of the first soldier in the Shearman and Taylors' pageant as a convincing connection with the Coventry tyrant.

For Davidson, it is impossible to interpret the tetralogy as an affirmation of the royalism promoted by the Crown. That Shakespeare's view of the English monarchy emerges as inconsistent and complex is no surprise to the author simply because he is a member of a "tradesman family with Roman Catholic connections in a Midland market town. Rather he wants to create a turbulent era as a backdrop to his own age." Although Shakespeare was not writing Mystery plays, features of his writing for the stage benefited from plays he probably saw at Coventry. Davidson reminds the reader, however, that only two extant Coventry plays were presented each year—the Shearmen and Taylors' pageant and the Weavers' plays. The former presented selected but important aspects of the Biblical story, and the latter were plays of the presentation in the temple and Jesus in the temple at the age of twelve, a limited knowledge, of course, of the story of history presented in the Coventry Corpus Christi cycle. With their limitations on the history of the world, the Coventry plays still grew from the context of the Creation and the Fall to the need for redemption and the Savior.

Davidson holds that the plays that Shakespeare probably saw while in school often included characters of power who often

Beatrice Batson xv

abused this power, and the lack of trust of those in authority who abused power emerges in the dramatist's plays, including the tetralogy, especially authority figures of the first three plays. What a reader immediately sees is that Davidson provides strong support for his position. By no means does he contend that Henry IV is immune from duplicity, but rather holds that by the end of *2 Henry IV*, Shakespeare "locates the new king on the side of law and justice." Yet the author of this cogently argued paper concludes with a straightforward note: casting the second tetralogy against the background of the Coventry plays that Shakespeare presumably saw in his youth surely indicates that Shakespeare "was not an absolutist."

Through an historical approach, Clifford Davidson uncovers new insights into the Elizabethan era, to the Coventry plays and their relationship to Shakespeare's second historical tetralogy. What is perhaps equally important is that he raises the probability of Shakespeare's Catholic faith, a subject commanding the attention of numerous Shakespearean scholars today.

In his historical and textual study, David George thoroughly scrutinizes his subject of "Sons Without Fathers" throughout the entire tetralogy. Before he moves from scene to scene in the four plays, George looks backward to the House of Plantagenet and Edward III to procure a deeper understanding of Richard II's fall. After examining the background and the play itself, George concludes that Richard II as king was either confused about or indifferent to the nature of fatherhood. Images of weak sons pervade the play, not only from history but from mythology such as the son, Phaeton, who was unable to drive his father's chariot across the sky. To George, the deposition of Richard is the point in the play when Richard must adopt Bolingbroke as his heir, the only "son" he has. It is true that Gaunt refers to England as "this teeming womb of royal Kings," but Richard is barren. Without question the play depicts some fathers and sons who succeed, but not Richard. George sees the success in "York allowing his duchess to save their son's life and Bolingbroke, having usurped the throne, finds his estranged son at last loyal," but he perceives *Richard II*, especially in its latter part, as the starting point at which Shakespeare "tentatively found his thread for the tetralogy: a King is part of a royal line, son and father of Kings."

xvi   *Introduction*

1 Henry IV clearly concentrates on fathers and sons. Oldcastle-Falstaff becomes the surrogate father of Hal, and Hal reveals himself as a loyal son to his father. That he became his men's "spiritual father" is depicted as Henry V the new King walks among his troops, advising them that they must seek their own salvation. By the play's end, George explains on the basis of his findings that as other fathers prove weak, the "cares of Hotspur, Mowbray, and Prince John end or fade away." The author also indicates that behind Hotspur stands a vacillating father who on the day of battle, and at a time when Hotspur badly needs him, fails to appear. Prince Hal has behind him a "ruthless and cunning" father, but the father of Bolingbroke, John of Gaunt, is a dependable father who George thinks was "elevated to a secular prophet." Near the end of his paper, David George concludes "... the grand sweep of these four plays presents us with a small gallery of sons whose fathers are absent or failing ... and with an heroic King who finds at the last he must be his own man, his own father, so to speak, and the father of his people."

Through an historical approach, George contends that Shakespeare altered history, added incidents that were not historical, and compounded history to make it more coherent and appealing to his audience. In addition, he holds that the dramatist also wanted to show the audience which human relationships were essential to balance and success in life and which ones did exactly the opposite.

An important part of George's methodology is his use of allusions, especially to the Bible. In these allusions, he uncovers abundant sources that lead to an understanding of the Christian dimension of the tetralogy.

Under the title "Dear Expedience: The Imagery of Shakespeare's Henry IV Tetralogy," John Rumrich turns from an historical approach to the study of imagery—walking imagery—in the tetralogy. One feature of this imagery, says Rumrich, is to demonstrate ways in which human beings cover ground but also to a significant degree how England moved from the kingdom of Richard II to that of Henry V.

The dramas build upon images of walking, or, as the author states, feet hitting the ground one at a time to arrive at one place and then another. To Rumrich, equestrian imagery is most appropriate in a play in which the plot turns on a contest for sovereignty

Beatrice Batson xvii

over a kingdom; it also had associations with continuity, as a means of "maintaining the possession of historical property and identity," and with changes in going across borders as well as with the changing and developing of character—see, for example, the growth of Prince Hal. Yet for Rumrich, the references to the earth as the "mother and grave" of soldiers and Richard's laments over the earth filled with wounds, calls for far more than "horseshoed hoofprints" to a reader's mind, particularly if one ponders the "bloody events after Shrewsbury and Agincourt."

To see and hear images and metaphors in the interpretation of a play would not have been at all unfamiliar to an Elizabethan audience. Those audiences would have been trained and nurtured, Rumrich contends, in poetic terms through "officially sanctioned and repeated interpretation of liturgical metaphors and accompanying festive rituals...." Scriptural references such as Ephesians 5:15–16 (undoubtedly relevant to Hal's soliloquy to redeem the time) and Colossians 4:5, equally relevant to the same soliloquy, would not have been lost on any group.

Crucial to understanding the entire tetralogy, however, is the way in which imagery expresses the dialectic of expedience that shapes and structures the dramatic action. To Rumrich, "dear expedience" (*1 Henry IV*.1.33) is usually glossed as meaning haste; for example, haste with which arrangements for the crusade to Jerusalem are to be made. In his view, the phrase signifies something of a "linguistic dwarf star" in which the form and images of the tetralogy are densely packed. This density, in his judgment, is partially due to the etymology of expedience. The word "expedire" primarily refers to extricating by the freeing of the feet as in Shakespearean usage, recalling the Latin word "expeditus," a fast-moving foot soldier. What is especially important is that Shakespeare depicts Henry IV as desiring to lead an expedition to the Holy Land to "free" himself from the guilt of the murder of a king.

One of the subtlest features of walking imagery in the essay is the dramatist's preoccupation with "boot" and "bootless"—words that become means of "defining history and unfolding character." Following the thinking of John Freccero in *Dante: The Politics of Conversion*, Rumrich also sees walking imagery as the incarnation of the act of choice and "feet" embodying its spiritual components of choice, pointing to the image of "Christ's feet walking over the Holy Land and then being nailed to the cross." He also sees this embodiment in the King's lengthy opening speech in *2 Henry IV*.4.

xviii   *Introduction*

The depicting of Falstaff as expedience, or expedience as inventing a way out of a situation, is most excellent and persuasive. What is also clear is that Rumrich holds that all who are sacrificed en route to the glorious moment of Hal's becoming Henry V are summed up in the rejection of Falstaff.

John Rumrich sees Prince Hal, the "nimble-footed madcap Prince of Wales" as an excellent, heroic king. Completely aware of critics who disagree, he builds a compelling case for Hal's valor and has no doubt that the drama unfolds "a measured approval of Hal's achievements."

In his essay "The Chronicles of Emptiness: Loss, Disappointment and Failure in Shakespeare's Second Tetralogy," Joseph Candido clearly states his own purpose on the first page, "... in wake of the recent spate of 'ironic' or 'deflationary' readings of the tetralogy, where every good intention has a machiavellian or materialist adder lying beneath it, we may wish to remind ourselves that Shakespeare's sense of history is just as powerfully informed by the pattern of Fall and Redemption depicted in the Medieval cycle plays." Candido further notes that the comic structure of the late medieval moralities, the Providential readings of history, the moral and religious teachings of the Homilies and the Christian concepts of forgiveness and reconciliation also inform the tetralogy.

To launch his purpose, Candido uses a challenging approach to the topic he expresses. Beginning his cogently argued study with references to James Black's essay "Henry IV's Pilgrimage" (*Shakespeare Quarterly*, 1983), Candido states that Black shows the references to travel by Henry throughout the tetralogy, and on the basis of his findings concludes that scholars are unable to discuss the references as exclusively Machiavellian. Harold Goddard, however, thinks of the journey as undertaken by a hypocritical man. Black sees the flaws of Henry but thinks of the death in Jerusalem Chamber as a "blessing conferred upon Henry," one Shakespeare would never have given to one completely Machiavellian.

What Candido contends is that Black's position, which sees Henry from a Christian perspective, is consistent with a view of one who undoubtedly frequently demonstrates a Machiavellian behavior, and he further contends that symbolically and substantially Henry finds rest from his travels through failure. It is true

Beatrice Batson xix

that he never reaches the distant Jerusalem, but he does discover what might be called a "spiritual" Jerusalem near him. To Candido, Henry's death need not be interpreted as "necessarily deflating" the spiritual paradigm of the death scene at which failure becomes success and loss gain is embedded in Christianity—a religion that embodies irony and paradox. To establish a perspective on failure and loss, he cites the deathbed sequence in *1 Henry IV* where Hal removes his father's crown and later returns it (5.1–224); the episode in *Henry V* in which the treason of Cambridge, Scroop and Grey is uncovered (2.12–181); and Hal's visit with his soldiers prior to Agincourt in *Henry V* (4.1.85–305).

Although he persuasively handles his thesis in the deathbed sequence in *2 Henry IV*, Candido admits that the episode of Cambridge Scroop and Grey is far more problematical than the other two episodes mentioned, due in part to "certain unspoken dynastic issues that lie beneath the characters' stated motives." After clearly examining the episode and admitting Henry's harsh treatment of the traitors, Candido, while showing the intricacies of the text as well as his own position, perceives the emergence of a redemptive and moral transformation. The author comes to the conclusion that in the statement of the three traitors, taken together as a "choice sequence on the virtue of repentance" is not unlike the homily of repentance contained in *The Second Book of Homilies*, a conclusion reached not through subjective opinion but through challenging argument. He knows that some critics will have strong aversions to his position, but he carefully shows that regardless of "jostlings for political survival that color its markings," the traitors episode is "a movement from earthly disappointment to religious assurance (on the part of the traitors, the King, and society at large) that resembles the similar pattern seen in Henry IV's 'failed' pilgrimage to Jerusalem and his mock 'deposition.'"

Continuing to engage in dialogue with other critics, Candido now addresses the night visit of Henry to his troops on the eve of Agincourt and finds this episode posits more serious problems than the one with the traitors. A sense of disappointment and aloneness all but overwhelms the King, due in part to his burdensome responsibility as well as his quarrel with his soldiers. Again, the writer charts his own position. He advises "Henry-haters" to consider this unusually "rare glimpse of Henry's conscience at this moment in the play," and urges a clear-eyed consideration of the speech on "ceremony," and the prayer in 4.1.289—a prayer which is not the prayer of a hypocrite. Although he admits that Henry's *xx*   *Introduction*

statement on the Agincourt victory being a demonstration of God's being on the side of the English is regarded by numerous critics as "jingoistic nonsense," he perceives another possibility. To see Henry's statement as "the perfectly logical response of a grateful penitent who may well have seen his improbable triumph as indicating God's clemency for his father's deposition of Richard as well as a divine ratification for his own kingship" is another possible way of heightening this awareness of the complexities of a Shakespearean text. The author does not ignore the complexities, nor as this chapter indicates, does he deem it wise for others to overlook them.

In an essay entitled "Spilling Royal Blood: Denial, Guilt and Expiation in Shakespeare's Second Tetralogy," Charles R. Forker primarily considers the drama *Richard II*, but his clear argument not only enriches a reader's understanding of *Richard II* but of the entire tetralogy or indeed of any Shakespearean drama embodying the rule of a monarchy. He shows early in his paper that "blood-spilling" and "king-killing" are prevalent in Shakespeare, but the two killings in *Richard II*—that of Thomas of Woodstock and Richard himself—represent special cases in that both murders are presented in such a way as to complicate the morality and politics of the tragedy. In addition, the ambiguities and uncertainties regarding Richard's murder resonate in the later plays of the tetralogy. Forker clearly states his focus: "a certain moral cloudiness surrounds these acts of violence ... and that the dramatist deliberately obfuscates the issues in the interest of dramatic and political complexity." He deals, for instance, at some length on Gloucester's death because it serves as an emblem of the moral and political issues that attend the murder of the king as well as illustrate the thematic technique in the later histories.

It is worth noting that after Bolingbroke's banishment and return, he never again mentions the murder of his uncle, and by the end of act 2, Shakespeare has dropped the subject of the murder as a major part of the play. Equally significant is that Richard gives several great speeches: the "hollow crown" speech, the murder episode, and the soliloquy at Pomfret Castle, all different attempts at self-assessment, but never once does Richard express the slightest hint of guilt for Gloucester's murder.

By the time he leaves his crown, Richard II has compared himself several times to Christ, implying that enemies of his rule are

Beatrice Batson   *xxi*

similar to Judas and Pilate delivering him to Golgotha, and although such comparisons are self-pitying, Forker says that we are asked to take them "in part as makers of the royal Christology on which the doctrine of divine right is founded." Believing that Shakespeare wants to suppress Gloucester's murder, Forker holds that the theme of guilt and denial persists through displacement. What the dramatist does, in the author's view, is to transfer the theme "from Richard who now functions as tragic victim, to his successor Henry IV who has just been redefined as the tragic perpetrator of a royal murder." With clear, subtle reasoning, the writer offers this position: "By accusing Mowbray, Richard's agent, of Gloucester's death and by arrogating to himself the task of avenging Abel's spilled blood, Bolingbroke identifies Richard by implicating him with Cain."

Ambiguities and "cloudiness" persist throughout the play. Forker draws the reader's attention to the killing of Richard at Pomfret Castle by Henry IV's "tacit permission" if not by his "explicit command"; the "symbolic roles are reversing. Henry IV repudiates Exton just as Richard had repudiated Mowbray," sending him to permanent exile, again ironically like the first murderer, Cain.

To scrutinize the murder of Richard is to find it, too, surrounded by ambiguity and uncertainty. Forker raises several troubling questions that refuse to yield clear answers: Did King Henry give a command to murder Richard? What part did he have in the murder? Forker knows that the play suggests that he disavows any direct part and exiles the one who actually committed the act. Whatever he said or meant to say, Henry begins his reign with a sense of guilt so burdensome that it calls for expiation. Plans for a pilgrimage to Jerusalem go away. Confession to his son concerning the "by-paths and indirect crook'd ways" through which he became king failed to alleviate his pain of guilt; and self-pitying rhetoric which identifies him with Richard gives no genuine relief.

It is appropriate to add that *Henry V* is not completely without a reminder of the guilty past. One of the clearest illustrations of this reminder is Henry's prayer prior to the battle of Agincourt. Undoubtedly, the epilogue at the close of *Henry V* reminds all readers that the burden of spilled blood, defeat and guilt has not yet run its full course.

Charles R. Forker's essay is clearly written, beautifully phrased, and scholarly documented. It offers a splendid historical argument and imaginative insights into the artistry of *Richard II.*

xxii   *Introduction*

In "Shakespeare and Religious Polemic: Revisiting *1 Henry IV* and the Oldcastle Controversy," Paul White immediately recognizes that the subject of religion is now commanding the attention of leading scholars, especially the interchange between religious culture and theater in modern England. Perhaps the New Historicism, suggests White, both "delayed and spawned" this critical interest. After briefly examining that possibility, he gives a clear statement of the direction of his paper: "connections among patronage, the London playing community and religion." What White accepts as his task is: "... how religion, politics, patronage, and theatrical entertainment all get entangled in the dispute over the Cobham family's most celebrated and controversial religious member, the fifteenth-century Lollard hero, Sir John Oldcastle." At what point Shakespeare changes the name Oldcastle to Falstaff is unclear, but White states that the revision appears in the first printed quarto of *1 Henry IV* in February 1598.

Whether Shakespeare and his company desired to parody the old Lollard martyr and, in turn, to insult the living Lord Cobham is the next question for White, and even more important is the way in which the portrayal of the Cobham family becomes entangled with religion. With clarity, White follows the knotty questions, unravels complexities and draws careful, documented responses.

In White's judgment, the Oldcastle controversy illustrates changes in theatrical patronage from the middle years of the sixteenth century. One of the major changes is that the Lord Chamberlain company, with Shakespeare as leader, managed possibly to "resist" or subvert any views of court patrons. On the other hand, Shakespeare's plays, especially history plays, were perhaps more vulnerable to topical controversy. For example, did Shakespeare and his company intend to satirize the Elizabethan Cobhams?

Paul White has written a well-documented essay that adds to our sense of the complexities of the Oldcastle controversy and why it has a religious connection. In treating his subject, he has raised important issues as he studies the primary text and as he engages in dialogue with other scholars.

John W. Velz begins his essay, "England as Eden in *Richard II*: The Implication for the Second Tetralogy," by quoting extensively from John of Gaunt's deathbed speech in the belief that it is crucial to an understanding of *Richard II* as well as to the tetralogy.

Beatrice Batson

Readers may think, in Velz's judgment, the speech to be only hyperbolic praise of England, but soon the garden imagery in subsequent parts of the play reinforces the fertility imagery. The latter, says Velz, is a moral alteration to the dying as well as to the barren and infertile. He finds support for his thinking in reference to the "bay tree all withered" (2.4.8.). Bushy, Bagot and Green are caterpillars of the commonwealth, with Bushy and Green in particular being the caterpillars who "feed on the foliage that is the nurture of the nation!" But Richard's responsibility is to care for the garden, and this he failed to do; moreover, just as Adam was banished from the Garden of Eden when he failed to perform his God-given responsibility, so also will Richard be deposed from the Eden of England because of his failure to care for his Eden.

Seeing the garden scene (3.4) as allegorical can be asked to "carry too much weight" in Velz's view, but it is a scene central to the play. In fact, he advises that this and another scene (4:1) need each other, the latter practically being a ratifying of the garden scene.

Readers should observe that Richard as England's failed garden is the basis for an interpretation of *Richard II* in which the "original sin of the play" is Richard's failure to accept his responsibility given him by God. On the other hand, the deposition of Richard is Bolingbroke's original sin, and it is from this view of original sin that the War of the Roses stem. Velz believes that such a view is supported by many allusions to crime and punishment throughout the subsequent plays of the tetralogy.

John W. Velz further contends that Richard ironically is both the sinner (Adam) and another's crime (Bolingbroke's original sin). To see Richard's sin as failed gardener is only one aspect of his sin; the author also discovers connections with the Cain and Abel story.

What is especially fascinating is to follow the view of the "plural sin" of two men in the play: Richard's possible murder of Woodstock and his exploitation of Gaunt's land; and Bolingbroke's challenging Richard's right to the throne through primogeniture and his responsibility for Richard's murder.

Velz raises the question of how original sin may be expiated and spends time on the question in various sections of the tetralogy. The subject of guilt receives some attention.

Not only does the author deal with the written text, but he also raises several questions on performance of the plays, especially *Richard II*. Whether writing on an interpretation or on perfor-

xxiv *Introduction*

mance, Velz obviously has his own sense of direction. At the same time, he is obviously unafraid to engage in substantive dialogue with other writers.

In "'Judge, My Masters': Playing Hal's Audience," Ellen Summers grapples with problems arising from Hal's statement to the audience in *1 Henry IV* (1.2.), "I'll so offend to make offense a skill, / Redeeming time when men think least I will." Recognizing that there is certainly more than one problem that might be addressed, she focuses on what she calls her desire "to link this moment of contact between an image of authority and an audience to a transformational process well underway in the 1590s in the relation between hearer and word, subject and authority, soul and conscience." She takes the position early that Shakespeare's histories participate in this transformational process.

In working through her subject, Summers carefully studies another part of the famous soliloquy: "I know you all." Who is the "you"? What audience is involved? Does it not include any or all of us who see the play? Are we the object of Hal's persuasion? Are we attending the theater for entertainment alone? Is Hal condemning the audience? Does he expect reformation from any audience? Questions such as these lead Summers to study the English controversy over the morality of attending plays. Homilies, Puritans, literary authors, and treatises all assist in helping sort out potential responses. If, then, we are part of the original audience, we, too, must heed the words which close the soliloquy. In Summers's words, "we in Hal's original audience become part of an operation to raise the perceived cultural value of theatergoing."

What the late sixteenth century did to improve the status of the theater is Summers' starting point, and her argument is persuasive. Might the possible resemblance of a play to a parable be worthy of consideration? In *1 Henry IV*, do we recognize ourselves? Yet the play presents us with a choice, and the audience is asked to judge. Summers completes her study with ways in which this particular play of the tetralogy enjoins the audience to attain salvation, both in the world to come and in this present one.

Ellen Summers has written a readable and provocative essay that raises numerous questions, but the reader-audience must "judge how readily the answers come."

Beatrice Batson xxv

The eight essays that follow indicate how the various critics work through the plays with their selected Christian approaches. Readers will undoubtedly observe that approaches include biblical allusions, iconography, allegory and emblems, plot construction, influence of thinkers, writers and practices of the Medieval and Reformation eras, imagery, and others. Each approach shows ways in which a reader may uncover Christian features. All approaches show that William Shakespeare is a consummate artist whose created poetic world of the Second Historical Tetralogy embody a Christian dimension.

Beatrice Batson, Editor
Coordinator of Shakespeare Institutes

Contributors

Beatrice Batson (editor), Professor Emerita of English at Wheaton College, holds the B.A., M.A. and Ph.D. degrees. She served as Chair of the Department of English for thirteen years and taught courses in Shakespeare for thirty-three years. Professor Batson is the author (or editor) of seven books and the author of numerous chapters in books edited by others. She has also written many articles for journals and magazines and scores of book reviews. During her teaching career, she was a frequent lecturer on college and university campuses in the United States and in Canada. At present, Professor Batson is the Coordinator of the Shakespeare Special Collection on Shakespeare and the Christian Tradition at Wheaton College, Illinois.

Joseph Candido is Professor of English at the University of Arkansas. He has published articles in *Shakespeare Quarterly, Shakespeare Studies, Philological Quarterly, Studies in Philology, SEL: Studies in English Literature, ELN, Anglia, English Studies, Religion and the Arts* and elsewhere, and has compiled two annotated bibliographies on Shakespeare's histories: *Henry V* in the Garland series (with Charles R. Forker), and *Richard II, Henry IV, I and II, & Henry V* for Pegasus Press. Most recently he has edited *Shakespeare: The Critical Tradition: "King John"* for the Athlone Press and published an article on "Teaching Texture in *The Alchemist*" in *Approaches to Teaching English Renaissance Drama* (MLA). He is currently editing the New Variorum *King John* with Charles R. Forker and Deborah T. Curren-Aquino.

Clifford Davidson is Professor of English and Medieval Studies Emeritus at Western Michigan University, where for more than thirty years he was an editor of *Comparative Drama* and director of the Early Drama, Art, and Music project in the Medieval Institute. As the recipient in 1985 of his university's prestigious Distin-

xxvii

xxviii Contributors

guished Scholar award, he has published widely on medieval drama and Renaissance literature as well as related topics. His next book, now in press, is *Deliver Us from Evil: Essays on Symbolic Engagement in Early Drama*, and he is presently collaborating on a new edition of *Everyman*.

Charles R. Forker, Professor of English Emeritus at Indiana University, Bloomington, has taught Shakespeare and Elizabethan drama at Indiana since 1959 and held teaching posts at the Universities of Wisconsin and Michigan, at Dartmouth College, and at Concordia University, Montreal. His work has appeared widely over the years in academic journals. *Skull beneath the Skin*, a major book on John Webster, appeared in 1986. Since then, he has published scholarly editions of Marlowe's *Edward II* (The Revels Plays, 1994) and of Shakespeare's *Richard II* (Arden series 3, 2003). An historical anthology of commentary on the latter play with an extensive analytical introduction came out in 1998 as a volume in the series entitled *Shakespeare: The Critical Tradition*.

David George is Professor of English at Urbana University, Ohio. He previously taught at Pomona College, Claremont, CA, the University of Minnesota and a mission school in Lesotho, Africa. David George is editor of *Shakespeare's First Playhouse* (1981), *Records of English Drama, Lancashire* (1991) and the Critical Heritage *Coriolanus*. His articles have appeared in *Shakespeare Quarterly* and *Shakespeare Survey*. He is co-editor of the New Variorium *Coriolanus* for MLA.

John Rumrich is Thaman Professor of English at the University of Texas at Austin and Editor (British Literature) of *Texas Studies in Literature and Language*. His books include *Matter of Glory: A New Preface to Paradise Lost* (Pittsburgh, 1987) and *Milton Unbound: Controversy and Reinterpretation* (Cambridge, 1996).

Ellen Summers is Professor of English at Hiram College. She served as co-editor of Robert Weimann's *Authority and Representation in Early Modern Discourse*, and her papers on Shakespeare and Shaw have appeared in such journals as *Studies in Bibliography* and *Deutsche Shakespeare Gesellschaft*. She is presently engaged in a study of doubling in productions of Shakespeare's plays.

Contributors

John W. Velz has published numerous articles on Shakespeare's inheritance from the medieval Christian dramatic tradition. In recent years in articles and public lectures he has examined the complex evidence for Shakespeare's personal religious commitments. He taught Shakespeare for nearly fifty years, thirty of them at the University of Texas.

Paul White is Director of Graduate Studies in the Department of English at Purdue University. He teaches courses in Medieval and Renaissance Drama and Culture. Cambridge University Press published his book *Theatre and Reformation: Protestantism, Patronage, and Playing in Tudor England,* Garland published a collection of critical essays entitled *Biblical Drama in Reformation England,* and AMS published a collection of critical essays called *Marlowe, History and Sexuality.* These three books were published in the 1990s. White has also published additional works, and other scholarly writing is in progress. He is also active in scholarly associations and frequently presents papers at national meetings.

Shakespeare's Second Historical Tetralogy
Some Christian Features

The Coventry Mysteries and Shakespeare's Histories

Clifford Davidson

The Coventry mystery plays, among the most famous in England, were at last suppressed after their final performance at Corpus Christi on 18 June 1579 when, as the Coventry annals explain, "the padgins were layd downe."[1] They had survived and perhaps even thrived in a city which, however reduced in population and importance after the economic crises of the early part of the century,[2] still regarded itself as the third city of the realm, only after London and Bristol. It saw itself as having a special relation with the Crown; as London depicted itself as the "king's chamber," so it declared itself to be the "prince's chamber"—terms which were intended to evoke the *sponsus-sponsa* imagery of the Song of Songs.[3] When Queen Margaret with her son Edward came to Coventry in 1457, she was welcomed "[t]o this conabull cite, the princes chaumbur" by a pageant at the city gates at which there was a Jesse tree and prophets praising Edward as one who had brought gladness to the realm "as mankynde was gladdid by the birght of Ihesus."[4] The nineteenth-century antiquarian Thomas Sharp pointed out in his 1825 monograph *Dissertation on the Pageants or Dramatic Mysteries Anciently Performed at Coventry* that as late as 1565 Sir John Throgmorton, the Recorder of Coventry, welcomed Queen Elizabeth I with the explanation that "this auncient Citie hath bine of longe tyme called the princes Chamber the iij^de Citie of youre Realme."[5] In its pageantry for Richard II's second entry into London which marked his reconciliation with the city in 1392, the city had affirmed its connection to the sacred when it envisioned itself as the image of the New Jerusalem descending from heaven.[6] Coventry in its presentation of religious plays at Corpus Christi nearly every year also would affirm its participation directly in sacred history even after its radical swing

4   *Clifford Davidson*

to Protestantism in the course of the sixteenth century and during a time when the feast of Corpus Christi had been officially suppressed.

Two facts are incontrovertible with regard to the topic at hand. One is that Coventry was only a short distance from Stratford-upon-Avon where Shakespeare spent his boyhood and that the larger city was still a commercial magnet for nearby villages and towns. For someone like the future playwright's father, the glover John Shakespeare, Coventry with its diverse guilds and crafts would have been a primary source for many of the things that he needed in his business and in his home. And especially useful would have been the wide availability of such things at the Corpus Christi fair held concurrently with the plays at Coventry each year. Indeed, the double attraction of fair and plays was reliably reported to have attracted people from all across England,[7] and the pageants even lured kings and queens to the city as spectators. Richard III and Henry VII saw the plays in 1485 and 1493 respectively, and the latter gave them "great commendacions."[8] Shakespeare, as a boy and youth destined to be an actor, playwright, and theater entrepreneur, would have had ample opportunity to see the plays on more than one occasion, for he was fifteen years of age at the time of their final performance.[9]

The second fact is that the Corpus Christi plays, presented on pageant wagons on stations in the streets of Coventry, began their progress toward the city center from Gosford Street, presumably with the first performance of each pageant there.[10] This location is identical to that chosen for the scene which provides the defining moment of Shakespeare's *Richard II*, for the city annals report that the combat arranged by the king between Bullingbroke and Mowbray was "to be fought at Coventre upon gosford green the 7th of September,"[11] a slip for the 17th, a Monday, and also misdating the event as occurring in 1397 instead of 1398. The day was the feast day of St. Lambert, which still appeared in the calendar in the 1562 *Book of Common Prayer*.[12]

The object of the present essay, then, will be to meditate on possible connections between the playwright Shakespeare's second tetralogy and the civic plays which we can expect that he saw in the streets of Coventry, not impossibly at the very location where King Richard II broke off the contest between Bullingbroke and Mowbray before banishing them from his kingdom. In this we must give special attention to Shakespeare's treatment of history and of kingship—matters which seem much more complicated

The Coventry Mysteries and Shakespeare's Histories   5

now than they did years ago when I was a graduate student contemplating a dissertation topic. It is currently impossible to interpret his plays as merely an affirmation of the royalism promoted by the Crown or a repetition of the Tudors' bending and shaping of history. To be sure, Shakespeare's view of the English monarchy emerges as inconsistent and complex, as we ought to expect from one who emerged from a tradesman family with Roman Catholic connections in a Midlands market town.[13] We must not expect him as a playwright to be a rigorous philosophical thinker, a political theorist, or, for that matter, a modern historian with a consistent view of the unfolding events of history. Instead, in his four plays on the reigns of Richard II, Henry IV, and Henry V he seems to have attempted as a dramatist to re-create and memorialize a period of turmoil which he undoubtedly saw as a backdrop to his own age. He was not writing mystery plays, but certain aspects of his writing for the professional stage benefit from close analysis in relation to the drama that he presumably saw when he was young in the streets of Coventry, where likewise the actors were concerned with some of the same problems and even in some cases the same characters that resonated in the work of the bard.[14]

In *A Midsummer Night's Dream* Shakespeare depicted a troupe of "rude mechanicals," tradesmen-actors, who seem verifiably to be caricatures of the men who performed in the Coventry Corpus Christi plays.[15] And in *Hamlet* he condemned acting and actors who overdo roles: "it out-Herods Herod" (3.2.13–14). Few would deny that the playwright had in mind the Herod of the Coventry Shearmen and Taylors' play who, according to the stage direction, "*ragis in þe pagond and in the strete also*" (729 s.d.). Even more convincing as a connection with the Coventry tyrant is the terrible threat by Henry V to the people of Harfleur:

> Your naked infants spitted upon pikes,
> Whiles the mad mothers with their howls confus'd
> Do break the clouds, as did the wives of Jewry
> At Herod's bloody-hunting slaughter-men.
> (*Henry V* 3.3.38–41)

"Who hard eyuer soche a cry / Of wemen thatt there chylder haue lost," remarks the first soldier in the Shearmen and Taylors' pageant (ll. 816–17).

Because the extant Coventry plays are only two in number—the Shearmen and Taylors' pageant of the Annunciation, Nativity, Magi, and Slaughter of the Innocents, and the Weavers' play of the

6   *Clifford Davidson*

Presentation in the Temple and Jesus in the Temple at Twelve Years of Age—the full treatment of history presented in this city's Corpus Christi cycle cannot be known. The dramatic records do indicate a complete set of New Testament plays but no evidence of the Creation, the Fall, and the other Old Testament plays such as those presented at Chester and York.[16] Prophets, however, are included as speaking characters in the extant Coventry plays, and the sweep of events from the Annunciation to the Ascension and the Assumption seems to have been maintained, though the latter, presented by the Mercers, would have been discontinued in Protestant times.[17] The Cappers' Harrowing of Hell and Resurrection play may have included a popular devil who served as the porter of hellgate at the entrance to the hellmouth specified in the guild's records.[18] Particularly unfortunate is the loss of the Smiths' Passion play, since from it Shakespeare could well have taken echoes for his presentation of Richard II during the course of his torment leading up to his murder. The cycle concluded with a Doomsday play presented by the Drapers, Coventry's most affluent guild—an extension of history to its final moments after skipping over everything between the biblical period until the appearance of some of the signs of the expected end as described in the influential *Golden Legend* of Jacobus de Voragine and other sources.[19] The records that are available for these lost plays may, however, be usefully compared to the texts available from the locales that had similar civic plays or with the plays in the N-Town and Towneley collections.

The extant Shearmen and Taylors' and Weavers' playtexts are probably the basis for the productions of these plays up to 1579 and represent the work of Robert Croo, a Capper, who in revising and writing out the plays in 1535 may have introduced something of a Protestant drift.[20] The fragments of an earlier text of the Weavers' pageant which Croo used (and on which he wiped his pen) inexplicably survived, but these do not tell us as much as we would like to know about his rewriting.[21] If one of his purposes was already at that early date to sanitize the plays to make them safe for Protestantism, the ultimate result was failure. Though in his highly partisan *Acts and Monuments* John Foxe described a weaver named John Careles who had been jailed for his Protestant activism but was let out of prison to play in the Corpus Christi plays, finally this same Protestantism would be the major force in causing the mysteries at Coventry to come to an end.[22] The mysteries had probably survived longer in Coventry than in York[23] be-

The Coventry Mysteries and Shakespeare's Histories 7

cause of the city's known Protestantism, which would have made the plays seem less dangerous, but at the last the plays were seen for what they were—remnants of Roman Catholic dramas which had brought religious topics onto stage. Already in May 1559 the queen had issued a proclamation which had forbidden "either matters of religion or of the gouernaunce of the estate of the common weale ... to be handled before any audience, but of graue and discreete persons,"[24] and the authorities became progressively more nervous over time.

The Coventry plays, though as we have seen they apparently lacked the plays of the early history of the world, nevertheless shared with the other extant English mystery plays a dependence on the context of the Creation and Fall to provide a need for redemption, which would, as the prophets knew, be forthcoming in the Savior whose entry into time was to culminate in his suffering in order to redeem the time. Hence the Shearmen and Taylors' pageant begins with a monologue by the prophet Isaye (Isaiah), who remarks on the "grett mesere" in which the human race is bound on account of the "sarpent" Satan in the garden (ll. 4–5). Speaking as if he were making his pronouncement prior to Jesus' birth, the prophet explains that this unhappy condition of the race will not need to continue indefinitely, since "myrthe and joie" (l. 8) will come through the one who will bring salvation. He will be born of a Virgin, and he will be the conduit of grace to make all people glad.

> Beholde, a mayde schall conseyve a childe
> And gett vs more grace then eyuer men had.
> (ll. 24–25)

Adam, lying in bondage in Limbo, and also those who come after the Crucifixion and Resurrection, including those who are in attendance at the play which is being presented, will be released from servitude.

Isaye's monologue serves as introduction to the scene of the Annunciation in which the angel Gabriel comes to Mary with words that verify her role as virgin and mother of the one who will "the fyndis powar dystroie" (l. 73). Upon Gabriel's departing, Joseph enters and registers his shock at seeing Mary already obviously pregnant—a scene, derived from apocryphal sources, that telescopes time, for several months have passed in a moment. Joseph is comic, a figure introduced here and also later in the Weavers' play to be the butt of laughter—but not, of course, hostile

8   *Clifford Davidson*

laughter. He is therefore less broadly dramatized than other comic figures in the religious vernacular drama such as the wife of Noah in the Towneley play, but he represents a precedent for comedy within a historical drama that we find in these plays. Unlike Falstaff, however, his presence in the play is ultimately benign, a sign of human fallibility without viciousness. In the Shearmen and Taylors' play Joseph's doubts are quickly corrected by the miraculous appearance of the angel, and the scene shifts, without a stage direction, to the shepherds who, on a cold night, share a meal and then hear the announcement of the birth of Christ in the singing of the angels. Croo's 1535 revision of the play thus moved quickly from its beginning in the speeches by Old Testament prophets through the necessary episodes of the rich Nativity sequence; already by line 269 the "Kyng of blys" will be born. The remainder of the play, totaling fewer than nine hundred lines in length, stages the coming of the Magi, the slaying of the Innocents, and, briefly, the flight to Egypt. The pageant, like the Weavers' play, is surprisingly theatrical and plays well, as those who have produced it or witnessed it as spectators have reported, and it is particularly well suited to amateur players who have a limited capacity to learn lines and master the gestures and movements required on stage. Both extant plays thus share radical differences from Shakespeare's histories and other plays, designed as the latter were for professional actors on the London stage. But Shakespeare's contributions for the theater have in common with the Coventry plays the effect of stimulating cultural memory, of bringing the past into the present in a way that will appeal in a deep psychological sense to the members of the audience. The Coventry mysteries were not so very different from the devotional and mnemonic plays that had been presented in pre-Reformation times, and though the devotional element was under suspicion by Protestants, the pageants still were participants in a memory theater with the serious purpose of making visible the scenes of history of the greatest significance for audiences to see.

At the time when Shakespeare was a schoolboy in the mid-1570s at the Stratford Grammar School he would already have been mature enough to see the Coventry plays with comprehension. It is sheer conjecture to say that his schoolmaster, Simon Hunt who was to leave Stratford for Douay in 1575 and would eventually be inducted into the Society of Jesus,[25] may have encouraged his pupils to attend this show of visible scenes from religious history, including the Smiths' Passion, the Cappers' Harrow-

The Coventry Mysteries and Shakespeare's Histories 9

ing and Resurrection, and the Drapers' Doomsday as well as the scenes shown in the plays of the Shearmen and Taylors and the Weavers. If we may judge from the other English plays of the trial and execution of Christ, the presentation of authority in figures such as Herod, Pilate, and the chief priests was highly problematic. Power is arbitrarily, wilfully, and selfishly displayed, and it is demonic. In the extant plays of the Passion from elsewhere in England, the procedural safeguards already in place in English common law were openly flouted, as scholars have shown. If the Herod of the Smiths' play was under better control than the Herod who attempted to betray the Magi or ordered the slaying of the Innocents, he nevertheless likewise established kingship as untrustworthy. The dramatic records indicate that Herod appeared either wearing a mask or with a painted face which would indicate his inherent evil, and that he held a falcion, a type of curved sword not indicative of justice.[26] In the visual arts, it was the weapon assigned to Saracens and pagans. A cast list from 1477 also included Annas and Caiaphas—the sinister high priests who traditionally were shown to have been willing to use any means to destroy Jesus and bring him to his death—and Pilate along with his wife Procula.[27] Procula's role likely would have been to serve as the devil's agent, as a temptress, comparable to her appearance in the York play, and also as a foil to her husband's legally irresponsible action in allowing the Crucifixion to go forward.[28]

The untrustworthiness of rulers and other authority figures is a quality that emerges time and again in Shakespeare's plays, including the second Henriad. Richard II, though not the thoroughgoing hypocrite of *Richard III*, nevertheless emerges at first as a false friend and as one capable indeed of unlawful acts of pillage and murder, if we accept that he was responsible for the death of his uncle Thomas of Woodstock. Wrapping himself in absolutist theory, he certainly highhandedly grasped as much wealth as he could squeeze from his realm through the issuing of his infamous blank charters and through confiscation of the property of John of Gaunt, and he was doing this in order to support his famously stylish court and his imperial pretensions.[29]

The ruler who usurps the throne and succeeds Richard fares no better. Henry IV's attempt to pass the blame for Richard II's murder onto those who physically performed it and his statement "They love not poison that do poison need" (5.6.38) are hypocritical, and Shakespeare in the subsequent play of *1 Henry IV* presents him as guilt-ridden, wishing to go on a pilgrimage to the Holy

10   *Clifford Davidson*

Land in penance for his sins against Richard and the realm. In *2 Henry IV*, John of Lancaster, Prince Hal's brother, deals with duplicity against the rebels led in the play by the Archbishop of York, Richard Scrope, the former Bishop of Coventry and Lichfield for whom there had been enough sympathy in pre-Reformation Coventry that he had been depicted as a saint in a window in St. Mary's Hall.[30] It is tempting to believe that this image disappeared from the window as part of the long Tudor campaign against rebellion which had declared Thomas à Becket to be no "sainct, but rather estemed to haue ben a rebell and traytour to his prynce"[31] and which we can gauge in the sermon *Against Disobedience and Wilful Rebellion* added to the *Book of Homilies* in 1574. Prince Hal is himself in Shakespeare's second Henriad certainly not immune from the charge of duplicity, though in *Henry V* he is more a king who alternates between cruelty (see especially the deplorable "Then every soldier kill his prisoners" [4.6.37]) and the mercy that we would expect of an ideal Christian monarch.

That which had been reflected on the pageant wagons of Coventry might be expected to have had a special resonance for a young person who had grown up in a family with strong ties to the Old Religion, particularly through his mother. Shakespeare's father's declining fortunes in the late 1570s were long blamed for his refusal to attend his parish church where he said he feared he might be served with a summons for debt, but this was a common excuse by those who wished to avoid Anglican services. Further, recent interest in his Spiritual Testament points to his renewed adherence to Roman Catholicism.[32] Peter Milward speculates that the Roman mission to the Midlands, beginning in the mid-1570s, had its effect on John Shakespeare's family,[33] though they must have conformed to the established Church until then. Already there had begun what would be for the Catholic community the period of terror and repression that was unleashed following the abortive and ill-timed rebellion in the North in 1569 and the Pope's bull *Regnans in excelsis* (1570) against Elizabeth which, declaring her illegitimate and a pretender to the throne, purported to release her subjects from their allegiance to her.[34] Over the following years the repression only intensified, with notable Roman Catholics imprisoned and executed according to the brutal fashion of the time.[35] Elizabeth's claim not to persecute for religion's sake but only for the secular crime of treason was hollow. Even possession of Mass vestments or Roman Catholic books could be dangerous in the extreme, as the case of the martyr Margaret Clitheroe of York would

The Coventry Mysteries and Shakespeare's Histories 11

prove.[36] We do not need to assume that Shakespeare, in the years before he emerged as part of the London theater scene, was necessarily himself either actively or passively a Roman Catholic—or that during the so-called "lost years" he had moved in Catholic circles in Lancashire, as Milward and Ernst Honigmann have suggested[37]—in order to imagine his discomfort with the ruling monarch. By the time he wrote the first Henriad, which would have given London audiences of the day what they wanted to hear, Shakespeare seems to have conformed, like his patron Southampton in later life[38] but over time with far less enthusiasm. If at the time of the writing of the second Henriad he was neither a Church Papist[39] nor a recusant, he certainly seems to have been nostalgic for the Old Religion—that is, favorable toward a more Catholic political and social order in which religious orders were not the object of ridicule and in which the Catholic Mass was not regarded as subversive.[40] But the likelihood is that earlier, prior to 1579, the young Shakespeare would have been unusually receptive to the civic religious theater and its Augustinian handling of history wherein secular and pre-Christian religious rulers are aligned with Babylon rather than the City of God.[41]

In *Richard II*, however, Shakespeare treats the king who has espoused an absolutist understanding of the monarchy with surprising sympathy *after* his deposition when he is taken off to prison, tormented, and murdered—a rehabilitation of the protagonist which makes the play more of a tragedy than a mere history play. As the pageants presented for Richard's second triumphal entry into London in 1392 indicated, this king was historically a political theologian who saw his role in the kingdom as sacred—that is, an affirmation of *sancta majestas* and of the king's role as "the vicar of the highest King."[42] Shakespeare would not have had access to the Wilton Diptych in which Richard, accompanied by his patron saints John the Baptist, Edmund, and Edward the Confessor, kneels with his hands raised in veneration as he is presented by them to the Virgin Mary and Child, who are accompanied by the angels of the court of heaven who wear his white hart emblem.[43] However, the playwright in his reading of his sources understood implicitly that Richard perceived the anointing of the monarch to be a holy act, a commissioning as God's representative not only for the city of London-Jerusalem and but also for the kingdom as a whole. The anointing at the king's coronation is not reversible, in his view: "Not all the water in the rough rude sea / Can wash the balm off from an anointed king" (3.2.54–55). But

12   *Clifford Davidson*

Shakespeare will inconsistently turn around any skepticism he might have had earlier in the play concerning Richard's absolutism and his *de jure* right to the throne when it suits him. Shakespeare hence is able to make of Richard's political theology a connection between the suffering of Christ whose representative Richard claims to be.

The Passion was, we can safely assume, vividly presented to the eyes of the spectators in the Coventry Smiths' play at the same time that the Elizabethan government and the Protestant hierarchy of the Church of England had tightened the iconoclastic screws against depictions in the visual arts.[44] Undoubtedly in response to official pressure, Shakespeare's father as Stratford chamberlain in 1563–1564 had supervised the partitioning off and whitewashing over of the wall paintings that included religious scenes in the Guild Chapel, from which the rood with its crucified Christ and attendant figures over the chancel arch were removed.[45] It may be that the father's guilt was shared by the son in that he felt his family implicated, if we see a personal statement in *Richard III* 2.1.123–24; here Edward IV speaks the words "... and defac'd / The precious image of our dear Redeemer." The Crucifixion and the events leading up to it, however, certainly had not been removed from the Coventry Smiths' play, as verified by the fragmentary guild accounts. A masked devil was recorded in the fifteenth century along with a pillar and four scourges for the Scourging.[46] Peter, who denied his Lord, was present, and the final accounts before the cycle was suppressed also included reference to Judas's hanging and the hook that was used for this act.[47] Judging from the other English plays of the Passion, we would expect that the play presented a great deal of brutality and blood. The plays of York and Chester as well as in the Towneley and N-Town plays establish a resemblance between the tormenting and execution of Jesus and the actual judicial cruelty and execution in sixteenth-century England.[48] Likewise, the terrible final scenes in *Richard II*, along with the politically sensitive deposition scene which was not allowed to see print in the early quartos, offer acts of extended cruelty directed to a king, whom official Elizabethan political thought had identified as God's viceregent in the kingdom. As in the Smiths' play, the audience's sympathy is directed to the victim, albeit in the case of Richard *not* one who is guiltless in the earlier part of the drama. The presentation of divine authority as at once humble and afflicted against the brutality of official power would seem especially to have had appeal for those who sympathized

The Coventry Mysteries and Shakespeare's Histories 13

with the adherents of the Old Religion who were suffering for their faith.

The two plays of *1 Henry IV* and *2 Henry IV* show the usurping king suffering from guilt and longing to go on a crusade to set free the Jerusalem where Jesus' feet had trod and where "for our advantage on the bitter cross" those same "feet were nail'd / For our advantage" (*1 Henry IV* 1.1.25–27); this would be an act of penance—a pilgrimage to a site, the Holy Sepulcher, which had been popular among English pilgrims before the Reformation. Unfortunately, Henry is faced with revolt against his authority in the West and North which forces cancellation of his plans. The official Tudor view was that the rebellions which occurred in England at this time were in divine retribution for his usurpation, and in the character of Henry IV Shakespeare offers a king who himself accepts this view. Henry V, appearing to agree, will attempt to expiate his father's "fault" by re-interring Richard's body and establishing prayers for his soul in Purgatory as well as founding two chantries "where the sad and solemn priests/ Sing still for Richard's soul" (*Henry V* 4.1.293, 301–02). Retribution is, however, also something with which Henry V must be concerned. The commoner William in *Henry V* speaks explicitly of the Last Day when the severed body parts of soldiers will be joined together again and when those who have not had a good death in battle will accuse the king who sent them into the fray (4.1.134–46). Seemingly on a different wavelength, the king before the battle at Agincourt on St. Crispin's day (25 October)[49] claims that the event will be remembered in connection with this feast "[f]rom this day to the ending of the world" (4.3.58). So too in one of Shakespeare's earlier histories, Henry is described as "blest" and as one who appeared to the French like the Judge at Judgment Day (*1 Henry VI* 1.1.28–30). In spite of the seeming contradictions here, there is no denying the shadow cast by the traditional view as expressed in the Coventry Last Judgment play—a view shared by Dante in the *Commedia*—that would not make rulers of either Church or State immune from judgment. The Chester Whitsun play of Doomsday, for example, has among the damned a pope, emperor, king, queen, judge, and merchant, while such wall paintings of the Doom such as the fourteenth-century example at the Church of St. Thomas of Canterbury at Salisbury might show high ecclesiastical and secular figures among the damned being rounded up and dragged off to hell by means of a red-hot chain.[50] In the Dance of Death iconography appearing in the wall painting which had been allowed to

14   *Clifford Davidson*

remain unobscured on the north wall of the nave of Stratford Guild Chapel when Shakespeare was a child, Emperor, King, Cardinal, Archbishop, and Bishop alike would receive the summons of Death as a prelude to the judgment of God.[51] We do not know if the Coventry Drapers' play included such secular or ecclesiastical officials among the "iij blank [black] Sowles" destined for hell— color-coded to provide immediate recognition and to distinguish them from the pure (white) souls of those about to be saved.[52] The eschatological thrust of the Coventry pageant, however, was congruent with what was in Shakespeare's mind when he was writing his histories.[53]

The Coventry Drapers' Doomsday play may have been the most spectacular of all the Last Judgment pageants in England. The play was apparently introduced by a sign, a pyrotechnic device in which a "world" was burned, at least at three stations where the drama was presented in the Coventry streets each year, in expectation that at the Last Day this actual world would be destroyed by fire.[54] The Drapers' financial records indicate that there were also an earthquake made by a barrel device, the sounding of trumpets, and the appearance of God descending from above by means of a windlass or similar mechanism.[55] He wore a gown of "Redde Sendall" and very likely, as in Chester's Whitsun plays and in various depictions in the visual arts, came with hands and side bleeding his sacred blood.[56] The use of these pyrotechnic and visual effects would have been all the more effective since the timing of the performance, coming at the end of the day, was almost certainly at dusk. The Coventry Drapers provided cressets and other forms of lighting, apparently in the event that the play would require them.[57] Nor was the topic of the play expected to be remote from the lives of those who watched as spectators. For the Protestant-leaning citizens of Coventry and also for traditional Christians at that time, the end of history was believed to be imminent and the Last Judgment at hand at any moment, but, even aside from the expectation of a conclusion to history, it should not be forgotten that individual human life was fragile and extremely unpredictable with regard to its ending. The anxiety of living in such a temporary world in such a temporary human body is an important element lying behind the presentation of character and event in Shakespeare's second Henriad as well.

In this transitory world, Hal's flirtation with Poins, Bardolf, and especially Falstaff will seem all the more problematic, however wonderfully amusing are the antics of the prince and his

The Coventry Mysteries and Shakespeare's Histories 15

friends. Hal's promise early in *1 Henry IV* to cast off his disguise of dissoluteness and to redeem the "time when men think least I will" (1.2.217) provides assurance to the audience that he will reform. But Falstaff, that misleader of youth, has also talked, in cadences like a Puritan, of psalm singing and reformation, and on his deathbed will be reported in *Henry V* to have been attempting (if Theobald's widely accepted emendation of the Folio's "a Table of green fields" is correct) to repeat the twenty-third psalm—a very ambiguous end. He is "that reverent Vice, that grey iniquity," as Prince Hal calls him (*1 Henry IV* 2.4.453–54)—an expansion of the vice figure into the fat knight from the examples which had appeared in earlier plays such as *Cambyses* but not in the mystery cycles. Falstaff's very name signifies his falsehood in private life and as a military adventurer when he emerges as nastily predatory. His ambition to be made Lord Chief Justice under King Hal is truly sinister, though it is of course amusing today as it must also have been in Shakespeare's time when judicial corruption was less unexpected.

However, Falstaff, designated humorously as "that old white-bearded Sathan" by Prince Hal in *1 Henry IV* 2.4.463, may stand alongside a set of characters that appeared in the Coventry plays. These are the devils that we know appeared in the Drapers' Doomsday play and whose role was to round up the wicked and to take them away to the entrance of hell, which appeared on stage as a gaping hell mouth. Perhaps they roared—an attribute of the "devil i' th' old play" identified in *Henry V* (4.4.71). The Drapers made payments to three "Demones" in c. 1539, and probably in the next year (the accounts are somewhat confused for this period) two "demens heds" or masks were painted and made new at their expense.[58] In c. 1567 only two demons were being retained, and two shillings were laid out "for a demonys face."[59] These devils were obviously grotesque, as illustrations in the visual arts from medieval Coventry and elsewhere demonstrate.[60] In 1572 the Drapers paid "for mendyng ye demens cotts and hose" and "for ij pound of heare for ye Same."[61] Falstaff's grotesquely fat body—a role played by the clown William Kempe—was not so far as we know hairy like the devils in the Coventry play, nor did he wear a mask; however, the mixture of comedy and anxiety that was connected with the appearance of demons on the medieval stage seems likely to have been present. Who, at least among the commoners watching Shakespeare's play, would have felt comfortable being conscripted into Falstaff's company of soldiers in prepara-

16 *Clifford Davidson*

tion for the battle at Shrewsbury? Who would appreciate having his horses taken as Falstaff and his friends race off from the West Country to be present at the coronation of Henry V? This is, of course, not to deny the great fun of the scenes in which Falstaff appears or the other dimensions of this character.

Among these other dimensions it seems necessary to interject attention to one of them, and this is the curious association which Shakespeare seems to have developed between Falstaff and Puritanism for which, as for example the figure of Malvolio in *Twelfth Night* indicates, the playwright had a dislike. Undoubtedly this was in part on account of the presumption with which the Puritans spoke of themselves as "saints," however much they worried about their own election, and their inflexibility. The left wing of the English Reformation made the role of the demonic seem much more serious and humorless, and the more extreme Puritans were as we know determined enemies of the theater where evil and human fallibility were displayed and judged.[62] Members of this party often tended, like their Calvinistic counterparts on the Continent, to be intolerant and hence were regarded by moderate Anglicans to be a source of dissension. In many towns they did in fact cause the community to split apart in something other than Christian charity, as Robert Whiting has shown in his study of the Southwest in the sixteenth century.[63] If Falstaff, originally identified as Sir John Oldcastle until the playwright was forced to change the name, is recognized as modeled upon the historical figure who was seen by John Foxe and others as a crypto-Protestant martyr, Shakespeare's strategy may be recognized as having an even broader bias,[64] but this matter will take us too far from our present subject.

The rejection of an upside-down world by Henry V—necessary if he is not to emerge as a criminal king—at the end of *2 Henry IV* locates the new king on the side of law and justice rather than misrule. The much-discussed conclusion of this play thus may be seen as only a very pale reflection of the Last Day of history when absolute justice will prevail among all the people who have ever lived on this earth. Of course, perfect justice also cannot be achieved in the next play, even with the king's "zero tolerance" for infractions among his soldiers that results in Bardolph and Nym's hanging for theft (*Henry V* 4.4.70–73). Doomsday is not yet, certainly, and this final play in the second Henriad takes the story in a different direction with the victory in 1415 at Agincourt and beyond. Together in these plays Shakespeare reveals that his view of

The Coventry Mysteries and Shakespeare's Histories 17

history, however inconsistent, is not to be merely identified with that of his sources, although he was not reluctant to make drama even out of some of the official political theories—and out of popular chauvinistic feeling—at his disposal.

If the foregoing discussion of the second Henriad against the background of the Coventry plays which Shakespeare probably saw in his youth—and of the social and religious context in which they had their being—proves nothing else, it should demonstrate that he was not an absolutist but rather one who saw monarchy very differently than those, among whom the most visible was Edmund Spenser, who fostered the literary cult of the Virgin Queen. The reality of rule in the realm was quite different, with the confiscation of property and confiscatory fines against Roman Catholic adherents as well as the imprisonment, torture, and even execution for those who celebrated the Roman Mass—or allowed such services to be celebrated—in private houses. Many of Elizabeth's clergy were time-servers or, worse yet, profiteers who allowed curates to do their work while they pocketed the larger share of the priest's stipend, and so the center of parish activity migrated from the church and churchyard to the alehouse. On the other hand, in some towns, intolerant Puritan clergy introduced a theology which emphasized the individual as saint or sinner, predestined sometimes even in the sense of double predestination,[65] with the effect of tearing communities apart. For those who, like Shakespeare, apparently looked back with nostalgia at a medieval past—though not with a nostalgia blind to the turmoil of the late Middle Ages—the Crown would need to bear responsibility for a great deal, including, we might suspect, the iconoclastic program that had destroyed so much beauty in so many churches and chapels, the program that had erased so many images of the Redeemer from the walls, chancel arches, and even windows. Shakespeare had made his peace—or at least had declared a truce—with the New Religion, as his knowledge of the liturgy and the homilies testifies, but there seems to have been no wholehearted acceptance of unlimited royal power, which could be either beneficent or demonic. Shakespeare could never have agreed with John Donne, the protégé of King James who was to be also the patron of the bard's acting company, the King's Men, that the king is a participant in God's divine power, and that God's power is not limited by law but only by his will.[66]

History, therefore, might work its way through periods of chaos and suffering, as during the rebellions in the time of Henry

18   *Clifford Davidson*

IV or during the Wars of the Roses, and through merit or grace might achieve stability and progressive improvement in the realm. So when Henry VII defeated the allegedly tyrannical Richard III at Bosworth Field and united the houses of Lancaster and York, he was regarded as a providential blessing to the land, though in fact his rule was marked by corruption.[67] And though the playwright's sympathies in the late play of *Henry VIII* were with Catherine of Aragon,[68] he nevertheless allowed the infant Elizabeth to emerge as destined for greatness. He was aware throughout that his characters represented people living in this world but in a period of grace—imperfect, sinful, capable of charity and malice, of acts of goodness and of terror. And those in high places could, as dramatized in the Coventry Corpus Christi plays, have an immense influence on history over long periods of time.

Likewise the interpretation of rebellion in Shakespeare's histories needs to be more nuanced when it is remembered that in the mystery plays it is Jesus who is accused of rebellion and treason. We do not know the playwright's mature attitude toward the 1569 rebellion in the North against Elizabeth which prompted the writing of the homily *Against Rebellion and Wilful Disobedience,* but a careful look at Archbishop Scrope's role in *2 Henry IV* suggests more sympathy than might be expected for his rising against a king who had sneaked his way onto the throne and along the way had deposed a legitimate ruler, however imperfect. The rebels are responsible for a "plot," an action which too is seen as illegal and in which not all the plotters have good motives, but from the Archbishop's point of view it is raised against the abuses of the new king which he has itemized ("[t]he parcels and particulars of our grief" [*Henry V* 4.2.36]) with the hope that these will be redressed, whereupon the Archbishop expects his submission will be sufficient to achieve reconciliation. His arrest and the arrest of his compatriots is indeed a breach of faith in spite of Prince John's words in defense of his action. Archbishop Scrope, a man noted for his holiness, was long the subject of local veneration in York where he was believed to be a "martir Christi,"[69] and a hagiography prepared in connection with the unsuccessful campaign for his canonization gives details of the grievances.[70] The historical account of the Archbishop's sentencing also is a demonstration of the cruelty of the king, who defied his own court and installed a pliant judge when the judge on the bench refused to convict.[71] If in Shakespeare's play the Archbishop's actions were nevertheless treasonous under normal circumstances—and if John of Lancaster's

The Coventry Mysteries and Shakespeare's Histories 19

duplicity was the sort of thing practiced by both sides in the Irish wars—the trick played on the Archbishop was hardly appropriate for the English subject of the English king. May not there also have been some sympathy among members of Shakespeare's family and their friends for the rebels in 1569 which was retained by him in adulthood? It is certainly of interest to turn to a play such as *Macbeth* in which a rebellion is raised against a man who has made himself king by duplicitous and criminal means. Here the rebellion against Macbeth is depicted as a holy crusade against evil.[72] To be sure, the idea of rebellion as presented in the second Henriad is hardly so simple, but however we interpret it we would do well to evaluate it in all its complexity against the treatment of rebelliousness against God in the mysteries presented at Coventry until the playwright was fifteen years old.

Notes

1. Ingram, ed., *Records of Early English Drama: Coventry*, 294; hereafter *REED: Coventry*.
2. See Phythian-Adams, 33–35, 281.
3. Kipling, 11–21.
4. King and Davidson, 154–55, 157.
5. Sharp, 148n; see also *REED: Coventry*, 233.
6. Kipling, 15–18.
7. Dugdale, 116.
8. *REED: Coventry*, 66, 77.
9. Davidson, *On Tradition*, 56–69.
10. See King and Davidson, 10.
11. Birmingham Public Library Manuscript, quoted in Burbidge, 217.
12. Clay, 452.
13. The arguments for Shakespeare's family's Roman Catholicism are set forth by Mutschmann and Wentersdorf; and Milward. Not all their conclusions have been accepted. Some other aspects of Shakespeare's handling of kingship are usefully explored by Tiffany.
14. A different approach to connections between the mystery plays and Shakespeare's work appears in Jones, and in Guilfoyle.
15. Quotations from Shakespeare's works are from *The Riverside Shakespeare*, 2nd ed., gen. ed. G. Blakemore Evans, and quotations from the Coventry plays are from King and Davidson.
16. The revised second edition of Dugdale's *Warwickshire* claimed Old Testament as well as New Testament subjects for the plays, but the records give no evidence for the former; see King and Davidson, 14–52.
17. King and Davidson, 44.

18. King and Davidson, 35–36.

19. Jacobus de Voragine, *The Golden Legend*, 1:8.

20. See King and Davidson, 52–53, and King, "Faith, Reason and the Prophets' Dialogue," 37–46. For the change in mentality during the Reformation, see Duffy.

21. For the text preserved in the fifteenth-century fragments, see King and Davidson, 150–53.

22. Foxe's account of Careles's release from jail is excerpted in *REED: Coventry*, 207–08. The classic arguments concerning the suppression of the mysteries are those of Gardiner, but his views have been modified in recent criticism. For discussion of the growing antagonism to the visualizing and playing of biblical scenes, see my contributions to Davidson and Nichols.

23. The York cycle was suppressed in 1580 when permission for it to go forward was not given by the ecclesiastical authorites. See Lancashire, 294; see the edition of the York plays by Beadle.

24. Chambers, 4:263–64.

25. Milward, 39; Mutschmann and Wentersdorf, 78.

26. *REED: Coventry*, 73.

27. Ibid., 59.

28. For discussion of Procula, see Woolf, 243–45.

29. See Mathew, 17 and *passim*.

30. Davidson and Alexander, 50, citing the early nineteenth-century local historian William Reader.

31. Borenius, 110.

32. Milward, 20–21. Milward suggests that John Shakespeare may have received the text of his Spiritual Testament from Edmund Campion, and that this could have happened "at the house of Sir William Catesby, who was related to his wife."

33. Milward, 19–20.

34. See the translation of this document in Hughes, 3:418–20.

35. For an example, see the description of the brutal treatment, including the most extreme torture, accorded to the missionary-poet Robert Southwell in Devlin.

36. Farmer, 84–85.

37. Milward, 40–42; Honigmann; Thomson, 18–20.

38. See Akrigg, 178–81.

39. For background, see Walsham.

40. See Hughes, 3:350–53.

41. Johnston, 225–46.

42. Quoted from the so-called "Laws of Edward the Confessor," as translated in O'Brien, 174–75. The term *sancta majestas* is from *2 Henry VI* 5.1.5. For the view that the polemical historian John Foxe was responsible for the "peculiar form" of "Sacred Monarchy" in Tudor England that replaced the earlier formulation of the theology of kingship and its relation to history, see Yates, 86.

The Coventry Mysteries and Shakespeare's Histories   21

43. See Wormald, 191–203.

44. Destruction of ecclesiastical art continued, though at the Queen's command sparing memorials and glass, which was too expensive to replace. The theologian William Perkins was hardly alone in claiming that even *mental* images of God were to be avoided: "So soon as the mind frames unto itself any form of God (as when he is popishly conceived to be like an old man sitting in heaven in a throne with a sceptre in his hand) an idol is set up in the mind" (William Perkins, *Warning Against Idolatrie* [1601], 107–08, as quoted by Aston, 453.

45. Savage, 128. See also the discussion and illustrations in Davidson, *The Guild Chapel Wall Paintings*.

46. *REED: Coventry*, 74.

47. *REED: Coventry*, 289.

48. See especially Tiner, 103–12, and, for the response to cruelty in the Crucifixion, Davidson, "Sacred Blood and the Medieval Stage," 436–58.

49. This feast too remained in the calendar in the Elizabethan prayer book (Clay, 453).

50. Lumiansky and Mills, 1:444–50 (Play 24.173–356); Hollaender, 359, pl. 3.

51. Puddephat, 29–35; and Davidson, *The Guild Chapel Wall Paintings*, 33–34, 51–55, figs. 19–20.

52. *REED: Coventry*, 217.

53. See especially Velz, 312–29.

54. See King and Davidson, 48–49.

55. *REED: Coventry*, 230, 474.

56. *REED: Coventry*, 230, and Lumiansky and Mills, 453 (Play 24.429 *s.d.*).

57. *REED: Coventry*, 465.

58. *REED: Coventry*, 466, 468.

59. *REED: Coventry*, 474.

60. An early sixteenth-century devil, now lost, appeared in painted glass in the church of St. John Bablake in Coventry which had an oversize head, extended nose, and shortened legs; see Davidson and Alexander, 17; fragments of the glass remained as late as 1930 and were reported by Harris, 232. For a general treatment of the appearance of devils, see Palmer, 20–40.

61. *REED: Coventry*, 259.

62. All the Puritan arguments against the stage are marshaled by William Prynne in his *Histrio-mastix*.

63. See Whiting.

64. Taylor, 85–100. The name "Oldcastle" is returned to *1 Henry IV* in the new Oxford edition of Shakespeare's works.

65. Double predestination, to hell as well as heaven, was advocated by a number of divines, especially at Cambridge, and was incorporated in the Lambeth Articles, which were never disseminated. See White, 101–10.

66. See Shuger, 169, 171, citing John Donne, 2:9.143, 7:1.555–61, 8:1.744–45.

67. The article by Gairdner in the *Dictionary of National Biography (s.v.* Henry VII) reports that the "chief blot on his reign" was extortion.

68. See Merriam, 461–64.

69. Bodley MS. Lat. Liturg. F.3, as quoted by McKenna, 618n.

70 See Maidstone; Latin text in Raine, 304–11.

71. See McKenna, 611.

72. *Macbeth* is of course a complex play on account of the historical moment when it was written; see the discussion in Davidson, "The Anxiety of Power in Shakespeare's *Macbeth*," 181–204.

Works Cited

Akrigg, G.P.V. *Shakespeare and the Earl of Southampton.* Cambridge: Harvard UP, 1968.

Aston, Margaret. *England's Iconoclasts I: Laws Against Images.* Oxford: Clarendon P, 1988.

Beadle, Richard, ed. *The York Plays.* London: Edward Arnold, 1982.

Borenius, Tancred. *St. Thomas Becket in Art.* 1932; reprint Port Washington, NY: Kennikat P, n.d.

Burbidge, F. Bliss. *Old Coventry and Lady Godiva.* Birmingham: Cornish Brothers, n.d.

Chambers, E.K. *The Elizabethan Stage.* 4 vols. Oxford: Clarendon P, 1923.

Cheney, C.R. *Handbook of Dates for Students of English History.* 1945; reprint Cambridge: Cambridge UP, 1996.

Clay, William Keatinge, ed. *Liturgies and Occasional Forms of Prayer Set Forth in the Reign of Queen Elizabeth.* Parker Society. Cambridge: Cambridge UP, 1847.

Davidson, Clifford. "The Anxiety of Power in Shakespeare's *Macbeth*." In *The Iconography of Power: Ideas and Images of Rulership on the English Renaissance Stage,* ed. Győry E. Szőnyi and Rowland Wymer. Szeged, Hungary: Institute of English and American Studies at the U of Szeged, 2000. 181–204.

———. *The Guild Chapel Wall Paintings at Stratford-upon-Avon.* New York: AMS P, 1988.

———. *On Tradition: Essays on the Use and Valuation of the Past.* New York: AMS P, 1992.

———. "Sacred Blood and the Medieval Stage." *Comparative Drama* 31 (1997): 436–58.

The Coventry Mysteries and Shakespeare's Histories 23

———, and Jennifer Alexander. *The Early Art of Coventry, Stratford-upon-Avon, Warwick, and Lesser Sites in Warwickshire*. Early Drama, Art, and Music Reference Series 4. Kalamazoo: Medieval Institute Publications, 1985.

———, and Ann Eljenholm Nichols, eds. *Iconoclasm vs. Art and Drama*. Early Drama, Art and Music Monograph Series 11. Kalamazoo: Medieval Institute Publications, 1989.

Devlin, Christopher. *The Life of Robert Southwell*. London: Longmans, Green, 1956.

Donne, John. *The Sermons*, ed. George Potter and Evelyn Simpson. 10 vols. Berkeley and Los Angeles: U of California P, 1953–62.

Duffy, Eamon. *The Stripping of the Altars: Traditional Religion in England 1400–1580*. New Haven: Yale UP, 1992.

Dugdale, William. *The Antiquities of Warwickshire*. London, 1656.

Farmer, David Hugh. *The Oxford Dictionary of Saints*. Oxford: Clarendon P, 1978.

Gardiner, Harold C. *Mysteries End: An Investigation of the Last Days of the Medieval Religious Stage*. 1946; reprint Hamden, CT: Archon Books, 1967.

Guilfoyle, Cherrell. *Shakespeare's Play within Play: Medieval Imagery and Scenic Form in Hamlet, Othello, and King Lear*. Early Drama, Art, and Music Monograph Series 12. Kalamazoo: Medieval Institute Publications, 1990.

Harris, Mary Dormer. *Some Manors, Churches, and Villages of Warwickshire*. Coventry: Coventry City Guild, 1937.

Hollaender, Albert. "The Doom-Painting of St. Thomas of Canterbury, Salisbury." *Wiltshire Archaeological and Natural History Magazine* 50 (1942): 351–70.

Hoenigmann, E.A.J. *Shakespeare: The Lost Years*. Manchester: Manchester UP, 1985.

Hughes, Philip. *The Reformation in England*. 3 vols. New York: Macmillan, 1954.

Ingram, R.W., ed. *Records of Early English Drama: Coventry*. Toronto: U of Toronto P, 1981.

Jacobus de Voraigne. *The Golden Legend*, trans. William Granger. 2 vols. Princeton: Princeton UP, 1993.

Johnston, Alexandra F. "*The Word Made Flesh*: Augustinian Elements in the York Cycle." In *The Centre and Its Compass: Studies in Medieval Literature in Honor of Professor John Leyerle*, ed. Robert A. Taylor *et al.* Kalamazoo: Medieval Institute Publications, 1993. 225–46.

Jones, Emrys. *Scenic Form in Shakespeare*. Oxford: Clarendon P, 1971.

24 *Clifford Davidson*

King, Pamela M. "Faith, Reason and the Prophets' Dialogue in the Coventry Pageant of the Shearmen and Taylors." In *Drama and Philosophy*, ed. James Redmond. Themes in Drama 12. Cambridge: Cambridge UP, 1990. 37–46.

———, and Clifford Davidson, eds. *The Coventry Corpus Christi Plays*. Early Drama, Art, and Monograph Series 27. Kalamazoo: Medieval Institute Publications, 2000.

Kipling, Gordon. *Enter the King: Theatre, Liturgy and Ritual in the Medieval Civic Triumph*. Oxford: Clarendon P, 1998.

Lancashire, Ian. *Dramatic Texts and Records of Britain: A Chronological Topography*. Toronto: U of Toronto P, 1984.

Lumiansky, R.M., and David Mills, eds. *The Chester Mystery Cycle*. EETS ss 3, 9. London: Oxford UP, 1974–86.

Maidstone, Clement. *The Martyrdom of Archbishop Richard Scrope*, trans. Stephen K. Wright. <http://arts-sciences.cua.edu/engl/maidstone/htm>

Mathew, Gervase. *The Court of Richard II*. London: John Murray, 1968.

McKenna, J.W. "Popular Canonization as Political Propaganda: The Cult of Archbishop Scrope." *Speculum* 44 (1970): 608–23.

Merriam, Thomas. "Queen of Earthly Queens." *Notes and Queries* 245 (2000): 461–64.

Milward, Peter. *Shakespeare's Religious Background*. Bloomington: Indiana UP, 1973.

Mutschmann, H., and K. Wentersdorf. *Shakespeare and Catholicism*. 1952; reprint New York: AMS P, 1969.

O'Brien, Bruce. *God's Peace and the King's Peace: The Laws of Edward the Confessor*. Philadelphia: U of Pennsylvania P, 1999.

Palmer, Barbara D. "The Inhabitants of Hell: Devils." In *The Iconography of Hell*, ed. Clifford Davidson and Thomas H. Seiler. Early Drama, Art, and Music Monograph Series 17. Kalamazoo: Medieval Institute Publications, 1992. 20–40.

Phythian-Adams, Charles. *Desolation of a City: Coventry and Urban Crisis of the Late Middle Ages*. Cambridge: Cambridge UP, 1979.

Prynne, William. *Histrio-mastix*. London, 1630.

Puddephat, Wilfrid. "The Mural Paintings of the Dance of Death in the Guild Chapel of Stratford-upon-Avon." *Transactions of the Birmingham Archaeological Society* 76 (1960): 29–35.

Raine, James, ed. *Historians of the Church of York*. Rolls Series 71. London, 1886.

Redmond, James, ed. *Drama and Philosophy*. Cambridge: Cambridge UP, 1990.

The Coventry Mysteries and Shakespeare's Histories 25

REED: *Coventry; see* Ingram.

Savage, Richard, ed. *Minutes and Accounts of the Corporation of Stratford-upon-Avon*. Dugdale Society I. 1921.

Shakespeare, William. *The Riverside Shakespeare*, gen. ed. G. Blakemore Evans. 2nd ed. Boston: Houghton Mifflin, 1997.

Sharp, Thomas. *A Dissertation on the Pageants or Dramatic Mysteries Anciently Performed at Coventry*. Coventry, 1825.

Shuger, Deborah Kuller. *Habits of Thought in the English Renaissance*. 1990; reprint Toronto: U of Toronto P, 1997.

Taylor, Gary. "The Fortunes of Oldcastle." *Shakespeare Survey* 38 (1985): 85–100.

Thomson, Peter. *Shakespeare's Professional Career*. Cambridge: Cambridge UP, 1992.

Tiffany, Grace. "Elizabethan Constructions of Kingship and the Stage." In *The Iconography of Power: Ideas and Images of Rulership on the English Renaissance Stage*, ed. Győry E. Szőnyi and Rowland Wymer. Szeged: Institute of English and American Studies of the U of Szeged, 2000. 89–115.

Tiner, Elza. "English Law and the York Trial Plays." *Early Drama, Art and Music Review* 18 (1996): 103–12.

Velz, John W. "'Some shall be pardon'd and some punished': Medieval Dramatic Eschatology in Shakespeare." *Comparative Drama* 26 (1992–93): 312–29.

Walsham, Alexandra. *Church Papists: Catholicism, Conformity and Confessional Polemic in Early Modern England*. Woodbridge: Boydell P, 1993.

White, Paul. *Predestination, Polity and Polemic: Conflict and Consensus in the English Church from the Reformation to the Civil War*. Cambridge: Cambridge UP, 1992.

Whiting, Robert. *The Blind Devotion of the People: Popular Religion and the English Reformation*. Cambridge: Cambridge UP, 1989.

Woolf, Rosemary. *The English Mystery Plays*. Berkeley and Los Angeles: U of California P, 1972.

Wormald, Francis. "The Wilton Diptych." *Journal of the Warburg and Courtauld Institutes* 17 (1954): 191–203.

Yates, Frances. "Foxe as Propagandist." *Encounter* 27 (1966): 191–203.

Sons Without Fathers:
Shakespeare's Second Tetralogy
David George

Imagine, if you will, a dramatist writing in this current year about the events of 200 years ago. He turns out four plays on George Washington, Benedict Arnold, the Marquis de La Fayette, Patrick Henry, Alexander Hamilton, and Thomas Jefferson, with some excellent battle scenes, and the wooing of Martha Dandridge. In addition, our dramatist avails himself of the story of the hatchet and the cherry tree and other details of the mythical life of George Washington by Parson Weems, and introduces a self-indulgent colonial soldier for some tavern scenes in Philadelphia just before the battle of Valley Forge in 1778. He also adds farcical and unhistorical details to that battle. The plays are extremely popular, but the academic critics are bitterly sarcastic, and finally descendants of the characters in the four so-called history plays decide to sue for damages.

Such was Shakespeare's situation in 1597 to 1599, except that there was no academic establishment that cared about plays, and only one family decided to make objections. These were the Cobhams, whose ancestor Sir John Oldcastle had evidently been turned into a comic butt. Thomas Fuller thought Shakespeare then changed the name to Fastolfe, but Fastolfe had distinguished himself at the battle of Agincourt and become governor of the Bastille. At any rate, Shakespeare settled on "Falstaff," and the objection blew over. No one seemed to care that Shakespeare altered history where it suited him.

Shakespeare altered history and added unhistorical incidents for two purposes. One was to compress history and thus to make it more coherent and entertaining, and the other was to create themes that would bind each play into a whole and show the current audience which human relationships make for balance and

28   *David George*

success in life, and which ones tend to destroy relationships, enterprises, and even life itself.

The three kings about whom Shakespeare wrote his second tetralogy reigned collectively from 1377 to 1422, a period of 45 years. However, Shakespeare did not interest himself in Richard II until the last two years of his life, 1398 to 1400, and he was not interested in Henry V's reign after 1420, when Henry married Catherine, the French princess. All in all, Shakespeare covered only 22 years, but they were some of the most exciting years of English medieval history.

Before studying the tetralogy, there is need to take a look backward. To understand the fall of Richard II, we must go back to the House of Plantagenet and Edward III. Edward, who reigned from 1327 to 1377, mounted five campaigns against France in an attempt to become ruler of a united England and France. This attempt had its origin in the Norman Conquest and later dynastic marriages of English and French royalty. Our chief interest in Edward is his numerous offspring, seven sons and five daughters. Five of those sons were important: Edward the Black Prince; Lionel of Antwerp, duke of Clarence; John of Gaunt, duke of Lancaster; Edmund of Langley, duke of York; and Thomas of Woodstock, duke of Gloucester. Edward the Black Prince, heir to the throne, wore himself out in France. Victor at Poitiers in 1356, aged only 26, he was dead twenty years later at the age of 46. He left behind him an eight-year-old son and only child, Richard, who was brought up by his mother, Joan, the Fair Maid of Kent. In 1377 Edward III died and Richard became a boy king, just ten years old. Joan died when Richard was 18, and so the young king was in the hands of advisers, Gaunt—virtual monarch in 1375—and men of his circle.

When Shakespeare decided to dramatize Richard's reign, he must have had in view its disastrous ending in 1398–1400. Shakespeare would have known about a play called *Woodstock*, also known as *I Richard II*, which dramatizes Richard's reign between 1382 and 1397. This play dates from 1591 to 1595, and is therefore almost certainly prior to Shakespeare's *Richard II*, which is commonly dated 1595. *Woodstock* may have been acted by the Chamberlain's men, Shakespeare's company after 1594. In this play the recurrent theme is Richard's relationship with his favorites, his financial exactions, and the attitude of graver persons, Richard's uncles Thomas of Woodstock and John of Gaunt, to his behavior. Shakespeare therefore decided to pick up Richard's reign in its last

Sons Without Fathers: Shakespeare's Second Tetralogy 29

two years and to probe those years for tragic potential. They were certainly years in which the hubris requisite for a tragic fall subsumed Richard: *The Dictionary of National Biography* says that he "took vengeance on his enemies and assumed despotic power in 1397."[1]

Shakespeare's main source was Raphael Holinshed's *Chronicles of England*, the second edition of 1586–87. Holinshed gives examples of Richard's "insolent misgovernance and youthful outrage," his acts of tyranny, his licentiousness, his "inordinate desires," his "lack of wit," his "evil government" generally; and York describes Richard as "an unadvised captain, as with a leaden sword would cut his own throat." The chroniclers of Richard's reign offered a king who was never very stable, a mercurial man with an explosive temper and changeable moods. For example, at the Salisbury Parliament of 1384, Richard, "white with passion," said to the earl of Arundel that if "it is supposed to be my fault that there is misgovernment in the kingdom, you lie in your teeth. You can go to the Devil."[2] A complete hush followed these words. When Richard's wife Anne of Bohemia died in 1394, Richard destroyed the palace at Sheen where she died. He was also fond of clothes, jewelry and lavish patronage. He made an unpopular second marriage with the seven-year-old Isabella, daughter of Charles VI of France, in 1396. The French connection was deeply resented in England. One chronicle describes Richard in 1398 and 1399 as sitting on a throne at court after dinner and requiring every man whom he glanced at to kneel.

Of course, Shakespeare would have known of Richard's courage in the Peasants' Revolt of 1381, when Richard (aged 14) met the rebels near London and managed to calm them down. Still, it seems clear that Shakespeare had decided Richard was a boy even at the age of 31, given to favoritism and of unstable temper. In 1387 five English nobles—Thomas Mowbray, Henry Bolingbroke, the earl of Arundel, Thomas Woodstock (the earl of Gloucester), and the earl of Warwick—marched on London and formally accused Richard's favorites of treason. These five revolutionaries were known as the Lords Appellant, and Richard shook them off in 1388. In 1397 he arrested Woodstock, Arundel, and Warwick in an arbitrary stroke of power, but Mowbray and Bolingbroke supported the king. It only remained for Richard to exile the two remaining Lords Appellant in 1398, and he had, as he declared, "the laws of England in his mouth." However, in May 1399

30   *David George*

the king made the mistake of sailing for an Irish campaign, taking all his most trusted advisers with him.

Richard II opens in April 1398 with the Court of Chivalry at Windsor hearing of Henry Bolingbroke's accusation against Thomas Mowbray concerning treasonable speech against the king. Mowbray maintains that Bolingbroke is "a slanderous coward." Bolingbroke adds further charges, that Mowbray has misused royal funds, that he has been a traitorous conspirator for 18 years, and that he has murdered the earl of Gloucester. The latter's blood cries out, like Abel's, for Bolingbroke's vengeance. While God took revenge on Cain for his fratricide, one would expect God's role to be filled by Bolingbroke's father, John of Gaunt, Gloucester's brother; yet Gaunt is too old to seek revenge. And should that revenge be upon Mowbray? The order for Gloucester's death came from Richard himself, and Mowbray, though probably transmitting the order to Gloucester's jailers, did not kill him personally. Richard's best move here is to dismiss the whole affair casually: "Forget, forgive, conclude, and be agreed; / Our doctors say this is no month to bleed" (1.1.156–57). The dispute is conveniently adjourned to trial by combat at Coventry, September 1398.

The second scene of the first act concerns Gaunt's reaction to his son's failure to deal with Mowbray. The Duchess of Gloucester reminds Gaunt that her husband was his brother, "one vial full of Edward's sacred blood," and that they shared "that mettle, that self-mold." Gaunt's failure to avenge Gloucester's death means "thou dost consent / In some large measure to thy father's death" since he was "the model of thy father's life" (17, 25–26, 28). In short, the Duchess is driving Gaunt to see himself as a parricide, a weak son. At the lists at Coventry, of course, Bolingbroke never gets the chance to destroy Mowbray. Instead he is banished for six years and Mowbray for life, and both swear never to conspire together against the king. The risk that Bolingbroke might unhorse Mowbray, widely suspected of being Richard's agent in Gloucester's murder, was too great; "popular feeling would have hailed it as a defeat for the king."[3] Gaunt, considering that he will never see his son again, says he should have argued more like a father than a judge for his son's sentence. No matter; Bolingbroke has already assumed a new kind of fatherhood, the popular patron who has wooed the common people, "As were our England in reversion his / And he our subjects' next degree in hope" (1.4.35–36). Richard, on the other hand, resorts to farming out the royal taxes, forcing cash gifts from the rich, and appropriating John of Gaunt's wealth.

Sons Without Fathers: Shakespeare's Second Tetralogy 31

It is important to note that by the end of the first act, there is a father who regrets his not acting like a father, and another father who shows a new kind of fatherhood—not toward a son.

In the first scene of the second act, Shakespeare takes us to early 1399, to Gaunt's great scene of dying prophecy, where he predicts that Richard will burn out and prey upon himself. His auditor is the duke of York with others, but not the king, who never hears what he is predicted to become. He learns only that Gaunt has been fasting in a manner, feeding on grief at being deprived of fatherhood. Accused by Gaunt of leasing out England like a landlord, Richard threatens to behead the old man. Only the memory of his father, Edward the Black Prince, restrains him. Gaunt reminds Richard he was not afraid to kill Gloucester, so that Richard's familial piety becomes tainted with disingenuousness here. Yet York assures Richard that Gaunt loves him as much as his son Harry. Richard's cynical reply ("as Herford's love, so his; / As theirs, so mine") means that Gaunt's love is no better than Bolingbroke's, and that his own love for the dukes of Lancaster is the same. When Richard proceeds to seize Gaunt's "plate, coins, revenues, and movables," York reminds him that Gaunt has a son entitled to these assets, and that Richard can teach others by this example that he can be deprived of his kingship. But Richard is set on paying for an Irish expedition.

By the second scene of the second act, the rebels have landed at Ravenspurgh, and the earl of Northumberland, his son Harry Hotspur, other lords, and the earl of Worcester have hastened to join him. The only defender is the duke of York, who is torn between his nephews Richard and Henry Bolingbroke. At Berkeley Castle, York has only 300 men, and so his best—and only—stratagem is to appeal to the past:

> Were I but now the lord of such hot youth,
> As when brave Gaunt, thy father, and myself,
> Rescued the Black Prince, that young Mars of men,
> From forth the ranks of many thousand French,
> O then how quickly should this arm of mine,
> Now prisoner to the palsy, chastise thee,
> And minister correction to thy fault!
>
> (2.3.98–104)

Here is a memory of a gathering of united fathers, both Bolingbroke's and Richard's. Bolingbroke's response—the old divide-and-conquer stratagem—is to outmaneuver York's appeal to solidarity by adopting him from that gathering as a surrogate father:

32   *David George*

> Look on my wrongs with an indifferent eye.
> You are my father, for methinks in you
> I see old Gaunt alive. O then my father,
> Will you permit that I shall stand condemned
> A wandering vagabond, my rights and royalties
> Plucked from my arms perforce, and given away
> To upstart unthrifts?
>
> (2.3.115–21)

In transforming York into his father Gaunt, Bolingbroke has fastened on York a bond stronger than York's duty to the king. But Bolingbroke also suggests that York think of the situation had he died and Gaunt survived: would not then Gaunt have acted as a father to Aumerle, York's son? York knows chop logic when he hears it: "To find out right from wrong—it may not be." A moment later, however, he drops to the status of neuter in the quarrel between his nephews. This seems primarily because he does not have the forces to stop the rebels, but his resistance is perfunctory anyway. The earl of Salisbury, John de Montagu, has come swiftly from Ireland and raised an army, but in 2.4, the Welsh captain, possibly Owen Glendower, announces that it has dispersed. So also has Richard's army collected for the Irish campaign. This scene surely sharpened the complexities of the subject "sons without fathers."

The following scene—Richard's landing on the Welsh coast—speaks volumes about his inner character. Peter Ure calls this new evolution of Richard's character "the expressive Richard."[4] Emotional over being in Wales again, Richard breaks into tears and smiles, "As a long-parted mother with her child / Plays fondly with her tears and smiles in meeting" (3.2.8–9). He then talks as a mother might to the earth, urging it to provide various poisons and harms to the rebel troops. The cynical, manipulative Richard of the first two acts has returned from Ireland a changed man—and Shakespeare provides no explanation for the change. Harry Berger finds that when Richard salutes the motherland as his child, "strange things begin to happen." In kissing the earth, "he seems to regress to childhood and rematernalize the earth, for he beseeches her in her traditional role of nurturant ... the tonal and the figural emphasis is on feminine vulnerability, softness, and weakness."[5] Strange things indeed happen: perhaps the effects of the shock of dispossession.[6] If Richard is the unmanly boy that the chroniclers present, and if he was never able to witness any deed of his brave father's, then he must of necessity turn to his mother's

Sons Without Fathers: Shakespeare's Second Tetralogy   33

model for dealing with a looming catastrophe. Hence his son, the dear earth, (another "fathers and sons" relationship), is going to make all well. To be sure, Richard will use other images to describe his new self, disclosing the accomplished actor's imagination beneath the autocrat he became in London.

Very puzzling is the swiftness of Richard's apprehension of death. This may be the vulnerable child's fear that comes when any serious menace threatens—with no protector to deflect the danger, the child apprehends the prospect of dying. Richard could have re-boarded his ship and sailed for Ireland or France, where his queen was born and where he might have found patronage. Yet he makes no plan, practical or otherwise, but instead thinks of "rainy eyes [that] / Write sorrow on the bosom of the earth" (3.2.146–47). This sounds like a small boy weeping into his mother's bosom after a terrible fright.

The Bishop of Carlisle tries to make Richard see that he lacks wisdom: "My lord, wise men ne'er sit and wail their woes, But presently prevent the ways to wail" (3.2.178–79). "Fearing dying," he adds, "pays death servile breath." Yet of course Richard does not intend to die if he can avoid it, nor to do anything to avoid it. He remains passive as Bolingbroke relentlessly advances. The showdown comes at Flint Castle, where Richard appears on the battlements like the sun in the cloudy east. Bolingbroke feigns submission provided he can get his lands back, but of course we shall see his son John do something similar at Gaultree Forest in 1305. The Bolingbrokes understand well the value of military psychology and betrayal. Richard again begins to anticipate, this time deposition, coming down into the base court "like glistering Phaeton, / Wanting the manage of unruly jades" (3.3.178–79). Again we have the image of the weak son; Phaeton was too unskilled to manage the horses of his father Apollo. Phaeton's name means "shining, radiant," and Richard would have matched this image if he wore the Yorkist badge of the sun. This glorious boy Phaeton persuaded his father to let him drive the chariot of the sun across the sky, but failed to keep the horses on a high course. They swooped too near the earth and scorched it; Zeus was obliged to destroy the driver with a thunderbolt to save the planet. Just so, Bolingbroke will destroy Richard for the good of England.

The fourth act, which has only one scene, depicts the deposition of Richard at London on 30 September 1399, almost exactly a year after the Coventry lists. The murder of Bolingbroke's uncle Gloucester must first be settled, and Bagot accuses Aumerle of the

34 David George

crime. This Aumerle was Edward Langley, the duke of York's eldest son, born about 1373 and hence not more than 23 or so when Gloucester was murdered in 1397. Yet since he denies the offense, the only solution is to bring back the banished Thomas Mowbray, duke of Norfolk, Bolingbroke's old opponent; but Mowbray is dead at Venice. The matter can safely be put off till "days of trial" now that Bolingbroke has successfully raised the possibility that Richard II had a hand in his uncle's death.

The actual deposition requires Richard to abdicate and adopt Bolingbroke as his heir, the more pitiful a requirement since Richard's two marriages had produced no child. Bolingbroke's role as Richard's son is only an empty form. Bolingbroke has nothing to learn from Richard and requires of him only that he assent to his deposition and admit his guilt. Richard never admits to any wrongdoing; instead, he attempts to identify himself with Christ, and to identify the nobles who are watching him surrender his crown with Pilate. None of them actually understands this allusion, and so Richard drops the idea that he is going to his cross. A few lines later he casts Northumberland in the role of fiend and himself in Faustus' role ("Fiend, thou torments me ere I come to hell"), but no one picks up on this either.[7] Richard ends up as an ordinary civilian prisoner in the Tower of London.

The fifth scene of the last act presents Queen Isabella, Richard's second wife, and Richard together. She was historically only a girl ten years of age when Richard was deposed, but Shakespeare depicts her as a young woman. Her questions about why Richard has done nothing to fight back against Bolingbroke are highly pertinent. She asks, "Wilt thou, pupil-like, / Take the correction mildly, kiss the rod, / And fawn on rage with base humility, / Which art a lion and the king of beasts?" (5.1.31–34). Richard is like a pupil, and he kisses the rod, an expression meaning to accept chastisement or correction submissively. Perhaps the action was sometimes performed before punishment in Elizabethan schools. At any rate, the submission explains a great deal about Richard; he looks for an authority figure to account to, and this is consistent with the willful but penitent boy within him.

The theme of a son's correction by a father pervades the next scene, this time with a touch of farce. Aumerle, the duke of York's youthful son, has entered into a plot to kill Bolingbroke at Oxford, sketched out at the end of 4.1. Old York finds an incriminating letter in Aumerle's doublet and immediately quarrels with his wife about the best way to save him. The Duchess suggests keeping

Sons Without Fathers: Shakespeare's Second Tetralogy   35

Aumerle at home, but the Duke wants him impeached. In the end, the Duke rushes to Bolingbroke to reveal the plot, but the Duchess pleads successfully for her son's life in 5.3. Happily, Aumerle managed to succeed his father as duke of York in 1402. Shakespeare has invented most of this episode; in fact the duchess of York was dead five years before Richard's deposition. Perhaps this duchess is Aumerle's stepmother even though she "explicitly and repeatedly designates Aumerle as 'my son.'"[8]

In the third scene of the last act, Shakespeare shows us Bolingbroke inquiring after his "unthrifty son" Henry, who was at this time only twelve, but in those days that was old enough for considerable independence from the parents. Bolingbroke does not see Hal's tavern-haunting and support of "so dissolute a crew" as evidence of manhood in any way, but rather as "effeminate." This is a special use of the word; the *OED* gives, as a third meaning, "self-indulgent, voluptuous." It is the exact same word that the multitude applies to Richard II in Daniel's *Civil Wars*, I, 69:

> And must we leave him [Bolingbroke] here, whom here were fit
> We should retain, the pillar of our state?
> Whose virtues well deserve to govern it,
> And not this wanton young effeminate [Richard].
> Why should not he in regal honor sit,
> That best knows how a realm to ordinate?
> (Book 1, Stanza 69, ll. 1–6)

As Isaac Asimov has noted, it is curious that Hal has been missing for three months, haunting the stews of London—the exact passage of time since Richard was deposed in September 1599. Hal perhaps finds distasteful what his father has done to his cousin, who after all was kind to Hal when Hal's father was in exile.[9] Hal, as Henry V, mentions his concern for Richard on the morning before Agincourt in *Henry V*: "I Richard's body have interred new, / And on it have bestowed more contrite tears / Than from it issued forced drops of blood. / ... More will I do" (4.1.301–03, 308).

The last we see of Richard is as a prisoner at Pomfret Castle in Yorkshire in 1400. He has on his mind intercourse between his father soul and mother brain, the two of them begetting many children thoughts. The better children are "thoughts of things divine," but the inferior ones are religious doubts. These doubts include "It is as hard to come as for a camel / To thread the postern of a small needle's eye," found in Matthew 19:24, Mark 10:25, and Luke 18:25. Richard seems to have been struck by the idea that he was a

36   David George

rich child who had no thought of salvation, and now falls under Christ's stricture that rich persons will have grave difficulty in knowing salvation. But at last Richard desires to be "nothing," not a saved soul or even a damned one. As Edward Dowden asked rhetorically, "Into what glimmering limbo will such a soul as that of Richard pass when the breath leaves the body? The pains of hell and joys of heaven belong to those who have serious hearts. Richard has been a graceful phantom."[10]

Phantom or not, according to Holinshed, but not modern historians, Richard died resisting violently. When a group of men bursts into his cell to murder him, Richard forces the bill-hook out of one murderer's hand and kills him, wishing him in hell. Bolingbroke is glad of Sir Piers Exton's murder of Richard but sends Exton away with only the reward of a guilty conscience. Bolingbroke will assuage his own guilty conscience by a journey to the Holy Land—or so he now thinks!

The lessons of Richard's character are not lost on Bolingbroke. Richard was mercurial, ironical, easily elated and easily depressed. Such could well be the characteristics of an adult whose childhood was insecure, spent among quarreling protectors. To the seventeenth-century mind, that meant a lack of valor. As one writer in 1652 said of a mercurial man, "He speaks too well to be valiant; he is certainly more mercurial than military."[11]

To Richard we owe some of the finest speeches on mortality in all of Shakespeare. Mortality must haunt the mind of a man who has no son and who has no memories of his father. Gaunt calls England "this teeming womb of royal kings" (2.1.51); it teemed for Edward III and will again for Henry IV, but Richard is barren. The play has fathers and sons who succeed where Richard fails; York allows his duchess to save their son's life, and Bolingbroke, having usurped the throne, finds his estranged son Hal at last loyal. Shakespeare had tentatively found his thread for the tetralogy; a king is part of a royal line, son and father of kings, and in that way he is harder to remove. Gaunt is the real kingly voice in *Richard II*; he had been effectively king in 1375, and his son Bolingbroke was one of the five appellant lords who ruled England in 1388–89. The isolated Richard cannot begin to match the power of this hegemony, and Gaunt tells him that Edward III would have bypassed him:

> O, had thy grandsire with a prophet's eye
> Seen how his son's son should destroy his sons,
> From forth thy reach he would have laid thy shame,

Sons Without Fathers: Shakespeare's Second Tetralogy 37

> Deposing thee before thou wert possess'd,
> Which art possess'd now to depose thyself.
>
> (2.1.104–08)

The man who supplanted Richard was officially called Henry of Lancaster, surnamed Bolingbroke. He was born in 1367 and therefore an exact contemporary of Richard. Henry was in fact Richard's cousin, but his claim to the throne was not the first after Richard's. That primacy lay with the Mortimers, descended from Edward III's second son, Lionel of Antwerp, by the marriage of Edmund Mortimer to Lionel's daughter Philippa.

Edmund and Philippa were the parents of Elizabeth, or Kate, wife of Harry Hotspur; and of Roger, who married Eleanor Holland, niece to Richard II. In 1385 Richard II named this Roger Mortimer heir presumptive to the throne, but he was killed in Ireland in 1398; his son Edmund was only seven when Bolingbroke usurped the throne. Edmund and his brother Roger remained in custody throughout Henry IV's reign, but their uncle, Sir Edmund Mortimer, would certainly have proclaimed young Edmund king if he could. Sir Edmund's marriage to Owen Glendower's daughter explains why Henry believes Edmund failed to defeat the Welsh.

Henry Bolingbroke lost his father in early 1399, but he was of course a mature man by then. As Shakespeare saw Henry, he was the opposite of his cousin Richard—rooted in family, practical and steadfast, but unfortunately cautious and suspicious, and perhaps cruel. Though Henry was a fruitful king, able to found a dynasty that lasted well into the fifteenth century, Shakespeare considered him a transitional man, mainly a supplanter of Richard and father of Henry V, and gave him therefore a minor role in the latter three plays of the second tetralogy. *1 Henry IV* and *2 Henry IV* are much more concerned with Prince Hal and his surrogate father, Sir John Falstaff.

Shakespeare's two plays on Henry IV are usually dated c. 1596 and c. 1597, and hence followed *Richard II* by at most a year or two. The two plays were highly popular; they were conflated into one by Sir Edward Dering sometime between 1613 and c. 1624, and the Falstaff scenes from Part 1 appeared in Francis Kirkman's *The Wits, or Sport upon Sport*. *Henry V* is dated firmly in 1599.

The Hal we meet in September 1402 in *1 Henry IV* was only fifteen historically, still shaping himself. Holinshed reported that certain of the king's servants claimed that Hal kept an evil rule at his house in London, and that more people came to his house than

38   *David George*

to his father's court. Shakespeare, finding that this portrait of a very young pretender did not quite suit his purpose, consulted John Stow's accounts in *The Chronicles of England* (1580) and *The Annales of England* (1592) for the story of highway robbery, and the anonymous play *The Famous Victories of Henry the Fifth* (c. 1583–86) for Hal's wild youth; hence we must suppose a young man whose teen years are behind him. *The Famous Victories* was printed in 1598, doubtless because of the success of the *Henry IV* plays. It features the prince's fellow roisterer Sir John Oldcastle and a really immature Prince Hal who wishes his father dead, gets drunk and smashes his pot against the tavern wall, and hits the Lord Chief Justice across the cheek. The Sir John Oldcastle of *The Famous Victories* is not old, nor alcoholic, witty, funny, untruthful, fat, or loquacious. Indeed, he has only about 250 words. The tavern has merely "a pretty wench that can talk well" but no Hostess. A.R. Humphreys has suggested that there was a better *Famous Victories* play than the 1598 one, which is at best some kind of memorial reconstruction from the plague years 1592–94. This better, lost original probably had a prominent Oldcastle.[12]

Still, it was Shakespeare who saw that Sir John Oldcastle— Falstaff—must play Prince Hal's surrogate father, and that Henry IV must be portrayed as a distant and distracted figure. This Prince Hal, despite being historically sixteen, must be sufficiently grown up to command the English forces against the rebels at Shrewsbury in 1403. His adversary Henry Percy, called Hotspur, though in reality 39, Shakespeare also made into a very young man, the same age as Hal. As Henry IV says, "Percy ... / being no more in debt to years than thou / Leads ancient lords and reverend bishops on / To bloody battles" (3.2.103–05).

Shakespeare begins with Henry IV "wan with care," and proceeds rapidly to show him ready to lead an English army east to Jerusalem, which he calls by metonymy "the sepulcher of Christ," whose cross was "bitter." However, this gloomy expedition is put off forever by Glendower's victory in Wales and Hotspur's intransigence over the prisoners taken at Holmedon. The second scene of the first act switches at once from Westminster to Eastcheap; Henry will need to look only a mile or two to the East to find his bitter cross. What we find there came as a surprise to W.H. Auden:

> What sort of bad company would one expect to find Prince Hal keeping when the curtain rises on *Henry IV*? Surely, one could expect to see him surrounded by daring, rather sinister juvenile delinquents and beautiful gold-digging whores. But whom do

Sons Without Fathers: Shakespeare's Second Tetralogy   39

we meet in the Boar's Head? A fat, cowardly tosspot, old enough to be his father, two down-at-heel hangers-on, a slatternly hostess and only one whore, who is not in her earliest youth either; all of them seedy, and, by any worldly standards, including those of the criminal classes, all of them *failures*. Surely, one thinks, an Heir Apparent, sowing his wild oats, could have picked himself a more exciting crew than that. As the play proceeds, our surprise is replaced by another kind of puzzle, for the better we come to know Falstaff, the clearer it becomes that the world of historical reality which a Chronicle Play claims to imitate is not a world which he can inhabit.[13]

Falstaff is "old enough to be [Hal's] father." Yet this fatherly companion is seeking work from his "son" and suggesting that Hal award him a judgeship, which Hal reduces to a hangman's post. Thus what we have is an inverted father-son relationship, not the usual relationship whereby the father gets his son a job. We divine that Hal went to the Boar's Head to seek his own version of fatherhood, but found instead an antic reprobate. Such wisdom as Hal has is from the Eastcheap streets; "wisdom cries out in the streets and no man regards it," he remarks, quoting Proverbs 1:20, 24. He has famously in view a "reformation" and, quoting the teasing phrase of Ephesians 5:16, the redeeming of time.

Still, Scripture and the streets are not Hal's only source of self-fashioning. In 1.3, we are introduced to the play's second drinker, Harry Percy, "drunk with choler." His deity is honor, a strange goddess who might live on the moon or be drowned in the ocean. In 2.4, Falstaff identifies Hotspur as "that … mad fellow of the North." Everyone recalls Falstaff's depreciation of honor at the end of 5.1: "What is honor? A word. What is in that word honor? What is that honor? Air." Hal, far more practically, looks upon Hotspur's worship of honor as something akin to the cultivation of a crop. The time to gather honor is at harvest, when a few strokes of the sword will yield handfuls of military prestige. "Percy is but my factor," Hal tells his father, "To engross up glorious deeds on my behalf" (3.2.147–48).

In the same scene (2.4.), Falstaff tries on fatherhood for Hal's benefit, attempting to be the "virtuous man" who might mentor the prince, a man whose fruit might suggest a good tree (Matthew 12:33, Luke 6:44). Hal will have none of this and takes the king's role himself—his own father's role. As Henry IV, Hal identifies Falstaff as a morality play Vice, that "father ruffian … that old white-bearded Satan" and hints that he is carrying Hal away from a state of grace. The style that Hal adopts is at once homiletic and

40   *David George*

colloquial, a style that will serve him well among his soldiers on the night before Agincourt. As the earl of Warwick explains to Henry IV in Part Two, "The prince but studies his companions / Like a strange tongue, wherein, to gain the language, / 'Tis needful that the most immodest word / Be looked upon and learnt" (4.4.68–71). This son-and-father role-playing marks the end of Hal's sonship; he makes Falstaff a captain of foot soldiers, while he himself is appointed to a junior command in the royal army.

Act 3 further explores the themes of fathers and sons. We may recall that Edmund Mortimer lost his father in 1398, when Edmund was only six. Now, in 1402 Edmund is still only ten, but Holinshed, confusing him with his 26-year-old uncle, also conveniently called Edmund, created a Mortimer with a claim to the throne and old enough to command an army. Shakespeare needed a young man of eighteen, just married to his lovely young Welsh bride. The resulting hybrid is another son in search of a father, whom he finds in Owen Glendower. While Hotspur finds Glendower "as tedious / As a tired horse," Mortimer warns Hotspur that Glendower "is a worthy gentleman / Exceedingly well read, and profited / In strange concealments" (3.1.153–54, 159–61). Mortimer was deceived in his confidence in Glendower, however; Glendower's cause sank slowly after 1404, and Mortimer perished miserably in the siege of Harlech Castle in 1409. Glendower stayed away and fought for his own nationalist cause in North Wales. A strange concealment indeed.

The pivotal scene of *1 Henry IV* (3.2) shows Hal as he becomes the true and loyal son of his father the king. In Holinshed Hal did not become reconciled with his father until nine years later, when Hal turned up at Westminster Hall in 1412 in "a gown of blue satin, full of small oilet holes, at every hole the needle hanging by a silk thread with which it was sewed. About his arm he wore a hound's collar set full of SS of gold, and the tirets likewise being of the same metal." Shakespeare moves the reconciliation back so that it will precede the battle of Shrewsbury. Henry begins, quite remarkably, suggesting that God sees father and son as one:

> I know not whether God will have it so
> For some displeasing service I have done,
> That in his secret doom, out of my blood
> He'll breed revengement and a scourge for me.
> But thou dost in thy passages of life
> Make me believe that thou art only mark'd

Sons Without Fathers: Shakespeare's Second Tetralogy   41

> For the hot vengeance and the rod of heaven
> To punish my mistreadings.
>
> (3.2.4–11)

At first we think that Henry believes Hal is the target of the hot vengeance and the rod of heaven, but then he adds "to punish *my* mistreadings." On whom will "the hot vengeance and the rod of heaven" fall? The answer is ambiguous: Hal is both a direct scourge to his father and also the one on whom the rod of correction will fall. Though both whippings punish Henry, father and son are alike under God's judgment. Henry then invites Hal to contemplate a vision of remote and reverend kingship, first holding up for contrast the vulgar Richard II, a ready companion of base characters; to which Hal responds, "I shall hereafter, my thrice gracious lord, / Be more myself" (3.2.92–93). To be himself means becoming like his father, becoming even more than his father—a royal warrior-saint. To effect this transformation, Hal will "wear a garment all of blood, / And stain my favors in a bloody mask, / Which, washed away, shall scour my shame with it" (3.2.135–37). This is indeed repentance and new life; Hal's sins will be covered with blood, which washed away, will take all shameful stain from his character. Yet the blood and the washing here are equivocations; they are human, not Christian.

The very next scene (3.3) opens with the dwindling of Falstaff, "withered like an old apple-john," and his intention to repent. The juxtaposition of Hal's repentance and Falstaff's dwindling is not accidental; Hal has now moved beyond his antic father, as he will move beyond his real father and on to self-fatherhood.

By contrast, 4.1 reveals to us a Hotspur at Shrewsbury deprived of his father Northumberland's army, "a perilous gash, a very limb lopped off." True to his worship of honor, a few moments later Hotspur is chopping logic: "I rather of his absence make this use: / It lends a luster and more great opinion, / A larger dare to our great enterprise" (4.1.76–78). Sir Richard Vernon, however, soon comes with news of the king and his son's armies, which outnumber the rebel forces two to one, a neat way of expressing the power of a father and son over a son without a father. 5.4 completes Hal's self-fashioning as a father. As the Scot, Douglas, comes close to killing the king, Hal intervenes and saves his life. Henry comments, "Thou hast redeemed thy lost opinion"; and then Hal adds to his name all of Hotspur's honors. Like Falstaff in 3.3, Hotspur shrinks, to "two paces of the vilest earth" (5.4.90).

42   *David George*

Both Richard and Hal are dangerously isolated, yet while Richard does not know that orphanhood is first kin to self-absorption, Hal goes in search of a father; finding his own father compromised by his usurpation, Hal must become his own man. To do so, he finds he will need the twin bases of warrior and saint.

2 Henry IV seems a planned sequel to Part One, and Samuel Johnson considered them "so connected that the second is merely a sequel to the first; ... two only because they are too long to be one." A.R. Humphreys points to five clues in Part One that adumbrate Part Two: (1) Hal's soliloquy at the end of 1.2 about casting off the clouds and shining forth like the sun; (2) Hal's promise in 2.4 to banish plump Jack; (3) the Archbishop of York in 4.4 writing to Scroop and Mowbray about further rebellion; (4) King Henry in 5.5 sending Westmorland and Prince John to deal with Northumberland and the prelate Scroop, and the King and Hal preparing to deal with Glendower; (5) Falstaff looking for promotion at Hal's hands after he has, at least by his own account, killed Hotspur. Perhaps, as Harold Jenkins has suggested, Shakespeare started out trying to get everything into one play, but discovered by act three of Part One that Henry IV's death, Hal's coronation, and Falstaff's rejection would require another play.[14]

Still, this raises the question of why Hal needs to be redeemed again in Part Two after his brilliant showing at Shrewsbury. Harold Jenkins believes Hal's second reformation is really a version of the first. For those who had missed Part One, the action starts again with the unredeemed prince; however, the redemptions take two forms, one a military reformation in Part One, and the other a character reformation in Part Two. A.R. Humphreys counters Jenkins' argument that Part Two came into being as an overflow play by pointing out that Part One never really had any chance of reaching Henry IV's death and its aftermath, no matter how compressed Shakespeare could have made it. So, Part Two may stand as a whole play by conception and also partially a reprise of Part One.[15]

In *1 Henry IV*, Hal dispenses with two fathers; one more father must appear on the scene to make Hal the kind of king who will be a father to his people. He still lacks the gravity and justice that will make him an able ruler, and to this end Shakespeare has built up the character of the Lord Chief Justice from only slight hints in Holinshed.

2 Henry IV opens after Shrewsbury and covers the campaign of 1405 (the betrayal of the Archbishop of York's army at Gaultree

Sons Without Fathers: Shakespeare's Second Tetralogy   43

Forest); the death of Northumberland in 1408; the death of Glendower in 1409 (see 3.1.103, where he is said to be dead before the action at Gaultree Forest; in actuality he died in 1415); the death of King Henry and Hal's accession in 1413. As Part Two opens, Northumberland, learning his son is dead, bursts into an appeal for the subversion of all order: "Let one spirit of the first-born Cain / Reign in all bosoms!" No longer a father, Northumberland calls on all brothers to murder their brothers until "darkness be the burier of the dead!" (1.1.157–60). Historically, Northumberland's loss of Hotspur left him without any sons, his two other sons Sir Thomas and Sir Ralph Percy having died earlier. Northumberland made his peace with the king by swearing an oath of fealty before Parliament in 1404. After all, Hotspur was 39 when he died, scarcely a youth. Yet Shakespeare chose to show the old earl as utterly bereft and vengeful after the news from Shrewsbury, and this seems dramatically the right psychological perception, given that Shakespeare had made Hotspur a youth about sixteen years old.

In the second scene of the first act, Shakespeare deals with Falstaff's impudence to the Lord Chief Justice, the man of civil authority who sounds the theme of what is to come in this play: "There is not a white hair in your face but should have his effect of gravity" (1.2.159–60). Without Hal to cover for him, Falstaff is soon facing arrest for failing to pay a hundred marks to Mistress Quickly, and must again face the gravity of the Lord Chief Justice (2.1). "You speak," he tells Falstaff, "as having power to do wrong; but answer in the effect of your reputation, and satisfy the poor woman" (128–30).

During the third scene, the dramatist deals with Hal's second repudiation of the Eastcheap group. He wonders whether Poins's bastard children will inherit God's kingdom, but the midwives say the babies are not at fault for their bastardy. Hal perhaps thinks of Ephesians 5, where Paul explains "that no whoremonger, neither unclean person, nor covetous person ... hath any inheritance in the kingdom of Christ or God.... Be not therefore companions with them" (5, 7). Falstaff's page soon identifies the Eastcheap crowd as "Ephesians ... of the old church," another allusion to Ephesians 5, the unregenerate Ephesians who indulged in wine-bibbing. Hal has more melancholy religious thoughts: "Thou thinkest me as far in the devil's book as thou and Falstaff, for obduracy and persistency. Let the end try the man" (2.2.43–45). Poins does not believe that the Prince can weep for his father's sickness; he thinks his tears are hypocrisy because "you have been so lewd, and so much

44   *David George*

engraffed to Falstaff" (58–59). As events turn out, however, Hal is capable of a full and feeling sorrow for his father's final illness.

The third scene takes the reader to Northumberland's castle, where Hotspur's wife Kate tells him that his intended rebellion against the king comes too late: "The time was, father, that you broke your word" to Hotspur. Northumberland's wife advises him to flee to Scotland and let the rebels take the same risk as Hotspur was forced to take. Northumberland thus passes up the opportunity to avenge his son, and meets an absurd offstage fate at Bramham Moor in Yorkshire, defeated and killed by "the shrieve of Yorkshire" (4.4.99). Twice Northumberland has failed to be Hotspur's father, each time through an unmanly combination of sickness, fear, and vacillation. If only Northumberland could have seen the recruiting in Gloucestershire in 3.2, he might have thought twice about fleeing to Scotland. Falstaff's recruits are very similar to the men he led at Shrewsbury in Part One.

In scene one of the fourth act, Shakespeare returns to the subject of sonship. Prince John of Lancaster (born 1389), was a mere sixteen-year-old at Gaultree Forest, but he was under the wing of the able Ralph Neville, earl of Westmorland. Westmorland was married to a daughter of John of Gaunt, and she was therefore the prince's aunt. Westmorland, a man of 41, ably tutors young Prince John in the use of military guile, as the episode at Gaultree shows well. Yet John is a quick study. Their opponents, the rebel Archbishop of York (Richard Scrope), and Thomas Mowbray II, son of the Thomas Mowbray exiled in *Richard II*, were in a similar kind of relationship. Mowbray was a mere 19-year-old, but his mentor in rebellion, Scrope, was 55. He strongly resisted the spoliation of the church by the "unlearned parliament" of 1404, but in the play, his reasons for rebelling are muted by a corrupt text at 4.1.93–96. He foolishly puts his "general grievances" on a sheet of parchment. Mowbray is at Gaultree because he believes that Richard II loved Mowbray's father and "was force perforce compelled to banish him." He further believes that Bolingbroke has been the source of the misfortunes in "all their lives / That by indictment and by dint of sword / Have since miscarried under Bolingbroke" (4.1.116, 127–29).

Shakespeare has here presented us with a youth betrayed by the sentimental judgment of an old man, and another youth shown the false advantages of military deception. Since Scrope and Mowbray have the larger forces, Westmorland is fairly certain to lose if he and the prince give battle. Prince John's hypocritical deference

Sons Without Fathers: Shakespeare's Second Tetralogy   45

to the Archbishop is shocking; we imagined, he says, you were "the voice of God himself," but now we find that you have abused God's substitute, Henry IV, by recruiting his subjects as soldiers. To unpack this casuistry, we must note how John first gives the Archbishop the role of God's surrogate, and then conveys it by sleight of hand to the king because only a peacemaker can have God's role. The Archbishop protests that "I am not here against your father's peace" (4.2.31). In good faith the Archbishop and Mowbray disperse their troops and are promptly arrested, which makes all the prince's talk of God absolutely disgusting. To rinse the bad taste of this deception out of our mouths, Shakespeare offers a comic version of it in 4.3., where Falstaff intimidates without much effort Sir John Coleville of the Dale, "a most furious knight and valorous enemy," or at least Falstaff claims he is.

As Henry IV approaches his death, Shakespeare writes the wonderful scene in which Hal tries on his father's crown, while talking of "tears and heavy sorrows of the blood, / Which nature, love, and filial tenderness / Shall, O dear father, pay thee plenteously" (4.5.37–39). The King, waking, calls for his other sons and misses the crown, feeling he has been murdered. The incident leaves "a bitter taste" in his mouth. This bitterness finds expression in accusing Hal of intending to introduce vanity, "apes of idleness," scum, and ruffians to the royal court as soon as he is crowned. Hal replies that he tried on the crown out of filial piety, "To try with it, as with an enemy / That had before my face murdered my father / The quarrel of a true inheritor" (4.5.166–68). Just as the king, as young Bolingbroke, acted as Gloucester's son might have done to avenge his murder, so now Hal acts in revenge against his father's enemy, Care. Henry approves of this, telling Hal to take the crown again, "That thou mightst win the more thy father's love" (4.5.179). Then the King gives the well-known advice to wage foreign wars in order to distract giddy English baronial minds. Henry has in mind the conquest of Jerusalem, but that goal is won only ironically when he dies in the Jerusalem chamber in Westminster Abbey.

There follows in the second scene the coronation procession, preceded by gloomy talk by Warwick and the Lord Chief Justice. Yet Hal, now Henry V, assures the troubled Justice and princes that "I'll be your father and your brother too" (5.2.57). Superficially, this means he will be to them like the old king and also like a new king. Yet the promise of fatherhood and brotherhood in one king will be fulfilled amply. The model will be the Justice himself.

46   *David George*

When Hal teases him with hints of revenge for jailing him after he struck the Justice, the Justice enters a serious defense: "I then did use the person of your father; / The image of his power lay then in me" (5.2.73–74). In striking the Lord Chief Justice, Hal struck his father, one of the most terrible sins in the Old Testament. As Exodus 21:15 says, "He that smiteth his father or his mother, shal dye the death." The Justice adds that if he did wrong, is Hal now contented "to have a son set your decrees at naught?" Hal's response is to speak his father's words, "Happy am I, that have a man so bold / That dares do justice on my proper son" (5.2.107–09). He then appoints the Justice "as a father to my youth." His own affections have gone with his father into the grave; and as compensation, his spirits survive soberly in Hal.

All this bodes ill for that white-bearded Satan, Falstaff. In his last scene at Shallow's house in Gloucestershire, he learns of Hal's coronation and bestows a lordship on Shallow, with more honors to come for Bardolph and Pistol. Falstaff will, of course, destroy the Lord Chief Justice. But the old father of lies must suffer retribution in the streets of Westminster. Hal delivers it in a 24-line speech of rejection and warning, with a monetary consolation. However, Falstaff and the Eastcheap group must first go to Purgatory in the Fleet prison, "till their conversations / Appear more wise and modest to the world" (5.5.100–01). As for Henry V, he will do what his father advised: make foreign wars "as far as France."

In the two parts of *Henry IV*, Shakespeare took up the theme of fathers and sons he had tentatively explored in *Richard II*. Hal moves through two fathers and at last settles on the grave Justice. As other fathers prove weak and unreliable, the careers of their sons Hotspur, Mowbray, and Prince John end or fade away.

As our focus turns to *Henry V*, we remember that one of the ironies of Henry IV's usurpation is that his son Henry had been taken under Richard's care in 1398 when Bolingbroke was exiled. Though Richard treated the 11-year-old boy well, Bolingbroke never mentions it. This and his many other failures are remedied when Hal becomes king, and some ecclesiastical writers alleged that he thereupon changed into another man entirely. His brief reign (1413–22) was England's most glorious from the point of view of medieval chivalry and arms, and his marriage to Catherine, the French princess, in 1420, the most powerful dynastic marriage Europe had ever seen. Shakespeare begins *Henry V* in 1415, the year of Agincourt, and ends his play in Hal's *annus mirabilis*

Sons Without Fathers: Shakespeare's Second Tetralogy   47

1420, leaving his last two years to any memories the audience had of his death in France and his wish to rebuild the walls of Jerusalem. Though covering only six years, the play encompasses epic materials; Samuel Daniel wrote in his *Civil Wars*: "What everlasting matter here is found, / Whence new immortal Iliads might proceed!" (Book 5, Stanza 5, ll. 1–2).

Henry, we recall, has undergone two reformations—at Shrewsbury and in the Jerusalem chamber—and at his father's death he evidently experienced an interchange of spirits with his father. Early in *Henry V*, the Archbishop of Canterbury returns to this deathbed scene and the mutual transmigration of father and son's spirit:

> The breath no sooner left his father's body,
> But that his wildness, mortified in him,
> Seem'd to die too; yea, at that very moment,
> Consideration like an angel came,
> And whipped the offending Adam out of him,
> Leaving his body as a paradise,
> T'envelop and contain celestial spirits.
> Never was such a sudden scholar made,
> Never came reformation in a flood,
> With such a heady currance, scouring faults.
> (1.1.25–34)

As J.H. Walter says, "this deftly intricate passage is based mainly on the Baptismal Service from the Book of Common Prayer"[16]; these quotations from the 1560 edition (rearranged to follow Shakespeare's order) show the parallels:

3   And humbly we beseech thee to graunt, that he being dead unto sin, and living unto righteousness, and being buried with Christ in his death, maye crucifye the olde man, and utterlye abolyshe the whole bodye of sinne.
1   Graunt that the olde Adam in this child may be so buryed, that the new man may be raised up in him.
2   Graunt that all carnall affections maye dye in him, and that all thynges belonginge to the Spirite may lyve and growe in him.

Hal had experienced some kind of conversion in 2.1 of *2 Henry IV*, but it was not as deep or permanent as the one he experienced in 5.2 of that play. Indeed, the Archbishop's account implies that Henry went to him and told him what had happened. The *Vita et Gesta Henrici Quinti*, written about 1550, reveals how Henry went secretly to a man of perfect life at Westminster and received

48   *David George*

absolution. Now it will be noticed that the present passage is managed without reference to Christ. The wildness mortified in Henry is buried with his father, not with Christ; the old Adam is not buried but whipped out of Henry by "Consideration," not spiritual regeneration; "reformation" just simply "came ... in a flood," whereas in the Book of Common Prayer "Jesus Christ in the River Jordan didst sanctifie Water to the mystical washing away of sin."

Though Shakespeare was almost certainly hinting that Henry was a completely regenerated man, he knew that Henry's destiny would be to conquer France, not conquer souls. Therefore Shakespeare has taken from the baptismal service what he needed but thoroughly sanitized it against any potential taint of blasphemy. The meaning of "consideration" is "intense spiritual contemplation and self-examination." Thus half the work of Henry's conversion is accomplished by the dead Henry IV, and the other half of the work by the living Henry V with the help of angel-like force. The implication is that Henry could easily be a prelate, a reverend father; and thus in finding cause for war with France, he is naturally guided by the Archbishop of Canterbury.

In order to contest the throne of France, Henry must show that his claim is better than that of Charles VI, the current French king. Henry's claim is based on his descent from the French king Philip IV (1268–1314) through his daughter Isabella, who married Edward II of England; and Edward II was Henry V's great-great-grandfather. Edward II's son Edward III was in line for the French throne when the French assembly declared in 1328 that "no woman, nor therefore her son, could in accordance with custom succeed to the monarchy of France." This was to prevent the daughters of Charles IV (1294–1328) from succeeding to the throne, and Philip VI of Valois inherited it instead. Yet "where Philip VI was grandson of Philip III, Edward III was grandson of Philip IV, a later king."[17] Philip of Valois' ascent to the throne angered Edward III and sparked off the Hundred Years' War (1337–1453). The French king in *Henry V* is Charles VI, who ascended the throne in 1380 at the age of 12, but he had been brain-damaged since 1392 when a fever set off seizures. Consequently the relationship between the royal father and his son Louis the Dauphin was virtually nonexistent. So, when in 1413–14 Paris was wracked by civil strife, Henry V saw his chance of conquering France. Only Louis stands in Henry's way, and Agincourt destroys him—he

Sons Without Fathers: Shakespeare's Second Tetralogy 49

died in 1415 two months after the battle, perhaps not more than 28 years of age.

By act 2, scene 1, Shakespeare brings in a newer crowd of Eastcheap disreputables, but they have no connection with Henry. Poins and Peto seem to have vanished; we have met Bardolph and Pistol before, but not Corporal Nym. These three useless military men prepare us for the three traitors who appear in the second scene, Richard Langley, earl of Cambridge; Sir Thomas Grey; and Henry Lord Scroop of Masham. Langley was married to Anne Mortimer, younger sister of Edmund Mortimer, imprisoned throughout Henry IV's reign, and next in line to the throne if Henry V died. Langley's grandson Edward eventually seized the throne from Henry's son. Scroop was nephew to the Archbishop of York executed in *2 Henry IV*. The three traitors find themselves involved in a version of the parable of the unjust servant in Matthew 19:23–35. This servant owes a great debt to his king, who forgives him the debt; but when he meets a debtor who owes him a small debt a little later, he throws him in jail. When the king discovers this fact, the unjust servant suffers the same fate. Shakespeare uses the tale in reverse; the three traitors condemn a man who railed against Henry, probably a drunk. Henry frees the man, and then levels against the three traitors the charge of conspiring to assassinate him. They appeal for mercy, but of course are denied as unmerciful men themselves.

Shakespeare disposes of the cast-off Falstaff in the third scene, appropriately in a London tavern. Like Lazarus in the parable of Dives and Lazarus, Falstaff has ascended into Abraham's bosom, or at least the Hostess thinks so, if we charitably allow "Arthur's bosom" to be in heaven and not in Avalon.

The fourth scene of the second act transfers us to France, where Charles VI is busy putting the French resistance in the hands of Charles of Orleans, his nephew, aged 21, and therefore necessarily an incompetent general. King Charles orders his son the Dauphin "to line and new-repair our towns of war / With men of courage and with means defendant" (2.4.7–8). The Dauphin decides he knows better, and that a general survey of "the sick and feeble parts of France" is in order. The preparations of King and Dauphin are apparently not satisfactory, for in the next act we watch the English take Harfleur.

Henry's famous speech of encouragement, apart from calling on his men to imitate the tiger, is an appeal to recall the fierce blood they have inherited. Their fathers, "like so many Alexan-

50   David George

ders, / Have in these parts from morn till even fought, / And sheathed their swords for lack of argument" (3.1.19–21). These sons can now prove that their fathers really were their fathers, that their mothers did not deceive them. Nym, Bardolph, and Pistol, however, are quite unable to prove their fathers were men; their boy decides that all three combined would not amount to one manservant of his, and so he will leave them. We meet this boy one more time in 4.4, where it appears he can speak French. He was originally the tiny fellow we met following Falstaff in *2 Henry IV*, now in 1415 some ten years older. It must have been Falstaff who saw to it the boy learned French.

Harfleur surrenders, as it did historically in late September 1415, after a siege of five weeks, without the bloody atrocities promised by Henry at 3.3.10–43. The march to Calais that followed in October was dreadful, a rain-soaked affair that made dysentery inevitable. Henry's greatest achievement was to march up the Somme some 54 miles and ford it there while the French army was elsewhere. The French finally caught up with the English at a bridge over the Ternoise some 40 or 50 miles from Calais. The English take that bridge in 3.6, and confront a superior French force at Agincourt, a village perhaps 40 miles from Calais. The Dauphin and the duke of Orleans, both in their twenties, spend the night of October 24, the night before the battle, discussing horses.

Henry, on the other hand, is moving among his men in disguise. For Bates, Court, and Williams, the matter of a good conscience is urgent since death seems imminent, and they think that good conscience is the responsibility of the king. Williams claims that "If these men do not die well, it will be a black matter for the king that led them to it" (4.1.146–48). Henry likens this claim to a son, who, sent by his father on overseas business, miscarries sinfully; the father is not responsible for the state of the son's soul at death since he did not know his son would die. Henry sums it all up with a version of Matthew 16:25: "where they feared the death they have borne life away, and where they would be safe they perish" (4.1.177–79): "For whosoever will save his life shall lose it; and whosoever shall lose his life for my sake shall find it." In short, it is up to a soldier to be prepared for the destination of his soul if he chances to die in battle. Such preparation is best done in the hours before the battle, and should a man survive, "it were not sin to think that, making God so free an offer, he let him outlive that day to see his greatness, and to teach others how they should prepare" (4.1.189–92). Thus Henry acts as his men's spiritual father

Sons Without Fathers: Shakespeare's Second Tetralogy 51

in the dark night before the dawn of Saint Crispin's day, assuring them that their salvation lies in their own hands: "every subject's soul is his own."

Alone, Henry must seek his own peace with God. God could use this day to even scores with Henry IV, and so Henry finds it essential to assure God that everything has been done to make reparation for Richard II's murder:

> Not today, O Lord!
> O not today, think not upon the fault
> My father made in compassing the crown!
> I Richard's body have interred new,
> And on it have bestowed more contrite tears
> Than from it issued forced drops of blood.
> (4.2.298–303)

Yet Henry is aware, like Claudius in *Hamlet*, that his penitence comes after all the gains of kingship, and that Richard's death is the foundation of his present ascendancy.

The early morning before the battle of Agincourt is the setting for the next scene; it is the feast of Saint Crispin and Saint Crispinian. Henry predicts that their feast day will acquire further significance as a day of victory for the English, and in fact it did. In England and Scotland the day was later celebrated both as the saints' feast day and as the anniversary of Agincourt; "the symbolical processions in honour of 'King Crispin' at Stirling and Edinburgh were particularly famous."[18] Thus Henry did in fact earn his saint's day because as he predicts, good fathers taught the battle of Agincourt to their sons.

In the fifth scene of the fourth act, the dramatist shows the destruction of the French army, which numbered about 30,000 to only 6,000 English troops. The slaughter was terrible, and Shakespeare could not or would not show it. The French lost 5,000 of noble birth killed, including the Constable of France, three dukes, five counts, and ninety barons; about a third of the French army perished. A thousand more were taken prisoner, among them Charles, duke of Orleans. The English lost only thirteen men-at-arms, including the duke of York, Edward III's grandson, and about a hundred foot soldiers. In all, modern historians estimate that English losses were fewer than 450. Hall and Holinshed, Shakespeare's sources, gave higher estimates. The French toll was increased because French prisoners' throats were cut in retaliation for the killing of the boys guarding the English baggage. Henry

52   *David George*

commands all the glory to be given to God by having his chaplains sing "Non nobis, Domine," and "Te Deum."

Shakespeare now begins to skip over periods as long as two years: 5.1 is two years after Agincourt, when Henry again mounted an invasion of France. The time was ripe since the Burgundians were besieging Paris, and Henry conquered a good deal of Normandy between July 1417 and March 1418. Act 5, scene 2, is set in 1420, by which time the French had suffered more losses. Paris fell to the English when the Burgundians abandoned it in 1419. At Troyes in the Champagne district, Henry met with the Burgundians to make a peace treaty, and the duke of Burgundy, Philip the Good, was more than willing to see Henry crowned king of France rather than the young Dauphin. Essential to Henry's designs on the throne of France is Katherine, the 19-year-old daughter of Charles VI of France. If her brother the Dauphin can be disinherited and if the Salic law can be set aside, Katherine's son will be the next French king. Of course, Henry wishes to be the father of that son: "Shall not thou and I, between Saint Denis and Saint George, compound a boy, half French, half English, that shall go to Constantinople and take the Turk by the beard? Shall we not? What sayest thou, my fair flower-de-luce?" (5.1.215–20). Crowning Henry's son as king of France and England entails disinheriting the Dauphin, which was done in 1420.

The son that Katherine gave to Henry was born in 1421, and lost his father before he was a year old. We have now come full cycle; here are the exact conditions which made Richard II such a mercurial king: a father victorious in France who left the son semi-orphaned, a lengthy period of rule by an aristocratic council during the boy-king's minority. The weaknesses of Henry VI's rule Shakespeare had already shown in his first tetralogy: the loss of France and the civil war in England that this fatherless and gentle child brought on. At the age of 50, Henry VI was murdered, perhaps by Richard of Gloucester, and Edward IV came to power.

Primarily *Henry V* is an epic play, but it is also the working out of the policy of Henry IV, who taught his son how to crush strong forces by speed and perseverance. The play also turns on a minor contrast with Charles VI of France, who allows his 28-year-old son to act like a boy with his first horse, or in today's terms, with his first car. The Dauphin is Henry's exact contemporary; Henry was 28 when he won Agincourt. His victory is the culmination, Shakespeare hints, of a tough seasoning in battle since Shrewsbury in 1403, and of a spiritual conversion upon his father's death in 1413.

Sons Without Fathers: Shakespeare's Second Tetralogy 53

William Butler Yeats did not care for Henry V, calling him a "vessel of clay," "the reverse of all that Richard [II] was," "that vessel of porcelain." Yeats, however, subscribed to a theory that one's life story is plotted in advance by some divine being.[19] Yet I think that the final impression Shakespeare's second tetralogy makes on us is what kingship does to character. Richard II is arbitrary, and therefore weak, and political nature abhors a vacuum. He does not know what to do when his back is to the wall except invent roles he might play, and so he is easily dispossessed by a resolute man. This father of this Bolingbroke, John of Gaunt, is shown to be a solid, dependable man who at the end is elevated into a secular prophet.

When Harry Hotspur attempts to do to Henry IV what Henry did to Richard, he fails. Behind him stands a vacillating father who on the day of battle fails to appear. His adversary, Prince Hal, has behind him a ruthless and cunning father, whose abilities Hal seeks to inherit but whose paternal performance he seeks to replace.

In the final play of the tetralogy, Henry V faces a French prince who exhibits all the weaknesses of a fatherless son even though his father sits on the throne. The outcome is Henry's most glorious year, 1420, and the peak of England's power for 450 years. Thus the grand sweep of these four plays presents us with a small gallery of sons whose fathers are absent or failing in one way or another, and with an heroic king who finds at the last that he must be his own man, his own father, so to speak, and the father of his people. Richard II became a byword for a pitiful and wronged king; Henry IV faded into the shadows; but Henry V remained at once England's saint and hero.[20]

Notes

1. Vol. 15, 846.
2. Goodman and Gillespie, 28.
3. *The Dictionary of National Biography*, vol. 16:1039.
4. *King Richard II*, lxix.
5. Berger, 80.
6. Berger, 87.
7. Berger comments at length on Richard's self-comparison with Faustus in 4.1, concluding that Richard's "Faustian subtext not only differs from its model, it subverts it, for Faustus wants to defer or evade the

54   *David George*

torments of the fiend while Richard's language vertiginously tempts them" (66).

8. Sharon Seelig devotes several pages of her "Loyal Fathers and Treacherous Sons" to York and his duchess' conflict over Aumerle (350–52). She notes that while the duchess designates Aumerle as "my son," "York calls his son 'boy' or simply addresses him without name or title" (350).

9. Asimov, 2, 310.

10. *Shakespeare: A Critical Study of His Mind and Art*, in Forker, 252.

11. OED, "Mercurial," 3.

12. Humphreys, ed., *The First Part of King Henry IV*, xxxiv–xxxvi.

13. "The Prince's Dog," *The Dyer's Hand and Other Essays*, 183.

14. Humphreys, ed., *The Second Part of King Henry IV*, xxii–xxviii.

15. Ibid., xxvi–xxviii.

16. *King Henry V*, xviii.

17. Asimov, 2, 459.

18. "Agincourt." *Encyclopaedia Britannica*.

19. In *Twentieth-Century Interpretations of Henry V*, ed. Ronald Berman, 97.

20. For an equivocal opinion of Henry's achievement, see Katharine Eisaman Maus, "Henry V," *The Norton Shakespeare: Histories*, 717–24. "As the stature of Henry's foes and associates diminishes, the ethical problems posed by his exploits are correspondingly aggravated" (722).

Works Cited

"Agincourt." *Encyclopaedia Britannica*, 11th ed.

Asimov, Isaac. *Asimov's Guide to Shakespeare*. 2 vols. New York: Avenel, 1970.

Auden, W.H. "The Prince's Dog." In *The Dyer's Hand and Other Essays*. New York: Random House, 1962.

Berger, Harry, Jr. *Imaginary Audition*. Berkeley: U of California P, 1989.

Berman, Ronald, ed. *Twentieth-Century Interpretations of Henry V*. Englewood Cliffs, NJ: Prentice-Hall, 1968.

Daniel, Samuel. *The First Fowre Bookes of the Civile Wars (1595)*. In *The Complete Works in Verse and Prose of Samuel Daniel*, vol. 2, ed. Alexander B. Grosart. 5 vols. London, 1885; reprint New York: Russell and Russell, 1963.

The Dictionary of National Biography. London: Oxford UP, 1937–38, 1967–68.

Forker, Charles, ed. *Richard II: The Critical Tradition*. London: Athlone, 1998.

Sons Without Fathers: Shakespeare's Second Tetralogy 55

Goodman, Anthony, and James Gillespie. *Richard II: The Art of Kingship.* Oxford: Clarendon P, 1999.

Greenblatt, Stephen, et al., eds. *The Norton Shakespeare: Histories.* New York: Norton, 1997.

Holinshed, Raphael. *Holinshed's Chronicles: England, Scotland, and Ireland.* 5 vols. London: Johnson, 1807.

Seelig, Sharon Cadman. "Loyal Fathers and Treacherous Sons: Familial Politics in *Richard II.*" *Journal of English and Germanic Philology* 94:3 (July 1995): 347–64.

Shakespeare, William. *The First Part of King Henry IV*, ed. A.R. Humphreys. London: Methuen, 1960.

———. *King Henry V*, ed. John H. Walter. London: Methuen, 1967.

———. *King Richard II*, ed. Peter Ure. London: Methuen, 1966.

———. *The Second Part of King Henry IV*, ed. A.R. Humphreys. London: Methuen, 1966.

Dear Expedience: The Imagery of Shakespeare's Henry IV Tetralogy[1]

John Rumrich

> Take hede therefore that ye walke circumspectly, not as fooles but as wise, redeeming the time: for the days are evil.
>
> (*Ephesians* 5:15–16)[2]

The historical distance between *Richard II* and *Henry V* has been theorized and debated at length, but the pertinence of the tetralogy's imagery to such discussions is rarely considered.[3] Scholars would profit from attending to the imagery of these plays, however, because it concerns ways in which human beings cover ground and thereby indicates, more articulately than might be expected, how England went from the realm of Richard II to that of Henry V.[4] Admittedly, such an account is limited to the linguistic practice of the characters of the drama, or in Harry Berger's formulation: "to ... the characterizing work done by clusters of images, topics, and tropes that twist and twine like rhizomes through the language of the play's speech community."[5] Yet it is difficult to see how literary critics can assess Shakespeare's representations of history without the foundation of such "characterizing work."

The plays build upon images of walking—feet hitting the ground one at a time to get from one place to another. Such imagery begins in *Richard II* and proliferates so extensively in the course of the tetralogy that it becomes fundamental to its dramatic idiom. Mowbray, for example, declares that he would accept any challenge to prove his loyalty and Bolingbroke's treachery: "were I tied to run afoot / ... / Where ever Englishman durst set his foot" (1.1.63–66). Both he and Bolingbroke are indeed sent abroad, but in exile, which Bolingbroke describes as "an enforced pilgrimage," a "sullen passage of ... weary steps" and "tedious stride[s]" (1.3.264–68). This is the first walk in Bolingbroke's history that fails to go according to plan, and it establishes the figure of ironic pil-

58   *John Rumrich*

grimage that characterizes the passage of his "banish'd and forbidden legs"—along "by-paths and indirect crook'd ways"—to the throne and beyond (*Richard II* 2.3.90; *2 Henry IV* 4.5.184). Once he "steps me a little higher than his vow" and seizes the crown, the crowds who had followed at his "admired heels" become cynical rebels "baying him at the heels" (*1 Henry IV* 4.3.75; *2 Henry IV* 1.3.105, 80). Eventually hounded by those rebels to his death, he still conforms to the trope, having "walk'd the way of nature" (*2 Henry IV* 5.2.4). In *Richard II*, however, despite Richard's claim that Bolingbroke's "every stride" on English soil is "dangerous treason," the danger is to Richard himself, even according to his musing that his "subjects' feet" will, once he is dead and buried, "hourly trample on their sovereign's head" (3.3.92–93, 156–57).

The idea of walking in these plays inevitably includes characterization of the territory that supports the walkers on their way—most famously, "this blessed plot, this earth, this realm, this England" (*Richard II* 2.1.50). Richard, despite his disdain for his native soil—"are we not high?" (3.2.87)—can also speak appreciatively of what he sometimes reviles:

> I weep for joy
> To stand upon my kingdom once again.
> Dear earth, I do salute thee with my hand,
> Though rebels wound thee with their horses' hoofs.
> . . . .
> [Do] annoyance to the treacherous feet,
> Which with usurping steps do trample thee.
>   (3.2.4–17)

Richard's encouragement of the earth as if it were an ally is supplemented by Carlisle's prophecy that if the legitimate king is uprooted and Henry crowned in his place,

> The blood of English shall manure the ground,
> And future ages groan for this foul act.
> Peace shall go sleep with Turks and infidels,
> And in this seat of peace tumultuous wars
> Shall kin with kin and kind with kind confound.
>   (4.1.138–42)

According to Carlisle, Richard's land is set to become "the field of Golgotha" (4.1.145), a site of sacrificial death that will see an end to so noble a man as Hotspur, who "had no legs that practiced not his gait," "walk'd o'er perils, on an edge," but unlike Bolingbroke

Dear Expedience ... 59

never managed "to tread on Kings" (*2 Henry IV* 2.3.23, 1.1.170; *1 Henry IV* 5.2.85). As it turns out, then, Richard's belief that "this earth shall have a feeling, and *these stones/Prove armed soldiers*" is not merely a compounded Ovidian fancy (*Richard II* 3.2.24–25; italics added). His deposition and murder induce the birth of strife prophesied by Carlisle. When we recall these plays' persistent identification of the earth as the mother and grave of soldiers, moreover, Richard's lament over wounds in the earth should call more than horseshoed hoof prints to our minds, especially at those astonishing moments when symbolic associations fuse with bloody reality: after Shrewsbury, for example, "many a nobleman lies stark and stiff/ Under the hoofs of vaunting enemies" (*1 Henry IV* 5.3.41–42); and after Agincourt, "wounded steeds/Fret fetlock deep in gore ... with wild rage/Yerk out their armed heels at their dead masters,/Killing them twice" (*Henry V* 4.7.78–81).

Classically, equestrian imagery, even more than walking imagery, suits a plot that turns on a contest for sovereignty over a kingdom.[6] Northumberland's description of civil insurrection as a riderless horse that "madly hath broke loose, / And bears down all before him" reflects the long philosophical tradition comparing horsemanship to government of either the individual or the state (*2 Henry IV* 1.1.10–11). The association of horsemanship with government derives from Plato's famous comparison of the soul to a chariot drawn by winged horses, an allegory that by Shakespeare's time had been translated into terms of walking imagery.[7] As John Freccero has amply demonstrated, "the association of the feet of the body with the wings of the soul" was a commonplace of Christian Neoplatonism.[8] The punitive translation of England into a war-torn, post-crucifixion Holy Land, however, involves more than Neoplatonic expression of divine-right typology.

In Shakespeare's time, and for centuries before and after, it was by "processioning," often and fittingly corrupted to "possessioning," that the extent and ownership of a community's land was marked. The official sermon for rogationtide, based on the verses that serve as epigraph to this section, insisted on a lesson that Holinshed and Shakespeare's Carlisle echo: "God in his ire doth root up whole kingdoms for wrongs and oppressions; and doth translate kingdoms from one nation to another, for unrighteous dealing."[9] Annually, on the three days before ascension Thursday, townspeople would proceed along the borders of their parish, inspecting them to insure that no one had encroached on community property, or contrived to enclose common wetland,

60   *John Rumrich*

forest, or pasture. Borders defined the community in many ways, not the least of them being for tax purposes and administration of poor laws. With these obvious and extensive practical implications, rogationtide perambulation, or "beating the bounds," was a religious ritual in which participation was nearly unanimous and unusually spirited. At significant points along the way, children would have the vital communal knowledge pounded into them: "boys were ... bent over marker stones and beaten, thrown into boundary ponds or clumps of nettles, or upended and 'bumped' where the borderline changed direction." Nor was this mnemonic reinforcement inflicted simply for the pleasure of abusing children. Men with axes and crowbars followed along to obliterate any false markers that had been erected in cunning attempts to steal land. Imprecatory verses from the law—"cursed be he that removeth his neighbor's landmark" (*Deut.* 27:17)—were pronounced by the parish priest.[10] Fights frequently broke out between processioners from neighboring villages when they met at disputed points. It was a religious holiday and community festival with its feet firmly on the ground of sacred property right, charged with the holy violence of marking territory. Hence, according to the *OED*, "walk" in Shakespeare's time could mean "a procession, ceremonial perambulation" (I.2.a) or a proprietary tract of land (2.10–12), as, for example, in the case of Caesar's "walks, / His private arbors, and new planted orchards" (*Julius Caesar* 3.2.259–60). By extension, it could also apply to an area "within which a person is accustomed to practice his occupation without interference from a rival" (*OED* 2.14), what a reporter or a policeman would call a "beat."

At the very heart of *1 Henry IV*, immediately after the great tavern scene and before Hal's interview with his father, comes the rebels' negotiation of the division of the land. Although the moment tends to go unremarked in recent criticism of the play, its relevance to an audience experienced in processioning would have been considerable:

> HOTSP.   See how this river comes me cranking in,
>   And cuts me from the best of all my land
>   A huge half-moon, a monstrous cantle out.
>   I'll have the current in this place damm'd up,
>   And here the smug and silver Trent shall run
>   In a new channel, fair and evenly;
>   It shall not wind with such a deep indent,
>   To rob me of so rich a bottom here.
> GLEND.   Not wind? It shall, it must! You see it doth.

Dear Expedience ...   61

MORT.	Yea, but mark how he bears his course, and runs me up
	With like advantage on the other side,
	Gelding the opposed continent as much
	As on the other side it takes from you.
WORCES.	Yea, but a little charge will trench him here,
	And on this north side win this cape of land;
	And then he runs straight and even.
HOTSP.	I'll have it so. A little charge will do it.
GLEND.	I'll not have it alt'red.
HOTSP.	Will not you?
GLEND.	No, nor you shall not.
HOTSP.	Who shall say me nay?
GLEND.	Why that will I.
HOTSP.	Let me not understand you, then; speak it in Welsh.

(3.1.95–115)

Although the rebels are here settling borders on a grand scale, their argument suggests certain similarities with what we know about rogationtide, especially as their festival mood quickly shifts toward violent disputes over the dislocation of property markers. The border skirmishes of an alternative future—for Shakespeare's audience, an altered present—are here projected, and Gaunt's vision of England as a single kingdom, bounded by the sea "against the envy of less happier lands," yields to the prospect of a kingdom riven by self-interested rebels (*Richard II* 2.1.49).[11] A successful Hotspur would not take long to erupt into battle with Glendower and the Welsh. For him even "a kingdom ... was too small a bound," at least according to the prince who defeats him, consigns him to "two paces of the vilest earth," and usurping his territorially aggressive spirit, goes on to trample France (*1 Henry IV* 5.4.90–91).

Richard, not Bolingbroke, initiates the unrighteous dealing that leads to this troublesome flux in established boundaries when he interferes with Bolingbroke's inheritance of his father's lands. J.H. Hexter has convincingly argued that Shakespeare forsakes the option provided by Holinshed—that of presenting Gaunt's son as a popular hero who overthrows a tyrant—to offer instead one "whose highest claim amounted to nothing more exalted than that he wanted his own property back."[12] Nor should we see this as a strategy for undercutting Henry IV's appeal; quite the reverse. The claim of liberation from tyranny would not automatically inspire trust or sympathy in an Elizabethan audience. But an audience accustomed to annual processioning to re-establish, by violence when possible, the boundaries of a community's inherited prop-

62   John Rumrich

erty could easily have identified with Henry's down-to-earth motives and even with his legalistic reasoning. Individual property rights stood on the same basis of time-honored custom and precedent as those of the community. These were in fact the state-prescribed principles for Elizabethan churchgoers' meditations as they walked their borders:

> Our walks on these days [are] to consider the old ancient bounds and limits belonging to our township, and to other our neighbors bordering about us; to the intent that we should be content with our own, and not contentiously strive for other's, by any incroaching one upon another, or claiming one of the other, further than that, in ancient right and custom, our fore fathers have peaceably laid out unto us for our commodity and comfort.[13]

Theoretically at least, not even the crown could interfere with the right to legitimately inherited property, and in the late sixteenth century this principle was being extended to include also "men's rights to hold what custom and their labor had made their own."[14] Hence common law was making it possible not only for copyholders, but also for those in inherited occupations threatened by crown monopolies, to imagine themselves in Henry's shoes against the encroachments of a "skipping King," (1 *Henry IV* 3.2.60).[15] A threat to inherited land or to one's established walk of life went beyond a threat to wealth; it struck at one's historical sense of self, rather as the enclosure of common lands destroyed historical communities. The judicial defense of historical continuity also justified the inheritance of kingship, which means that in usurping Bolingbroke's property, as various of his noble subjects repeatedly warn, Richard undoes himself.[16]

In sum, for Shakespeare, the figure of wise walking would have been inseparably associated with property rights and observance of boundaries over time, and would have been so during a period of momentous transition in these ideas, when notions of rights and boundaries were becoming less exclusively literal and so an integral part of a great revision of relations in and among communities. The very means by which changes in possession were regulated was itself changing, thereby testifying to the impossibility of rigidly maintaining the status quo. Walking thus would have had associations both with continuity, as a means of maintaining the possession of historical property and identity, and with change, in crossing borders or developing character. It is Hal's peculiar virtue in these plays to be able to balance the dialectic that walking implies, and he does so in part by carefully

Dear Expedience ... 63

unfolding his own character. In any case, though battles over property had begun to be transferred to the courtroom, with its more abstract definitions of boundary, rogationtide perambulation was still the practical norm and would long continue as such. Metaphors of boundary and of walking, moreover, did and still do express and influence the linked ideas of interest, identity, and possession—turf.[17]

As we have seen, then, an Elizabethan audience would have been trained and nurtured in these ideas through officially sanctioned and annually repeated interpretation of liturgical metaphor and accompanying festival rituals of great practical consequence. Educated auditors, furthermore, might also have registered them in the allegorical terms of Christian Neoplatonism. Aside from serving as the main text for the official rogationtide sermon, *Ephesians* 5:15–16 is familiar as a source for the conclusion of Hal's pledge to redeem the time. A similar passage, perhaps even more directly relevant to Hal's famous soliloquy, comes from *Colossians*: "walk in wisdom toward them that are without, redeeming the time" (4:5). Here Paul speaks directly to the issue of relations between Christians and non-Christians and the appropriate behavior of the former toward the latter. In Hal's case, however, those "that are without" applies to his idle companions, especially Falstaff, whom he will finally dispossess of his company by drawing and enforcing a distinct boundary around himself, charging the Chief Justice and others concerned to maintain the borders.

> 2. What man ordeineth, God altereth at his good will and pleasure not giving place more to the prince, than to the poorest creature living, when he seeth his time to dispose of him this waie or that, as to his omnipotent power and divine providence seemeth expedient.
>
> The king had great regard of expedition and making speed for the safetie of his own person.[18]

Following the ironic historical pattern described by Holinshed in the first passage above, the *Henry IV* plays establish what it is that "seemeth expedient" to various characters. Then the providential playwright "at his good will and pleasure" thwarts them. Thus when rebels "stand out in Ireland," Green counsels Richard to make "expedient manage" of the situation, which Richard indeed attempts to do, setting in motion the events that lead to his downfall. As we shall see, specific instances of walking imagery express—at the elemental level, as it were—the historical dialectic

64   *John Rumrich*

of expedience that shapes and structures the dramatic action of the entire tetralogy.

1 Henry IV opens with a long, rhetorical set speech. Because it will frequently be cited in what follows, I quote all of it here:

> So shaken as we are, so wan with care,
> Find we a time for frighted peace to pant,
> And breathe short-winded accents of new broils
> To be commenc'd in stronds afar remote.
> No more the thirsty entrance of this soil
> Shall daub her lips with her own children's blood;
> No more shall trenching war channel her fields,
> Nor bruise her flow'rets with the armed hoofs
> Of hostile paces. Those opposed eyes,
> Which like the meteors of a troubled heaven,
> All of one nature, of one substance bred,
> Did lately meet in the intestine shock
> And furious close of civil butchery,
> Shall now, in mutual well-beseeming ranks,
> March all one way and be no more oppos'd
> Against acquaintance, kindred, and allies.
> The edge of war, like an ill-sheathed knife,
> No more shall cut his master. Therefore, friends,
> As far as to the sepulcher of Christ—
> Whose soldier now, under whose blessed cross
> We are impressed and engag'd to fight—
> Forthwith a power of English shall we levy,
> Whose arms were molded in their mother's womb,
> To chase these pagans in those holy fields,
> Over whose acres walk'd those blessed feet
> Which fourteen hundred years ago were nail'd
> For our advantage on the bitter cross.
> But this our purpose now is twelve month old,
> And bootless 'tis to tell you we will go;
> Therefore we meet not now. Then let me hear
> Of you, my gentle cousin Westmorland,
> What yesternight our council did decree
> In forwarding this dear expedience.
>
> (1.1.1–33)

Despite Henry's intention to chase pagans in holy fields and so contradict the prophesied consequence of supplanting Richard, "frighted peace" will, as Carlisle had predicted, reside among "Turks and infidels" and leave England to the "furious close of civil butchery." Henry's long speech also recalls *Richard II* as it evokes the horrors of intestine war: maternal English soil drinking

Dear Expedience ... 65

her own children's blood and being bruised by war horses' hoofs; kindred slaughtering each other. Even Richard's poetic fancy of the earth giving birth to soldiers is revisited in Henry's richly ambiguous attribution of "arms ... molded in their mother's womb" to English infantry.[19] All this violence tears the land presumably because Henry's "treacherous feet" still "trample" on the soil Richard forbade him, and over Richard's head lying beneath it.

In encouraging the sacrifice of Richard for the sake of his political interests, Henry has at best followed the wisdom of Pilate. The bald fact, which Shakespeare makes manifest but leaves implicit, is that Bolingbroke goes beyond his justifiable goal of regaining his inheritance and takes what belongs to Richard. His obsessively planned crusade is initially presented as restitution for his crime (*Richard II* 5.6.49–50). This time the profit of Henry's efforts is to go to Richard, or at least to Richard's prototype, whose feet "were nail'd/For our advantage on the bitter cross." The ambiguity of "our advantage," however, characteristically superimposes Henry's pious motivation over his self-interested one. Ostensibly, he refers to the benefit that accrued to all Christians from the crucifixion, but, given Richard's reincarnation of the sacrificed Christ, we may also think of the benefit that accrued uniquely to the newly minted royal we from Richard's death, and that Henry similarly hopes will accrue from an expiatory crusade. Henry dangles the prospect of Jerusalem to quiet his subjects, persuading them to "march all one way and be no more oppos'd," their giddy minds occupied with the death of infidels.

Coming at the end of line thirty-three, perhaps not coincidentally the speech's final line, the phrase "dear expedience" is usually glossed as signifying the haste with which arrangements for the crusade have been made. Bevington's note, for example, has "urgent expedition." But "dear expedience" is also something of a linguistic dwarf star, in which the form and figures of the *Henry IV* plays are densely packed. This density owes in part to the etymology of "expedience." *Expedire* primarily means to extricate, literally by freeing the feet (*ex ped-*, *pes*), and extends to making convenient arrangements or to anything advantageous. "Expedience" in Shakespeare's usage also recalls the Latin *expeditus*, a fast-moving, lightly armed foot soldier—hence, the common Shakespearean meaning of "expedition" as armed men in motion. Henry seems to envision a symbolic reversal of his sin. Leading a crusade to the holy land will undo his former crime, un-nailing the blessed feet of Christ's/Richard's from the cross so that he can be free to walk the

66   *John Rumrich*

holy (Eng/land) and say, in Richard's words upon returning from Ireland, "I weep for joy / To stand upon my kingdom once again" (*Richard II* 3.2.4–5). Although the impossible reversal envisioned by the speech may amount only to an empty gesture, Henry, I think genuinely, does wish his own death. As many of his subjects eventually do, he seems to prefer Richard alive again at the expense of his own demise: "O earth, yield us that king again / And take thou this!" (*2 Henry IV* 1.3.97, 106–7). If such a switch could come about, Carlisle's prophecy would also be undone: war removed to the real holy land, peace returned to England, the rightful king in place, and the usurper dead in exile. Even dead, Richard's presence shapes the rest of Henry's life, whether through various premonitions about Hal's resurrection of Richard's ways, or, metonymically through the death-dealing crown.[20]

On the other hand, unconscious wishes aside, Henry proposes the crusade as an attempt to free no one's feet but his own, as is later made explicit (*2 Henry IV* 4.5.209–12). The pagans he chases are those of his countrymen who refuse to accept his legitimacy. Such an expedition, as Hal later puts it, entails much "waste in brief mortality" (*Henry V* 1.2.28), and the waste of "friends," whose "stings and teeth" threaten the king, comprises a good part of "our advantage" (*2 Henry IV* 4.5.204–5). Henry's intentions for his "friends" are darkly reflected in Falstaff's for his ragged foot soldiers. Their amputation from the body politic will boost its economic health, thus fostering domestic tranquility, and Falstaff will profit from arranging that they rather than others fill a pit.[21] Nor need compulsive talking about a crusade to the Holy Land register as "bootless," if it keeps the court preoccupied and assuages Henry's own guilt and fear, allowing him to fight rebellion. It is by precisely this strategy of misdirection—the fullness of and engagement with what is "bootless"—that these plays define the direction of history and unfold character. They also manage thereby to render what is being sacrificed in the move forward, whether that sacrifice is the legitimacy of the monarchy, Hotspur's intrepid valor, or Falstaff's ingratiating wit.

Although "bootless" in the sense of "absence of footwear" plays no part in Henry's speech and is almost unheard of elsewhere in Shakespeare, puns on boot as profit/footwear occur often enough in these plays that they seem to intrude even when uninvited. For example, Falstaff jabs at Poins for wearing "his boots very smooth, like unto the sign of the Leg" (*2 Henry IV* 2.4.246–47).

Dear Expedience ... 67

Though perfectly straightforward, the line at first sounds infected with the double sense. In *Henry V*, the priests' comparison of soldiers to bees, who "make boot upon the summer's velvet buds," while engaged with both meanings, sets one wondering if this instance would even be noticeable elsewhere (1.2.194). As king, Henry V refuses robbers such as Bardolph, "smooth boots"—i.e., easy profits, but in *1 Henry IV* the possibility appears open that Hal's thieving companions, their boots "liquor'd" by his compromised justice, could in effect "walk invisible" as they rob pilgrims of crowns (2.1.86–88). In initiating the pun on "boot," Gadshill ties the word into the complex of imagery we have already examined, explaining that he and his fellow thieves—"no foot land-rakers"—will "ride up and down on [the commonwealth], and make her their boots" (2.1.74, 82–83). Soon thereafter Hotspur adapts "bootless" to the Gadshill wordplay, responding to Glendower's boast that he sent Bolingbroke "bootless home": "Home without boots, and in foul weather too! / How scapes he agues?" (3.1.64–65).

The tetralogy is inhabited by characters obsessed with "boot" both in the sense of profit or expedience and in the sense of protection for their aggressive self-interest, regardless of what boundaries they trespass. But the dramatic action repeatedly denies them their expected profit and distributes instead disappointment and loss. Their supposed "boot" is revealed to be no more substantial than that on the sign of the leg. The pun on "boot," though confined mainly to the low plot, italicizes the sense of disappointment and disillusionment that in these plays inevitably attends what characters think will be expedient. Hence the key instance of the ambiguity of "boot," and the setup for the plays' consummate disillusionment, occurs near the end of *2 Henry IV*. Falstaff responds to news of Henry IV's death by repeatedly shouting the much punned-upon term: "Boot, boot, Master Shallow.... Let us take any man's horses; the laws of England are at my commandment" (*2 Henry IV* 5.3.131, 136–38). By "boot, boot," Falstaff may mean nothing more than "get on your shoes," but we hear more. His cries recall Gadshill and again invoke the now familiar constellation of boot, horse, and disregard of property and law.[22] Yet even in the Gadshill confusion over "boot," Hal's ulterior motive for participation in the robbery was the exposure of Falstaff, a process with which the victim seemed almost willing to comply, as if orchestrated scenes of public humiliation—not indulgence—were the real reward of his relationship with the

68   *John Rumrich*

prince. Such ironic coincidence of opposites displays the dialectical form of Shakespeare's dramatic design, most notoriously in Falstaff's case, but also in the progress of almost every character except Hal. By the conclusion of Falstaff's first humiliation, the prince, acting the part of king, says he will banish plump Jack, even if it means banishing all the world. On this later occasion, then, Falstaff's excited command to, and expectation of, "boot" leaves us with the uncomfortable feeling of waiting for the other foot to drop.[23]

Though it may seem merely clever to speak of Falstaff's second banishment as the other foot dropping, the idiom applies rather precisely to what happens repeatedly in *2 Henry IV*. Others have detailed the way in which most scenes in the second part recall in a darker and diminished fashion scenes from the first, and the growing sense of increasingly weary and anxious waiting. The feeling aroused is that of the past closing in and determining the shape of the present. We feel the harsh fall of that other foot early, as Northumberland reacts to news that the son he forsook has been slain, as Lady Percy laments the heavy loss of her husband. By the time we get to part two, the choices have all been made it seems; what is left is the aftermath.

If nothing else, *2 Henry IV*, even in its title, mercilessly exposes the lie of the fresh start. One does not require the allegorization of the feet as the wings of the soul to understand that the act of walking can be taken as "quite literally the incarnation of the act of choice, for walking was simply choosing brought down to the material plane."[24] Choices are made: one road is taken, another not. It is terrifyingly simple. Yet, this natural symbol had also been more arcanely elaborated in terms of faculty psychology: "thoughts and desires produced by the intellect and will are reproduced, in the act of walking, by the succession of right and left."[25] The traditional interpretation of feet as embodying the spiritual components of choice, as Freccero informs us, had indeed been so well established in theological vocabulary that the wounds in Christ's feet were often allegorized as the ignorance and concupiscence associated with original sin.[26] This returns us to the king's long opening speech and its prominent images of Christ's feet first walking over the holy land and then being nailed to the cross for "our advantage." In these plays, characters' past concupiscence—ignorantly conceived as "expedience"—costs them dearly and eventually renders them volitionally immobile. They are nailed to the cross of their past "mistreadings" (*1 Henry IV* 3.2.11).

Dear Expedience ... 69

Our first glimpse of Northumberland in part two shows him supporting himself with a staff, and though he throws it away and promises to fight this time, he is soon persuaded again to inaction by reason of his former inaction (1.1; 2.3). Our first sight of Falstaff similarly reveals him halting—from the gout or the pox (2 *Henry IV* 1.2.243–44). Soon thereafter the aptly named Snare is set upon him for the repayment of past debts (2.1). But Henry IV suffers most for the past, finding himself impeded by what earlier he accused Mowbray of suffering—"the clogging burthen of a guilty soul" (*Richard II* 1.3.200). In his first speech of part two, the king restlessly laments the burden of the crown (3.1.4–31).[27] For some these protestations are hypocritical, but from that point on—though present for two more full scenes totaling more than 370 lines—Henry never walks on stage again but appears either carried in a chair or bedridden (2 *Henry IV* 4.4; 4.5). According to Stow, to whom Shakespeare is more indebted than is generally recognized, "he was diseased and might not go."[28] And in Shakespeare's depiction, part of his "disease" is that still he plans obsessively, futilely, even ridiculously, his crusade. For Jerusalem means death to Henry and to Jerusalem—"by [his] scepter, and [his] soul to boot"—he desperately would go (1 *Henry IV* 3.2.97). An usurper who believes in legitimacy, he is eager for an expiatory death. From a vortex of repetition, Henry calls himself to his end, and does so with a compulsive sense of fate.[29]

Though incorrect, Henry's fearful and often repeated premonition that Hal will in one way or another be "the rod of heaven, / To punish [his] mistreadings," is an excellent guess (1 *Henry IV* 3.2.10–11). Hal has been or will be at the heart of every other character's disappointment in the desire for boot, and he is his father's main symbol of the reversal he at once fears and desires—his own death and Richard's resurrection.

Henry's fateful expectation of his son is what makes the episode of Hal's removing the crown from the unconscious king's head so poignant. In the rush to prove Hal a villain, recent criticism has tended to focus on the differences between what the prince really says to the crown when he takes it from his apparently dead father, and what he says he said. But leaving aside Hal's "damnable iteration," the more intriguing doubleness of this scene is the way it conflates Gadshill and Shrewsbury by pivoting on the theft of a crown from an apparently dead man (1 *Henry IV* 1.2.89). Although Richard—like Hotspur but unlike Falstaff—cannot return from death, despite Henry's unconscious wish, Henry

70   *John Rumrich*

himself does, and when he does, Hal actually manages to perform Henry's impossible wish, restoring the usurped crown to the resurrected king, even though that means performing yet once more the "double labor," despised by Falstaff, of paying back what has been stolen (*1 Henry IV* 3.3.179–80). "Thy wish was father ... to that thought," says Henry of Hal's supposing him dead (*2 Henry IV* 4.5.92). But that wish for Henry belongs to Henry, and his son is only its external representative.[30] Hal's theft and restoration of his crown gracefully undoes the king's crime in his heir, rendering their dynasty legitimate, for the time being.

Before his death, the king shows himself particularly acute in apprehending an alternative future in which Hal would kill his brothers, or they him—an unspoken fear but one nonetheless discernible in his advice to Thomas of Clarence (*2 Henry IV* 4.4.19–48).[31] Nor can Hal's reassurances after his father's death be heard without menacing recollections of the ironic geography of these plays: "This is the English, not the Turkish court; / Not Amurath an Amurath succeeds, / But Harry Harry" (*2 Henry IV* 5.2.47–49).[32] If these were plays driven only by nemesis along a high Hellenic plotline, the bloody succession Henry dare not name would be entirely apt and unavoidable. Of the various possible futures envisioned in these plays—a divided kingdom with Hotspur the main man, a return of Richard's lawless irresponsibility, and so on—it is the darkest. If, as Auden claimed, the poignancy of Christian as opposed to Greek tragedy resides in the awareness that things could have happened otherwise, then so certainly must part of the thrill of those brief moments of success that the Christian view of history allows. An underappreciated part of Shakespeare's genius in these plays is to have found so many ways to suggest how different, and, at least from his audience's point of view, how much worse, things could have been. *2 Henry IV* thus doggedly pursues the deterministic plotline, and has both Harrys adumbrate it, so that Hal's redemption of time from an otherwise automatic and inexorable cycle of sin and punishment will seem all the more remarkable, even miraculous. Perhaps the moral prerequisite for this respite is that Henry IV's repentance is more genuine than not. His fears for England finally and distinctly go past mere self-interestedness and so escape the cruel dialectic of boot. We know, and Shakespeare reminds us, that the dark version of the future will take hold soon enough after Henry V's death. But Hal is not merely a delay; he is a signpost to the future. He is a kind of destiny.

Dear Expedience ... 71

Though it is no longer fashionable to think so, Henry V is undoubtedly conceived as a hero who manages if not to break, then to interrupt and point beyond the bloody cycle begun by Richard, and he does so in part by banishing from his government Falstaff, who, among many other things, represents the temptation for Hal to become another Richard. This also means, as many have lamented, that he thereby banishes Shakespeare's representative of the capacity to see the world under the aspect of alterity, a capacity that, if generally underappreciated in the *Henry IV* plays, has been effusively celebrated in this single character. Falstaff is a kind of chaos. As an endless stream of commentators can testify, jumbled elements of the past and future characterize him—medieval vice, decayed nobility, hypocritical puritan, and so on. Unfortunately for Falstaff, Hal when he becomes king must sort out the confusion, must establish the way things will be for him and for England.[33] Of all Shakespeare's great modern critics, only Empson, whose appreciation of Falstaff was profound, has had the pragmatic wits and clear-sightedness to recognize this: "Hal deserved his moment of triumph because he had shown the right way [i.e., toward a "gradual unification of his own islands"] or at any rate seen things in their right proportions, before his time. That is the 'religious' or 'patriotic' feeling about Hal (one can hardly say which), and I feel it myself; it is a real enough thing."[34] Crucial to a fair assessment of Hal and of Falstaff is the realization that none of the alternative futures hinted at in the tetralogy would have been felt as preferable to the present lived by Shakespeare's audience and to which Hal pointed. The heroism he represents is the establishment of a united England out of the possible worlds that lie before him, one that will survive if only as a vision, and an ideology, for the future. Desire for unity should not, however, be reduced merely to ideological posturing or Tudor propaganda, though of course it also serves these purposes. "It is a real enough thing," as Empson says, and in the political world "real" things can be used to liberate or oppress. My point is that in becoming a heroic symbol of unity Henry V is not reduced to a creature of ideology; he too is real enough. Granted, the future that Henry V represents is also shot through with aggressive violence and a kind of piety that sounds like hypocrisy. As Nietzsche observed, the outbreak of the "classical ideal" of nobility in the millenia of Christianity is an uncanny and confusing phenomenon.[35] But Hal is an example of it. We taste nothing purely, and though Hal is one of the noblest humans Shakespeare invented, he is still human.

72   *John Rumrich*

All who are sacrificed in the *Henriad* en route to Hal's glorious moment on the throne—including Richard II, Henry IV, and Hotspur—are summed up in the rejection of Falstaff. Nor can the ignorance and concupiscence that in one way or another afflict them all be indulged if Henry V is to succeed in becoming the first national, and insistently native-speaking, king of England instead of a "bastard Norman" (*Henry V* 3.5.10).[36] In spite of the complexity and variety of Falstaff's character, his function in the plot is therefore quite simple, as many have observed—to be sacrificed so that Hal can achieve heroic stature. His secular martyrdom is ironically emphasized by the non-identification of him with Oldcastle, the continual parodies of religious language and attitudes in which he delights, and the descriptions of him "sweat[ing] to death" on Gadshill, "lard[ing] the lean earth as he walks along" (*1 Henry IV* 2.2.107–8). Although he may be compared to them, Falstaff is not quite Christ, Socrates, or any of the other martyrs with whom he has been identified.[37] Listing examples of Falstaff's ignoble viciousness has never quieted the enthusiasm of his advocates, however, even though the list includes leading "ragamuffins" unable to bribe their way free to where they can be quickly "pepper'd," or mutilating a corpse for personal gain (*1 Henry IV* 5.3.35–36). Nor has it helped to present evidence of a dramatic design that insistently unveils the increasing ugliness of what had originally seemed good-natured, inept troublemaking and charming disrespect for authority. Doll's arrest for helping Pistol beat a man to death occurs abruptly before the banishment scene. It comes there for a reason, as does Falstaff's promise to Pistol immediately prior to his banishment: "I will deliver her" (*2 Henry IV* 5.5.39).

It would be foolish to go to the other extreme and deny the genius or immense appeal of Falstaff, not only "witty in [him]self, but the cause that wit is in other men" (*2 Henry IV* 1.2.9–10). Yet scholars have tended to blow up that second clause into an allegorical reading of Falstaff as a harmless and somehow sacred spirit of comedy. If he is the embodiment of wit, it should be remembered that in these plays wit usually means verbal aggression, and he embodies both sides: its dazzling thrust and fluidity, and, as that second clause insists, its target: "man is not able to invent any thing that intends to laughter more than I invent or is invented on me" (*2 Henry IV* 1.2.7–9). Falstaff excels both at striking and at being the target. Indeed, the best scene in the tetralogy, one of the great scenes in all of Shakespeare, is the tavern scene after Gadshill. It has the pace and rhythm of a swordfight out of an epic

Dear Expedience ... 73

swashbuckler—and not the "fencing grace" of some later skirmishes "tap for tap, and so part fair" (*2 Henry IV* 2.1.190–91). In escalating rounds Falstaff is apparently caught, then loose; on the palpable verge of being skewered, then suddenly free—slipping his opponents' lunges and wheeling into the next clash. If he is a quasi-allegorical representative of anything, it is of expedience as extrication, of inventing a way out so that he can strike as well as play the target again. No one better prolongs the time or manages the tension before the other foot drops. But as his attitude toward Justice Shallow makes explicit, the game of wit he plays is like a food chain: "If the young dace be a bait for the old pike, I see not reason in the law of nature but I may snap at him" (*2 Henry IV* 3.2.330–31). Compunction and sympathy for others occur to him, but never influence his behavior. Nor is there any doubt that this fat Proteus exploits his incredibly flexible wit so that he might one day gain advantage by abusing his friendship with Hal. But heroes must master Proteus, not be mastered by him, if they are to succeed.

Yes, Hal is heroic. Shakespeare clearly portrays him that way and, as prince and king, he has been so received by centuries of audiences who nevertheless were most entertained by Falstaff. This rather straightforward and lifelike instance of ambiguity and ambivalence has been increasingly difficult for our most subtle critics to accommodate. Instead, the tendency to become sentimental over Falstaff has been complemented by the denigration of Hal. Stephen Greenblatt, most notably, for whom the prince is Kurtz by-the-Thames, breaks briefly from his grim and contemptuous account of Hal as a "conniving hypocrite" and "juggler," to savor in Falstaff the "irresistible embodiment" of, strange though it may sound, that which is "quintessentially" Shakespearean—the ability to awaken "a dream of superabundance."[38] On the contrary, if Falstaff may be said to embody any one thing, it is what Simone de Beauvoir called "immanence," the acceptance of things as they are, a willingness to rest content in the pastness of the status quo.[39] Falstaff is aggressively immanent and would perpetuate the past order, or in this case disorder, by manipulating others, at any cost to them, so that he can continue as he was at least in his own eyes—the favorite whose excesses the prince indulged. As Empson remarks, Falstaff is the first joke against the class system, "a picture of how badly you can behave and still get away with it, if you are a gentleman."[40]

74   *John Rumrich*

The many and varied excellences of "the nimble-footed mad-cap Prince of Wales" are for our purposes rather neatly summed up just prior to the battle at Shrewsbury:

> I saw young Harry, with his beaver on,
> His cushes on his thighs, gallantly arm'd
> Rise from the ground like feathered Mercury,
> And vaulted with such ease into his seat
> As if an angel dropp'd down from the clouds
> To turn and wind a fiery Pegasus,
> And witch the world with noble horsemanship.
> (4.1.95, 104–10)

Here, at the crucial moment, the displaced wings of the soul return with a vengeance, appearing not only on a winged horse but also on an angelic Hal's Mercury-like feet. The passage is an extraordinarily powerful one and has been repeatedly quoted as moving lyrical testimony to the prince's virtues, quoted even by scholars harshly critical of Henry V. The image is repeated in the chorus's description of Henry's troops, following their king "with winged heels, as English Mercuries" (*Henry V* 2.chorus.6). The comparison of Prince Hal to wing-footed Mercury taming Pegasus is particularly apt, bringing to mind heroes like Perseus and Bellerophon and of course the messenger god himself. The god of crossroads and borders, Mercury sponsors eloquence and oratory, travel and thievery—all activities with some bearing on Hal's character. Eschatologically, he was supposed to guide souls to their final resting-places, a function that Hal fills first in his generous tribute to the defeated Hotspur and later by virtue of his role as a warrior-king leading troops into battle. Henry V may argue that "every subject's soul is his own," but he never disputes that many meet their souls' destinies in following the king (*Henry V* 4.1.176).[41]

Primarily, though, Mercury is best remembered for mediating the destiny of heroes in epic literature, a kind of destiny that usually requires terrible sacrifice. Although in the passage above the myths of Perseus and Bellerophon are glanced at, the more tempting analogues are those concerning Hector and Achilles, Calypso and Odysseus, and Aeneas and Dido. In each case, Mercury persuades one of the parties to give up someone, in Achilles' case, Hector's corpse, so that the hero might fulfill his destiny and Jupiter's be accomplished. Others have pointed out the similarity between Hal's rejection of Falstaff and Aeneas' of Dido, and even resemblances between the fat knight and Cleopatra, which would make Hal a renovated Antony.[42] Regardless of the precise nature

Dear Expedience ... 75

or depth of the bond between them, the rejection of Falstaff clearly represents the decisive step in Hal's becoming the great English hero. Also, the absence of supernatural machinery explicitly demanding this sacrifice—Hal is his own, deliberate Mercury—has made many readers disgusted with the prince for his cold heart: "for miracles are ceas'd / And therefore we must needs admit the means / How things are perfected" (*Henry V* 1.1.67–69). On the other hand, Mercury is not a figure noted for warmth but rather for rhetorical prowess, a perfect sense of timing, and the unfailing ability to accomplish the tasks set for him. Hal's perfection pertains not to love or friendship, but to valor and policy, which constitute between them the "noble horsemanship" of successful government, allowing him to rein in "a fiery Pegasus," which in the past repeatedly and "madly hath broke loose." These plays do not ignore the human cost of Hal's successes, and they are both clearsighted and ironically bracing in their representation of the political realm. Yet in its cultural context the imagery that underwrites the dramatic design of these plays indicates their measured approval of Hal's achievement.

Notes

1. This essay substantially repeats my "Shakespeare's Walking Plays," although the present version is revised and incorporates new evidence.

2. References to scripture follow *The Geneva Bible*. Palmer, as he works to untangle the web of biblical allusions in the Henry IV plays, glances at the ironic use of walking imagery in Henry IV's vow to march "in the path of his Redeemer" (320).

3. Some recent, representative contributions, more engaging theoretically than for their insights into the tetralogy, are Rackin; Belsey; Pugliatti; and Cohen.

4. See Velz, who persuasively argues that Shakespeare's characteristic concern in his histories is "Janus-like." Like Virgil, he is preoccupied with periods of transition in which the past is present along with the future as one era shifts into the next. Velz's case seems to me especially convincing in light of the sometimes violently transitional nature of Shakespeare's own time.

5. See Berger, who is a notable exception to the usual practice of scholars concerned with Shakespeare's representation of history.

6. For Berger, images involving horses are more primary than those concerning walking (56).

76   *John Rumrich*

7. "The soul resembles the combined efficacy of winged steeds and charioteer.... Of these horses he finds one generous and of generous breed, the other of opposite descent and opposite character. And thus it necessarily follows that driving ... is no easy or agreeable work" (Plato, 237). Although imagery of wings is typically replaced in the Henry plays by that of feet, wings do appear in the characterization of Hal by his father and in a way that suggests the Neoplatonic background of the image: "thy affections ... do hold a wing / Quite from the flight of all thy ancestors"; "O, with what wings shall his affections fly / Towards fronting peril and oppos'd decay!" (*1 Henry IV* 3.2.30–31; *2 Henry IV* 4.4.65–66). For observations on the tradition of horsemanship as a symbol of rule and its relevance to the tetralogy, see Watson, "Horsemanship in Shakespeare's Second Tetralogy." Watson is particularly convincing in discussing Henry IV's usurpation of Richard's "roan Barbary" (see *Richard II* 5.5.78).

8. Freccero, 38. I am indebted to Eric Mallin of the University of Texas for recommending this source to me.

9. *Sermons*, 342.

10. Kightly, 48. David Riggs of Stanford University, after reading an earlier draft of this essay, suggested that I investigate walking rituals and so led me to consider rogationtide in relation to the tetralogy.

11. Even those critics with no great love for the Lancastrians have noted that by comparison the rebels show a distinct lack of concern for the interests of England. For example, see Auden, 162.

12. Hexter, 12.

13. *Sermons*, 339–40.

14. Hexter, 16. There is room for inconsistency here, one that proves vital to the interest of these plays, but to which Hexter in his advocacy of Bolingbroke does not attend. While *Henry V* makes a great fuss, ironically or not, about England's rightful possession of France by inheritance, Henry V himself sits on the throne not by the "ancient right" stressed in the Rogationtide sermon but by the new legality of protecting his father's "labor" in stealing the crown. The inconsistency is plain and often remarked. The underlying irony, though Shakespeare ignores it, is that the right of possession through the female line, by which Henry has legal claim to France, would set up "down-trod" Mortimer as the legitimate king of England (*1 Henry IV* 1.3.135).

15. Hexter, 14–16.

16. Hexter, 19–22.

17. On boundary metaphors and how they shape the modern western sense of self and community, see Nedelsky. Her chief criticism of boundary metaphors in contemporary society is that they tend to obscure the role of the community in guaranteeing rights and thus foster an illusory sense of independent autonomy. One could argue in her terms that Hal is a prime example of modern selfhood simply by the fact that in establishing himself as king, he sets boundaries around himself that others (Falstaff in particular, but through him "all the world") must not violate—though

Dear Expedience ... 77

of course these bounds depend on community cooperation. On the other hand, rogationtide processioning seems a remarkably effective way of reminding citizens of the fact that observance of boundaries is something contingent on the will of the community.

18. Holinshed, 3:57.

19. The earliest quartos and the first folio of course use no apostrophe for "mothers" in line 23, "Whose arms were molded in their mothers womb." Folio 4, which I follow, has "mother's." Bevington's less than adequate text of the play, following Theobald's, has mothers', though "womb" is left in the singular. The Ovidian image of soldiers born from the earth, like so many others in the middle plays, is capped in *Henry V*: "good yeomen, / Whose limbs were made in England, show us here / The mettle of your pasture. Let us swear / That you are worth your breeding" (3.1.25–28).

20. Shakespeare does not explicitly use Holinshed's report that the rebellions against Henry were generally accompanied by sightings of Richard alive. See, for example, the marginal note in *The Historie of England*: "King Richard once againe alive" (Holinshed, 3:29).

21. The ironic wartime connections between Henry and Falstaff continue in *2 Henry IV* when the rebels, without a fight, agree to "stoop tamely to the foot of majesty" and Falstaff bluffs Colevile into surrender, envisioning the event immortalized as "Colevile kissing my foot" (4.2.42; 4.3.48).

22. Falstaff's cries of "boot" may even hearken back to York's repeated cries for his boots as he hastens to tell the newly crowned Henry IV of Aumerle's treachery, despite the fact that Aumerle is, in the play at least, his own son (*Richard II* 5.2.77, 84, 87). Obviously, in terms of the dichotomy of interest versus justice, York is precisely opposite to Falstaff.

23. A final irony will occur when Hal himself succeeds in making France his "boots." It is perhaps what Branch Rickey called the "residue of design" that the historical record dates his great victory as coming on the feast of Crispin and Crispian, patron saints of shoemakers.

24. Freccero, 42.

25. Freccero, 42.

26. Freccero, 44. Greville exemplifies the use of metaphors involving travel by foot to convey the linkage of reason and will: "[Henry the Third's] favourites, ... were let loose to run over all the branches of his kingdom, misleading governors, nobility and people from the steady and mutual rest of laws, customs and other ancient wisdoms of government into *the wildernesses of ignorance and violence of will*" (my italics). See Greville, 107.

27. Holinshed says Henry cannot sleep because, hated by both courtiers and commons, he fears assassination (3:18–19). In Shakespeare, he cannot sleep for the same reason that he wishes he were in Jerusalem, i.e., dead. He possesses the crown and is thus his own assassin.

28. Stow, 543.

78 *John Rumrich*

29. The dialectic of expedience can be understood in Freudian terms as the working out of *thanatos* through the efforts of *eros*. For Freud the compulsion to repeat (*Wiederholungszwang*) signals the death drive.

30. "Fate compulsion" (*Schicksalszwang*) is, again, Freudian terminology, signaling behavior in which one's fate, though conceived of as external necessity, is actually arranged by oneself. See Freud, 21.

31. A fear of conflict between Hal and his brother Thomas is expressed in Stow's account of Henry's dying advice to his son (545). That in the drama Henry advises Thomas on this matter, not Hal, and deems him a peacemaker between the brothers is not so important as the fact that Stow has Henry fearing another usurpation of the crown, this time from within the family.

32. Hal's mention of Amurath and the intent of Henry IV's advice to Hal's brother Thomas have been remarked in Watson's psychoanalytic reading, "The Henry IV Plays." After discussing the Oedipal conflict between Hal and his father, Watson raises the fratricidal possibilities of the next generation (413–15). Hal and the plays must work out a way to short-circuit the pattern set by Henry IV's usurpation: "Shakespeare and Hal virtually conspire to find an escape from the vicious cycle of Oedipal justice"; Hal finds "a plausible way ... to fulfill his role as the nemesis generated by Henry's violations, without incurring a similar nemesis of his own" (417).

33. Various critics have noted the sense of narrowing possibilities that accompanies Hal's progress toward the throne and have particularly criticized him for losing so much of himself in becoming King. See, for example, Barish. It is impossible to deny the facts of such observations. Unlike Barish and others, however, I would deny that we are shown the "dehumanization" of Prince Hal (285). On the contrary, the process he undergoes is inevitable—for every living thing in time—and is the basis of human meaning. It does not strike me as very damning to note that, in effect, Hal is not Peter Pan.

34. Empson, 63.

35. Nietzsche, 53–54. Henry V is often scorned for attacking France under the cover of a trumped up claim to that land. It was, however, a valid claim that many Elizabethans took as matter of fact. See, for example, Greville's *Dedication to Sir Philip Sidney*, where various French cities are cited as "part of [Elizabeth's] ancient domains lineally descended from many ancestors" (56). Greville also mentions Henry IV as a monarch who remedied "all unjust combinations or encroachments" (63). It can easily be argued that Henry V's claim to France was better than his claim to England.

36. On Henry's use of English and the probable sensitivity of Shakespeare's audience to having been conquered and ruled by the French, see Empson, 59–62.

Dear Expedience ... 79

37. Auden's essay is a classic example of this identification in its portrayal of Falstaff as Christian charity made flesh and of Hal as "the Prince of this world" (176–80).

38. Greenblatt, 41, 62, 42. It is not possible here to deal at length with Greenblatt's famous essay on the tetralogy and its incarnation of contemporary suspicions regarding political power. Nor is it necessary to do so. He admits that the plays cannot be performed as he interprets them, an impossibility that is construed as validation of his general thesis of subversion and containment. What is more, the moral standard by which he measures Hal is admitted to be historically inappropriate for Shakespeare's time, and the better world in which more of the essay's readings would seem apt rather than contorted is "deferred" to some unknown future (62–63). The implication is that a reader who does not share in the disapproval of Hal is a dupe or evil, even though that category seems to include all of Shakespeare's audiences past, present, and foreseeable future.

39. de Beauvoir, xxxiv.

40. Empson, 46.

41. By virtue of uniting solar and lunar principles, Mercury is also the god associated with alchemy, and, in the Renaissance, with monarchy because of his role as the intermediary between gods and men and association with concord. Spenser identifies Elizabeth with Mercury. See Brooks-Davies, 2–25.

42. Walter, xxiv–xxv.

Works Cited

Auden, W.H. "The Prince's Dog." In Bevington, pp. 162–80.

Barish, Jonas. "The Turning Away of Prince Hal." In Bevington, pp. 277–88.

de Beauvoir, Simone. *The Second Sex*. Trans. H.M. Parshley. New York: Knopf, 1952.

Belsey, Catherine. "Making Histories Then and Now: Shakespeare from *Richard II* to *Henry V*." In *Uses of History: Marxism, Postmodernism and the Renaissance*, ed. Francis Barker, Peter Hulme, and Margaret Iverson. Manchester: Manchester UP, 1991. 24–46.

Berger, Harry. "The Prince's Dog: Falstaff and the Perils of Speech-Prefexity." *Shakespeare Quarterly* 49 (1998): 40–73.

Bevington, David, ed. *Henry IV, Parts I and II: Critical Essays*. New York: Garland, 1986.

Brooks-Davies, Douglas. *The Mercurian Monarch: Magical Politics from Spenser to Pope*. Manchester: Manchester UP, 1983.

80 *John Rumrich*

Cohen, Derek. "History and the Nation in *Richard II* and *Henry IV.*" *SEL* 42 (2002): 292–315.

Empson, William. *Essays on Shakespeare*, ed. David B. Pirie. Cambridge: Cambridge UP, 1986.

Freccero, John. *Dante: The Poetics of Conversion*, ed. Rachel Jacoff. Cambridge, MA: Harvard UP, 1986.

Freud, Sigmund. *Beyond the Pleasure Principle*. Ed. James Strachey et al. Standard Edition of the Complete Psychological Works of Sigmund Freud, Vol. 18. London: Hogarth, 1966.

The Geneva Bible: A Facsimile of the 1560 Edition. Madison: U of Wisconsin P, 1969.

Greenblatt, Stephen. "Invisible Bullets." *Shakespearean Negotiations*. Berkeley: U of California P, 1988. 38–64.

Greville, Fulke. *A Dedication to Sir Philip Sidney*. In *The Prose Works of Fulke Greville, Lord Brooke*. Ed. John Gouws. Oxford: Clarendon, 1986.

Hexter, J.H. "Property, Monopoly, and *Richard II.*" In *Culture and Politics from Puritanism to the Enlightenment*, ed. Peter Zagorin. Berkeley: U of California P, 1980. 1–24.

Holinshed, Raphael. *The Historie of England*. 6 vols. London, 1587; London, 1808.

Kightly, Charles. *The Customs and Ceremonies of Britain*. London: Thames and Hudson, 1986.

Nedelsky, Jennifer. "Law, Boundaries, and the Bounded Self." *Representations* 30 (1990): 162–89.

Nietzsche, Friedrich Wilhelm. *On the Genealogy of Morals*. Ed. Walter Kaufmann. New York: Random House, 1967.

Palmer, D.J. "Casting Off the Old Man: History and St. Paul in *Henry IV.*" In Bevington, pp. 315–36.

Plato. *Phaedrus*. Trans. J. Wright. In *Five Dialogues of Plato Bearing on Poetic Inspiration*, ed. Ernest Rhys. London: J.M. Dent & Sons, 1910.

Pugliatti, Paola. *Shakespeare the Historian*. New York: St. Martin's P, 1996.

Rackin, Phyllis. *Stages of History: Shakespeare's English Chronicles*. Ithaca: Cornell UP, 1990.

Rumrich, John P. "Shakespeare's Walking Plays: Image and Form in 1 and 2 *Henry IV.*" In *Shakespeare's English Histories: A Quest for Form and Genre*, ed. John W. Velz. Medieval and Renaissance Texts and Studies 133. Binghamton, NY: MRTS, 1996; Tempe: Arizona Board of Regents for Arizona State U, 1997. 111–41.

Sermons or Homilies Appointed to Read in Churches in the Time of Queen Elizabeth of Famous Memory. London, 1604; London, 1815.

Stow, John. *The Annales of England*. London, 1592.

Dear Expedience ... 81

Velz, John. "Cracking Strong Curbs Asunder: Roman Destiny and the Roman Hero in *Coriolanus*." *ELR* 13 (1983): 58–69.

Walter, John H., ed. "Introduction." *The Arden Edition of Henry V*. London: Methuen, 1954. i–xlvii.

Watson, Robert N. "The Henry IV Plays." In Bevington, pp. 387–422.

———. "Horsemanship in Shakespeare's Second Tetralogy." *ELR* 13 (1983): 274–300.

The Chronicles of Emptiness:
Loss, Disappointment, and Failure
in Shakespeare's Second Tetralogy
Joseph Candido

I

Viewed from one perspective, Shakespeare's so-called Henriad may be seen as presenting a single, great, and overarching dramatic action—the rise of the supposed wastrel Henry of Monmouth from unpromising youth to the triumphant hero of Agincourt. But unlike Marlowe's *Tamburlaine*, for example, which chronicles a similarly spectacular ascent from oblivion to greatness, Shakespeare's tetralogy repeatedly diverts us from the upward thrust of Henry's career with a series of "downward" movements that cut sharply across it. As Henry fulfills the plan of magnificent ascent he had orchestrated for himself as early as his opening soliloquy in *1 Henry IV* (1.2.195–217), characters like Bullingbrook, Falstaff, Hotspur, Lady Percy, Northumberland, Hostess Quickly, Bardolph, Doll, Shallow, Silence, and, at times, even Henry himself, must submit to feelings of rejection, isolation, loss, failure, disappointment, and defeat, that turn their fortunes downward, and in so doing, impart the deep sense of irony and failure that so many critics see as severely modifying, even undermining, the heroic dimensions of the second tetralogy.[1]

My intention in this essay is not to romanticize this sense of loss and disappointment in the Henriad by seeing it as inevitably linked to a sense of Christian fulfillment or gain; Shakespeare's rich and capacious vision of political life in these plays clearly resists such conveniently reductive thinking as that. But in the wake of the recent spate of "ironic" or "deflationary" readings of the tetralogy, where every good intention has a Machiavellian or materialist adder lying beneath it,[2] we may wish to remind ourselves

84 *Joseph Candido*

that Shakespeare's sense of history is just as powerfully informed by the pattern of Fall and Redemption depicted in the medieval cycle plays; by the comic structure of the late medieval moralities; by the Providential readings of history propounded in such Tudor apologists as Polydore Vergil and Hall; by the carefully articulated moral and religious teachings of the Homilies; and by the Christian values of forgiveness and reconciliation explicit in the Bible and the Book of Common Prayer, as it is by purely Machiavellian or materialist notions of society and of the self. Although there are enough Bardolphs, Bushys, Bagots, Greens, Dolls, Pistols, Shallows, and Silences—not to mention the boys and the luggage in *Henry V*—to remind us of Bosola's memorable sentiments in *The Duchess of Malfi* that as human beings we are no more than "fantastical puff-paste" whose lives end merely "in a little point, a kind of nothing" (Brown, 4.2.126; 5.5.7), there are also enough moments of personal triumph and spiritual gain in these plays to suggest, as Ferdinand affirms in *The Tempest*, that "some kinds of baseness / Are nobly undergone and most poor matters / Point to rich ends" (3.1.2–4).[3] Just how richly these ends are expressed in the second tetralogy and—more pertinently—to what extent we may want to see them in a Christian perspective and as occupying an important place in Shakespeare's conception of history, is the subject I should like to pursue in this essay.

II

I intend to take as a sort of paradigm for our discussion a useful yet often overlooked article by James Black, suggestively entitled "Henry IV's Pilgrimage." Black examines Henry IV's obsession with a voyage to the Holy Land—which, of course, many critics see in an unremittingly cynical light—calling it "a pilgrimage not just of remorse or of politics, but of the heart" (19). He traces each reference to travel by Henry from *Richard II* through *2 Henry IV*, noting that Henry tends habitually to think in terms of expiatory pilgrimages involving weary travel, hard marching, and compelled wandering. For Black, these references are too powerfully entrenched in Henry's imagination to be dismissed as expressions of Machiavellian policy alone; rather the king's obsession with the Holy Land creates a verbal and psychological context in which his death in the Jerusalem Chamber can be seen as expressing, instead of ironic futility, a king and a kingdom finally at peace. The sense

The Chronicles of Emptiness   85

of ironic failure that critics from Harold Goddard on have seen in
the circumstances of Henry's death—Goddard maintains that
Henry has arrived in Jerusalem "neither literally nor spiritually"
(198)—appears to be belied by Henry's own words:

> Laud be to God! Even there my life must end.
> It hath been prophesied to me many years,
> I should not die but in Jerusalem,
> Which vainly I suppos'd the Holy Land.
> But bear me to that chamber, there I'll lie,
> In that Jerusalem shall Henry die.
>
> (4.5.235–40)

Henry accepts his death, what he referred to moments earlier as
the "period" of his "worldly business" (4.5.230), with praise for
God and the sense of a spiritual journey fulfilled. The Jerusalem
that he had struggled unsuccessfully to attain, *both* to distract his
enemies from problems at home *and* in expiation for his sins, God
provides for him in the Jerusalem Chamber adjacent to Westminster Abbey. What Goddard sees as a journey to "Jerusalem" in
only the most "bitterly ironical sense," undertaken by a man of
hypocrisy and mendacity (198), Black reformulates into "a blessing
conferred upon Henry," and one that he believes that Shakespeare
never would have accorded a man whose motives were exclusively duplicitous or Machiavellian (Black 25).

It is important to recognize here that Black's position, as thor-
oughgoingly "Christian" as it may be, is nevertheless perfectly
consistent with a clear-eyed view of Henry that fully acknowledges his famously Machiavellian behavior. If it is only proper to
acknowledge that Henry throughout the tetralogy has been a man
with one eye fixed intently on the world, it is surely just as proper
to recognize that with the other he looks with equal steadfastness
toward heaven. Henry's symbolic expiration in the Jerusalem
Chamber, then, might well remind us that the peace the troubled
king finds there is intended for precisely such inwardly divided
souls, "shaken" and "wan with care" (*1 Henry IV*, 1.1.1) as he. Extremely important also for our purposes is the fact that symbolically and substantively Henry finds rest from his wearisome
earthly travels (and travails) through failure; he never reaches the
distant Jerusalem toward which he has so longingly inclined (for
whatever complex of motives), but he nonetheless—against his
will and expectations yet somehow strangely in fulfillment of
them—finds just as comforting a spiritual "Jerusalem" near at
hand.[4]

86   *Joseph Candido*

Shakespearean irony can cut two ways; hence its undeniable presence in the scene of Henry's death (and elsewhere in the tetralogy) need not be interpreted as *necessarily* deflating. The spiritual paradigm that the scene depicts—where failure becomes success and loss becomes gain—is, of course, deeply embedded in Christian thought and practice. Christianity, as we all know, is a religion that insists upon such mystifying ironies. Jesus's paradoxical admonition that "He that will save his life, shall lose it, and he that loseth his life for my sake, shall save it," could hardly put the matter more succinctly; and the statement appears with only slight variations in all four gospels (Matthew 10:39; Mark 8:35; Luke 9:24 and 17:33; and John 12:25).[5] We also find the principle affirmed in any number of other biblical passages and rhetorical formulations, from Jesus' pronouncement that "many that are first, shall be last, and the last shall be first" (Matthew 19:30; and Mark 9:35 and 10:31), to the related narratives of the story of the wedding banquet at which both the proud and the modest seat themselves inappropriately at table and are ordered by their host to exchange places, and the story of the proud Pharisee who prays to God with assurance while the abashed Publican dares not even lift his face as he begs for mercy. In each of these instances Jesus again states the Christian paradox with simple and unambiguous clarity: "For whosoever exalteth himself, shall be brought low, and he that humbleth himself, shall be exalted" (Luke 14:11; and 19:14). Also worth noting for our purposes is the similarly paradoxical notion of *felix culpa* (the idea that the Original Sin of Adam and Eve actually becomes a "happy fault" when we consider that their transgression necessitates the Incarnation), in literary works as diverse and temporally removed from one another as "Adam lay ybounden," the Corpus Christi plays, and *Paradise Lost*.

With this very basic pattern of Christian irony and paradox in mind, let us look at three other episodes in the second tetralogy as a starting place for us to consider just how far we can go in attempting to establish a Christian context for the repeated instances of disappointment and defeat that Shakespeare gives us in these plays. Each episode is characterized by royal speeches of considerable length and plaintiveness that give us similarly resonant perspectives on failure and loss, and in each sequence the name and presence of God are explicitly evoked. The episodes are, in chronological order, (1) the long deathbed sequence in *2 Henry IV* where Hal removes his father's crown and then restores it (4.5.1–224); (2) the episode in *Henry V* during which the treason of Cambridge,

The Chronicles of Emptiness   87

Scroop, and Grey is brought to light (2.2.12–181); and (3) Hal's nocturnal visit with his soldiers on the eve of the Battle of Agincourt in *Henry V* (4.1.85–305).

III

The scene between Henry IV and Hal (4.5) presents us with one of the most finely expressed ironies in the second tetralogy as Henry, the kinsman who deposed Richard II and forced the king to suffer the deep sense of isolation and rejection that comes with the loss of his crown, experiences something of the same treatment at the hands of his son. The deposer of Richard II, for a long and painful moment, discovers what it is like to have the crown snatched from him, to suffer a kind of metaphorical "deposition," not just at the hands of a kinsman, but at the hands of his own son. He goes to sleep a king and awakes uncrowned—or, to use Richard's apt term for it—"subjected" (*Richard II*, 3.2.176) to an ambitious blood relation who apparently cannot wait to wrest his royal inheritance from his father until after his death. "Here, cousin, seize the crown" (*Richard II*, 4.1.181) were Richard's artfully reproachful words to Bullingbrook; and now the old and dying king, experiencing the same sense of helpless demise that plagued his royal predecessor, must feel exactly what it is like to be on the receiving end of such a callously self-interested action. Like Richard, Henry expresses his suffering in strikingly Christological terms; his remorseful statement to Hal after he thinks that his son has taken the crown prematurely, "What, canst thou not forbear me half an hour" (4.5.109), strangely echoes Christ's reproach to Peter and the disciples in the Garden of Gethsemane: "What? Could ye not watch with me one hour?" (Matthew 26:40; and Mark 14:37). The parallel is intriguing, not only because it reminds us of the poignant sense of alienation and emptiness that inevitably attend the death of an abandoned king (earthly or divine), but also because it delicately and obliquely invests Henry—if only for a moment—with a dignity in his aloneness that associates him with the suffering God. And again like Richard, that most self-consciously Christological of all Shakespearean kings, Henry must experience the horror of seeing his own Body Politic (the political extension of his Body Personal as stipulated in the religio-political doctrine of The King's Two Bodies)[6] veering toward nihilism:

88   *Joseph Candido*

> For now a time is come to mock at form.
> ....
> For the fift Harry from curb'd license plucks
> The muzzle of restraint, and the wild dog
> Shall flesh his tooth on every innocent.
> O my poor kingdom, sick with civil blows!
> When that my care could not withhold thy riots,
> What wilt thou do when riot is thy care?
> O, thou wilt be a wilderness again,
> Peopled with wolves, thy old inhabitants!
>
> (4.5.118; 130–37)

What Henry also experiences, however, is a redemptive moment utterly denied to Richard—an immediate reconciliation with his usurper during which he is allowed to see his "loss" as a clear and explicit avenue to spiritual gain. When Hal returns and finds his father still alive he delivers his long apology and then immediately returns the crown to him, invoking the name of God as he does so: "There is your crown; / And He that wears the crown immortally / Long guard it yours!" (4.5.142–44). Henry responds fully in the manner of a man experiencing the joy of spiritual peace and reconciliation, even to the extent of seeing a clear connection between his momentary feelings of estrangement and his newfound joy in Hal. Moreover, Henry sees the whole episode as divinely ordained:

> O my son,
> God put it in thy mind to take it hence,
> That thou mightst win the more thy father's love,
> Pleading so wisely in excuse of it!
>
> (4.5.177–80)

Shakespeare delicately emphasizes Henry's powerful sense of reconciliation with Hal here through the dying king's use of such familiar terms as "son" and "father," as well as by the rather touching gesture that this particular father, who from the opening scene of *1 Henry IV* (1.1.77–91) has felt so emotionally distanced from his son, makes with the artless simplicity that always seems to accompany real feeling:

> Come hither, Harry, sit thou by my bed,
> And hear (I think) the very latest counsel
> That ever I shall breathe.
>
> (4.5.181–83)

As Hal re-positions himself physically by moving closer to his father, we sense a corresponding shift in their emotional relationship

The Chronicles of Emptiness 89

as well. The moment represents not only a complete interior reversal for Henry but also what amounts to a psychological wish-fulfillment for the father who, as far back as *Richard II*, had agonized over his physical and psychological separation from his son ("Can no man tell me of my unthrifty son? / 'Tis full three months since I did see him last" [*Richard II*, 5.3.1–2]). The old king's frustration over Hal's prolonged absence, his repeated negative comparisons of his son to Hotspur, his nagging sense of doom over Hal's eventual kingship, his dismay over the prince's apparent "relapse" in *2 Henry IV* back to Falstaff (the rival father) and away from the authentic one, all seem to evaporate in a moment as Henry experiences the joy of a freshly renewed intimacy with his son. The episode is by far the most unguarded that either Henry or Hal ever allows himself, yet Shakespeare averts any headlong rush toward sentimentality with one of the most disconcerting moments in the whole tetralogy. With his dying breath Henry cannot resist giving Hal the infamous advice "to busy giddy minds / With foreign quarrels" (4.5.213–14). Such a piece of stark Machiavellianism may easily give pause to even the most ardent of Henry's sympathizers, as indeed it has animated so many of his severest critics. We might do well to remind ourselves, however, that in Shakespeare's second tetralogy policy and piety can often occupy, perhaps incongruously but not always contradictorily, the same psychological space. There is nothing in Henry's admittedly pragmatic admonition to Hal that need cancel out the dying king's genuine longing for personal or spiritual renewal. A penitent—especially a royal penitent—may feel remorse for his past transgressions even as he concerns himself with the practical concerns of those he leaves behind ("How came I by the crown, O God forgive, / And grant it may with thee in true peace live!" [4.5.218–19]) in just the same way that a beleaguered king may decide on a military action in a distant Jerusalem that he hopes will bring peace both to his kingdom and to his troubled soul.

What follows, of course, is Henry's acquiescent death in the Jerusalem Chamber—an event that, as we have seen, may be regarded as further imparting a quality of joyous reconciliation to the whole sequence, or, at the very least, be seen as casting it in a not altogether cynical light. Even the old king himself, in confessing the unseemly "by-paths and indirect crooked ways" by which he had acquired the crown, recognizes that his impending death somehow "Changes the mood" (4.5.184–85; 199). Henry is brought low—"deposed" so to speak—only so that he may experience a

90   *Joseph Candido*

reconciliation—through the acknowledgment of his political transgressions and his accompanying feelings of loneliness and abandonment—first, with his son, and finally with his God. That he feels that he must do so while also casting a chill political eye upon the future welfare of Hal and of the nation only underscores the tragic divisions that Shakespeare everywhere recognizes lie so vexingly at the heart of kingship itself.

IV

The episode with Cambridge, Scroop, and Grey in *Henry V* (2.2) is far more problematical than the father-son episode in *2 Henry IV*, since implicit in it are certain unspoken dynastic issues that lie beneath the characters' stated motives. In a fine essay on what he calls "the conspiracy of silence" in *Henry V*, Karl P. Wentersdorf points out that the real cause of the conspiracy (the claim to the throne of Richard, Earl of Cambridge through his wife, Anne Mortimer, the sister to Edmund Mortimer who was designated as rightful heir by Richard II) gets almost totally suppressed in the scene.[7] Instead Shakespeare emphasizes the corrupting influence of monetary gain as the primary motive for the conspiracy—"the gilt of France" as the Chorus so baldly puts it (Chorus 2.26).[8] Wentersdorf attributes this silence regarding the dynastic issue on the part of both Cambridge and Henry to their separate interests in concealing the matter: Cambridge suppresses his true dynastic motives after his treason is discovered because he wants to ameliorate the king's anger as much as possible in order not to endanger the rights of his heirs to his title and lands, and Henry keeps silent on the question because he doesn't want to call attention to his own weak claim to the throne. Is it possible amid this swirl of dynastic cross-purposes and political maneuvering to see some measure of Christian peace and reconciliation emanating out of the bitter defeat of the traitors and Henry's harsh administration of justice?

Much of our interpretation of the episode, of course, depends upon how we respond to the behavior of the king. Most readers agree that there is something morally unpleasant (even smarmy) about the *coup de grâce* that Henry administers to the traitors—especially to Lord Scroop, a man of impeccable reputation for whom he professes a deep and sincere personal friendship. After baiting his adversaries with the story of his intended clemency toward the

The Chronicles of Emptiness 91

drunken man who "rail'd against [his] person" (2.2.41), Henry seems to delight in the trap he springs for the traitors after they counsel him against mercy:

> We'll yet enlarge that man
> Though Cambridge, Scroop, and Grey, in their dear care
> And tender preservation of our person,
> Would have him punish'd....
>
> (2.2.57–60)

And he continues in the same vein of unctuous irony after handing the traitors their death warrants, which they mistakenly suppose to be their "commissions" for the invasion of France:

> Why, how now, gentlemen?
> What see you in those papers that you lose
> So much complexion?—Look ye how they change!
> Their cheeks are paper.—Why, what read you there
> That have so cowarded and chas'd your blood
> Out of appearance?
>
> (2.2.71–76)

This is not merely the voice of justice, but rather the attitude of a man who enjoys seeing his fish dangle on the hook before he hauls them in. But Henry also speaks with another voice in the scene, that of the faithful friend struck to the quick by the betrayal of a trusted confidant. And in so doing, he not only implies a reason, perhaps, for the immoderation of his former behavior; he also begins to sound a good deal like his plaintive father:

> But O,
> What shall I say to thee, Lord Scroop, thou cruel,
> Ingrateful, savage, and inhuman creature?
> Thou that didst bear the key of all my counsels,
> That knew'st the very bottom of my soul,
> That (almost) mightst have coin'd me into gold,
> Wouldst thou have practic'd on me, for thy use?
> (2.2.93–99)

How are we to reconcile these two voices of the king? One way, of course, is to regard Henry as a royal hypocrite of the first order—audacious and mendacious—who can slip in and out of whatever moral register he pleases to suit changing political circumstances. But his plaintive reproach to Scroop, occupying some fifty lines, has the ring of real pain to it—it is the voice of Richard II and of Henry IV on those occasions when they have had to en-

92   *Joseph Candido*

dure similar feelings of disillusionment at the falling off of trusted friends:

> O, how hast thou with jealousy infected
> The sweetness of affiance! Show men dutiful?
> Why, so didst thou. Seem they grave and learned?
> Why, so didst thou. Come they of noble family?
> Why, so didst thou. Seem they religious?
> Why, so didst thou....
>
> (2.2.126–31)[9]

If we regard Henry's two separate voices here as rhetorical expressions of the two separate yet united aspects of the King's Two Bodies, we need find no necessary incompatibility between the two. The first voice is that of the royal head of state, who must impose the harshest and most indifferent justice upon traitors whatever their personal closeness to the king, and the second that of the man who, in Richard II's memorable words, "feel[s] want" and "taste[s] grief" (*Richard II*, 3.2.175–76). The two voices blend delicately—and I would say *not* hypocritically—in Henry's reply directed, first, to Scroop, and then to the traitors collectively:

> I will weep for thee;
> For this revolt of thine, methinks, is like
> A second fall of man. Their faults are open,
> Arrest them to the answer of the law,
> And God acquit them of their practices!
>
> (2.2.140–44)

As a man touched by the "fall" and subsequent betrayal of a friend, Henry weeps; as a royal figure who is the embodiment of Law, he condemns the traitors to death. And, as was the case during his father's mock "deposition" scene, we sense here, in the aftermath of Henry V's feelings of isolation and loss, the emergence of a redemptive—and explicitly religious—sense of moral transformation. Precisely the distinction that Henry makes between insisting upon the penalty of earthly law while at the same time invoking the comfort of divine forgiveness gets repeated by the traitors as, one by one, they echo the king's sentiments exactly. Scroop openly and, with apparent sincerity, acknowledges God's justness in revealing his traitorous purposes, repents his fault, and asks for the king's forgiveness. Cambridge follows suit, thanking God explicitly for aborting the plot, rejoicing in his own capture, and beseeching God and Henry to pardon him. Grey ends the litany of repentance in a similar vein, expressing joy at the discov-

The Chronicles of Emptiness 93

ery of his treason and asking Henry to pardon his fault but not his body.

It is, of course, possible to regard the traitors' sudden burst of repentance here as no more than a hollow bit of political grandstanding, cynically orchestrated as a last-ditch attempt to obtain princely pardon, or, in a similarly pejorative vein, as a mere cultural formality, the *de rigueur* behavior of sophisticated young aristocrats fashioning a last magnanimous and ostentatiously public farewell. The memorable scaffold speeches of Sir Thomas More, Lady Jane Grey, the Earl of Essex, and Sir Walter Raleigh, all attest to the prevalence of such a practice in sixteenth- and seventeenth-century England, and also give abundant evidence of how powerfully behavioral paradigms like the *ars moriendi* tradition informed such studiously self-reflective moments of earthly loss or defeat. And, as Wentersdorf points out, behind the traitors' ready acquiescence to Henry's justice lies their undoubted desire to ameliorate, in whatever way they can, the king's potential severity toward their families' titles and possessions (281).

But it is also possible to see the public repentance of the traitors as more than just conventional adherence to a culturally accepted code of aristocratic behavior or as a last, desperate attempt to protect the rights and privileges of their heirs. In his study of pain and the spectacle of punishment from the Middle Ages through the Renaissance, Mitchell B. Merback points out how important it was morally and socially for condemned malefactors to make a so-called "good death" in public (142–50).[10] Although Merback refers in his discussion to the behavior of criminals in the moments immediately preceding their public executions, his remarks are equally applicable to the situation of the traitors in *Henry V* who, like the condemned in such circumstances, make highly ritualized declarations of their guilt and repentance in full view of their auditory. Merback notes that an essential moral component of episodes such as these is the fact that the condemned are to be *seen* confessing their crimes, thus imparting both to the criminal and to the spectators a sense of emotional comfort and release:

> the community insisted that the spectacle be edifying, not as a lesson in the majesty of the law but as a drama of Christian repentance, purification and salvation. When, in their own eyes, a community had "paved the way to eternal life for a soul seemingly beyond redemption," the event may well have convinced spectators that redemption was possible for them as well. (144)

94   *Joseph Candido*

Such a therapeutic moral purification—what Merback calls "the communal need for social and moral order" (145)—invests each member of the auditory with a renewed sense of "the Christian values of community" (146).[11] In addition, the public "good death" of the condemned criminal also has the effect of "purg[ing] the community of its blood-guilt" while at the same time metaphorically and psychologically canceling out the "bad death" of the malefactor's real or intended victim (146). Such a death was "bad" because it was in most cases violent and sudden, took the victim unprepared for the life to come, and, most importantly, left the murdered person bereft of the last rites of the Church ("Unhous'led, disappointed, unanel'd" as old Hamlet's Ghost so aptly puts it [1.5.77]). Worth noting here is the fact that precisely the situation the Ghost describes would have existed if the traitors' plot to kill Henry had succeeded. Interesting too in this regard is the language the Chorus uses to characterize the conspirators' proposed murder: "And by their hands this *grace* of kings must die, / If *hell* and treason hold their promises" (Chorus 2.29–30, italics mine). Perhaps most significant, however, is the fact that, according to Merback, a strange sort of communality develops at the moment of public repentance between the condemned person and those who witness his or her punishment:

> ... popular sentiment sided with the condemned and urged him or her on to make a good repentance. Atonement rituals often included an *amende honorable*, or public acknowledgement of guilt, and a proclamation of repentance; although the ritual was designed mainly for citizens, culprits of all kinds were sentenced to perform it, and many did so upon the very ground where they committed their crimes. Addressing the crowd in this way, felons might recount their life stories, implore the judges for mercy, or ask the spectators for their prayers. (147–48)

> ... a "good death" inoculated the community from the threat of the vengeful returning dead: just as no one wanted to contemplate a sudden, unprepared death (*mors improvisa*) for themselves, the loose ends of the criminal's biography had to be tied tight, with everyone lending a hand. (146)

Clearly the traitors' sudden moral transformation in *Henry V*, despite the unquestioned political self-interest that lies behind it, acquires a richer social and spiritual significance when seen in the light of such an understanding of what it means for a condemned person (and the society in which that person lived and died) to participate jointly in a "good death." Thus the episode with the

The Chronicles of Emptiness   95

traitors depicts more than just a trap set for conspirators who then try to preserve their inheritances once they are caught; it also functions dramatically (and symbolically) to "clear" Henry, at least in part, of the weight of moral duplicity we might be inclined to ascribe to him even as it helps to draw together into a morally unified whole the English army that he takes with him to France.

Buttressing this complex of attitudes toward the "good death," and serving to bring it even more sharply into focus for a specifically English audience such as Shakespeare's, is a carefully articulated tradition of public repentance repeatedly affirmed in Anglican instructional and theological literature of the day. The two books of homilies published in 1547 and 1573 were, of course, well known to Elizabethans by virtue of the fact that they were read in all churches on rotating Sundays throughout the year. The Second Book of Homilies, printed twelve times from 1573 to 1600, contained the "Homilie of Repentance, and of True Reconciliation Vnto God," which, in its anticipation of Richard Hooker's remarks on repentance in *Of the Laws of Ecclesiastical Polity* (1594),[12] makes a clear distinction between two separate types of confession. The first form of confession is made privately to God, and the second, "another kinde of confession, which is needefull and necessary," is made openly to those individuals whom the sinner has offended:

> And of the same doeth Saint Iames speake, after this maner, saying: Acknowledge your faults to one another, and pray one for another, that yee may bee saued. As if hee should say: Open that which grieueth you, that a remedie maye be found. And this is commanded both for him that complayneth, and for him that heareth, *that the one should shew his griefe to the other. The true meaning of it is, that the faithfull ought to Acknowledge their offences, whereby some hatred, rancour, ground, or malice, hauing risen or growen among them one to another, that a brotherly reconciliation may be had....* (italics mine)[13]

The point that "we ought to confesse our weaknesse and infirmities one to another" is reiterated twice more in the homily, and is unmistakably related to the "true parts and tokens of Repentance" that the text later enunciates:

> ... heartie contrition and sorrowfulnesse of our hearts, vnfained confession in word of mouth for our vnworthy liuing before GOD, a stedfast faith to the merites of our Sauiour Christ for pardon, and a purpose of our selues by GODS grace to renounce our former wicked life....

96   *Joseph Candido*

The statements of Cambridge, Scroop, and Grey, taken together as a unified choric sequence on the virtue of repentance, could almost serve as a textbook example of precisely the sort of public confession the homily enjoins. Not only do all three traitors immediately acknowledge their transgressions to Henry in the hearing of the full assembly, they do so in a fashion explicitly in keeping with the homily's "true parts and tokens of Repentance": (1) hearty contrition and sorrowfulness of heart; (2) confession "in word of mouth"; (3) petition for Christ's pardon; and (4) renunciation of their former transgressions:

> *Scroop.* Our purposes God justly hath discover'd,
> And I repent my fault more than my death,
> Which I beseech your Highness to forgive,
> Although my body pay the price of it.
>   *Cam.* For me, the gold of France did not seduce,
> Although I did admit it as a motive
> The sooner to effect what I intended.
> But God be thanked for prevention,
> Which I in sufferance heartily will rejoice,
> Beseeching God, and you, to pardon me.
>   *Grey.* Never did faithful subject more rejoice
> At the discovery of most dangerous treason
> Than I do at this hour joy o'er myself,
> Prevented from a damned enterprise.
> My fault, but not my body, pardon, sovereign
>   (2.2.151–65)

Unless we want to see the scene in the most unremittingly ironic light (and this would mean that we would have to regard all three traitors as shamelessly trying to save their skins by drenching themselves in religious pieties for reasons of self-interest *alone*, and Henry, despite his own undoubted political motives, as not believing a single word of moral righteousness that he utters), what Shakespeare gives us here are three malefactors who not only repent their evil along the lines specifically prescribed in the homily, but actually rejoice in their capture and praise the king who condemns them to death—and a king who truly sees his near escape from treachery as an act of divine intervention.

I should make absolutely clear here that I am not contending that the political complexities and dynastic politics that underlie the episode should be soft-pedaled or brushed aside. These "silent" yet palpable aspects of the scene are clearly crucial to our understanding of the behavior of Henry and that of the traitors,

The Chronicles of Emptiness

and may well be seen as imparting to Henry that odor of hypocrisy that so many critics see surrounding him as he goes about busying giddy minds with foreign quarrels. I should also like to suggest, however, that such negative considerations, as powerfully as we may wish to see them operating in the episode, also collide with other, more positive, considerations equally as powerful. The whole sequence, for example, in its admittedly preternatural note of acquiescence to Divine Will as embodied in the justice of the king, helps invest Henry with that sense of miraculous accomplishment and moral punctiliousness that makes him, in the famously provocative words of the Chorus, "the mirror of all Christian kings" (Chorus 2.6). And just as we would be remiss to overlook the dynastic issues that lie behind the scene, we likewise should not ignore the fact that in its emphasis upon ritual speechifying, ostentatious repentance, and public acceptance of death, it deftly superimposes the tradition of the socially and morally therapeutic "good death" upon the behavioral norms explicitly prescribed in the "Homilie of Repentance."

What follows is Henry's stern justice; and although his sentencing of the traitors is admittedly severe, no one, and most particularly not the traitors themselves, voices the slightest doubts regarding its moral, social, or theological correctness. We may wish, with Wentersdorf and others, to see such behavior on the part of the traitors as proceeding in the main from political self-interest, but Shakespeare's studied "silence" regarding the dynastic issue may just as easily be seen as functioning dramatically here to de-emphasize the political dimension of the scene and bring into sharper relief the sense of providential good fortune that seems always to accompany Henry's enterprises. And unless we wish to regard Henry as an ironist on something of the order of Richard III, it seems to me that we must take his repeated hopes that God will pardon the traitors at face value, as well as his exultation that

> We doubt not of a fair and lucky war,
> Since God so graciously hath brought to light
> This dangerous treason lurking in our way
> To hinder our beginnings. We doubt not now
> But every rub is smoothed on our way.
> Then forth, dear countrymen! Let us deliver
> Our puissance into the hand of God,
> Putting it straight in expedition.
>
> (2.2.184–91)

98   *Joseph Candido*

Whatever aversion we as modern readers might have to public expressions of this sort, the miraculously successful campaign of the king in France seems to give them credence. Henry does appear to be associated throughout the play with preternatural acts of courage, good fortune, and political acumen. What the episode with the traitors can be seen as presenting, then, despite the jostling for political survival that colors its workings, is a movement from earthly disappointment to religious assurance (on the part of the traitors, the king, and the society at large) that resembles the similar pattern seen in Henry IV's "failed" pilgrimage to Jerusalem and his mock "deposition." In all three cases poor earthly matters—loss, disappointment, and frustration—point to rich spiritual ends. Henry's exclamation "Cheerly to sea! The signs of war advance! / No king of England, if not king of France!" (2.2.191–92) may sound offensively jingoistic to our ears, but in the aftermath of an episode that may have been seen by Shakespeare's audience—no strangers to public displays like those of the traitors' repentance—as an act that purified and re-ordered English society along lines specifically endorsed by social custom and ratified by the "Homilie of Repentance," it may well have sounded like the fit exultation of a prince newly-justified to himself, his people, and his God.[14]

V

Henry's nocturnal visit with his soldiers on the eve of the Battle of Agincourt (4.1) posits even more problems—and more serious ones—than the episode with the traitors. As Anne Barton points out, the motif of the disguised king who converses with his subjects was a familiar one in late Elizabethan history plays as well as in popular ballads of the day. In each of these instances the king is presented as just and tolerant, and the meetings result in harmony and understanding—the premise being that the king is a man like all men and sensitive to the problems of others. Barton sees Henry's meeting with Bates, Court, and Williams as evoking this naive notion only to reject it as falsely romantic; rather the episode demonstrates the wide gap that divides monarch from subject as well as the high price Henry pays for subordinating his individuality to the role of king. For Barton, this variation on the theme of the "King's Two Bodies" even appears in the wooing of Katherine (5.2), where we see the dilemma of a man whose "personal rela-

The Chronicles of Emptiness 99

tions" become severely inhibited by his "corporate self" (107)—a condition that contributes to "tragic" rather than to "comical" history.

Barton is, of course, absolutely right. The king who seeks to bond with his soldiers on the eve of his most terrifying military trial finds instead the sense of alienation, disappointment, and aloneness that seems everywhere to dog the royal personages of the second tetralogy. Henry's attempt to clear his conscience on the eve of battle results not only in the heavy burden of responsibility that Williams places upon him for the untimely deaths of those he leads into harm's way, but also to an open quarrel with one of the very soldiers with whom he seeks connection. "O heavy burthen" laments Claudius in *Hamlet* (3.1.53), another of Shakespeare's kings who also must deal with the loneliness and moral paralysis of guilt. But whereas Claudius cannot pray, "though inclination be as sharp as will" (3.3.39), Henry does—and does so readily. I would like to suggest that the contrast is instructive. The Henry haters—and they all come out for this episode—would do well to consider that Shakespeare gives us an extremely rare glimpse of the inner workings of Henry's conscience at this moment in the play, first in his famous speech on ceremony (another of those long, plaintive utterances that reminds us of his father and of Richard II at their most isolated and abject), and second, in the prayer he utters just after the brief interruption by Sir Thomas Erpingham (4.1.230–84; 289–305). No scene in all of Shakespeare's histories gives us a king under more strain—personal, moral, political, or religious—than does this one. Guilt-ridden, alone, fearful for the day to come, faced with apparently insurmountable odds and almost certain military disaster, Henry turns to God:

> O God of battles, steel my soldiers' hearts,
> Possess them not with fear! Take from them now
> The sense of reck'ning, if th' opposed numbers
> Pluck their hearts from them. Not to-day, O Lord,
> O, not to-day, think not upon the fault
> My father made in compassing the crown!
> I Richard's body have interred new,
> And on it have bestowed more contrite tears,
> Than from it issued forced drops of blood.
> Five hundred poor have I in yearly pay,
> Who twice a day their wither'd hands hold up
> Toward heaven, to pardon blood; and I have built
> Two chantries, where the sad and solemn priests
> Sing still for Richard's soul. More will I do;

100   *Joseph Candido*

> Though all that I can do is nothing worth,
> Since that my penitence comes after all,
> Imploring pardon.
>
> (4.1.289–305)

To my ears, at least, this private prayer (following in the wake of the long, private speech on the burdens of ceremony) is not the statement of a hypocrite. Like Henry's earlier reproach to Scroop, it has the ring of real sincerity. And, as in the earlier episode with the traitors, here Henry's deep sense of disappointment and isolation leads in due course to a positive conclusion—in this case the miraculous victory at Agincourt.

It is, of course, fashionable to regard Henry's public pronouncements after the battle that God was on the side of the English as jingoistic nonsense—the unseemly stuff of political mythmaking at its most self-serving (not to mention politically incorrect)—but such statements can also be seen as the perfectly logical response of a grateful penitent who may well have seen his improbable triumph as indicating God's clemency for his father's deposition of Richard as well as a divine ratification of his own kingship. (We might recall here that the English saw the similarly miraculous defeat of the Spanish Armada in very much the same light; i.e., as a divine endorsement of the reformed Anglican Church and as a sign of the moral and religious legitimacy of Elizabeth's reign.) For those of us who feel a bit queasy about the facile blending of politics and religion these days, Henry's ostentatious appropriation of God might strike just the wrong religio-political note. But it is important to recognize that such statements as the following, along with the singing of the *non nobis* and *Te Deum*, form a rhetorically apposite capstone to Henry's earlier prayer to "the God of battles":

> Praised be God, and not our strength....
>
> (4.7.87)

> O God, thy arm was here;
> And not to us, but to thy arm alone,
> Ascribe we all!
>
> (4.8. 106–08)

> Take it [i.e., the victory], God,
> For it is none but thine!
>
> (4.8.111–12)

> … be it death proclaimed through our host
> To boast of this, or take that praise from God
> Which is his only.
>
> (4.8.114–16)

The Chronicles of Emptiness 101

... God fought for us.

(4.8.120)

This whole sequence of ostentatious piety is, to Henry's mind at least, an appropriately religious expression of thanks for a prayer answered and a kingship apparently ratified by God. In this context even the texts of the *Non nobis* and *Te Deum* are significant. The psychological sincerity of Henry's praises to God on the occasion of the miraculous victory at Agincourt may be gauged by how closely his sentiments (in tone as well as in substance) seem to echo those of the holy texts that come immediately to his mind and that he orders his soldiers to sing (4.8.123). The *Te Deum*, for example, is replete with passages glorifying the awesome might of God;[15] and the king's encomiums to God after the battle, quoted above, amount to a virtual translation of the opening lines of the *Non nobis*:

> Not unto us, O Lord, not unto us, but unto thy Name
> give the glory, for thy loving mercy and for thy truth's sake.

Significant, too, is the introductory rubric preceding the *Non nobis* (i.e., Psalm 115), which may be seen as shedding further benign light on Henry's prayers both before and after the battle. Indeed, the words of the rubric express an uncanny applicability to Henry and his war in France, especially when we recall that Shakespeare's audience might well regard the play through the lens of post-Reformation views of the French who were, of course, still officially devoted to Roman Catholicism:

PSAL. CXV.

A prayer of the faithful [i.e., the Israelites] *oppressed by idolatrous tyrants against whom they desire that God would succor them.... Trusting most constantly that God will preserve them in their need, seeing that he hath adopted and received them to his favor.... Promising finally that they will not be unmindful of so great a benefit, if it would please God to hear their prayer, and deliver them by his omnipotent power.*[16]

VI

None of this, of course, need be seen as *completely* whitewashing the character of Henry. The modifying characteristics of the king and the play that so many critics see as undermining the heroism

102   Joseph Candido

of the tetralogy are unmistakably present—and unmistakable elements of Shakespeare's complex picture of political man. But so is the notion of Christian redemption, where a soul steeped in loneliness and isolation (for whatever reason) locates a spiritual good in what seems to be a terrible sense of disappointment or defeat. In an article several years ago, I argued that the mark of the Bastard's political and moral superiority in *King John* is that, in a play obsessed with the polar opposites of purity and adulteration, he stands for a sort of synthetic compromise between the two—what I called "wholesome impurity or 'good' adulteration"—that is, an attitude toward life that enables him to find a meaningful good even in a manifest evil ("Blots, Stains, and Adulteries," 123). What I had in mind here is not some notion of moral relativity, but the idea—it seems to me so eloquently expressed throughout Shakespeare's career—that we are all a perplexing mixture of evil and of good, and that Shakespeare's most enlightened thinkers—the Prosperos, Faulconbridges, and Henry Vs of the world recognize the fact—and that his sadly deficient characters like Angelo, Jacques, and Malvolio do not. To say that Henry V exploits his religion for all that it is worth politically is fair enough; but to say that his belief is insincere or cynical for that reason, as many critics seek to do, seems totally off the mark. In Shakespeare's second tetralogy poor matters certainly point to rich ends—to the fact that we can sometimes locate God just as intensely in our deficiencies as we can in our moments of greatest spiritual assurance. But they also point out the fact that the people who experience such transformations are hardly perfect, nor should we expect them to be so. The Bullingbrooks, Richard IIs, Falstaffs, and Henry Vs of Shakespeare's histories all have flaws enough to encourage the most cynical readings of these plays, and also flaws enough to invite the most comically Christian ones as well.

Notes

1. For a sampling of the range and variety of this sort of criticism see Belsey; Greenblatt (21–65); Macdonald; Burckhardt (144–205); Goddard (148–268, but especially 215–268); Hodgdon (127–211); Winny (48–214); and Rackin (especially 67–70; 117–42; and 164–68).

2. See, especially, Greenblatt (21–65); Mallett; Cox (104–27); Pye (13–42); Traub (50–70); Spencer; and Dollimore and Sinfield.

3. All references to Shakespeare are to Evans' *Riverside* edition.

The Chronicles of Emptiness 103

4. The point is made with even more emphasis in Shakespeare's source for the scene, Holinshed's *Chronicles* (1587). See Bullough (IV:278), where the passage from Holinshed reads as follows: "... At length, he [Henry] recovered his speech, and understanding and perceiving himselfe in a strange place which he knew not, he willed to know if the chamber had anie particular name, whereunto answer was made, that it was called Jerusalem. Then said the king; Lauds be given to the father of heaven, for now I know that I shall die heere in this chamber, according to the prophesie of me declared, that I should depart this life in Jerusalem."

5. All citations of biblical passages are to Berry. When parallel biblical passages are cited, as in this instance, the quotation is always from Matthew. When parallel biblical passages are quoted from the same gospel, the quotation is always to the first reference cited. *The Geneva Bible* is most likely the version that Shakespeare consulted during the period 1596–1599, when he was writing the *Henry IV* plays and *Henry V* (Berry 20). For all quotations I have modernized spelling but retained the original punctuation.

6. For the definitive explanation of the doctrine of The King's Two Bodies see Kantorowicz (especially 24–41).

7. I am also extremely indebted to Professor Charles R. Forker for his helpful information and advice on the dynastic issues underlying this scene.

8. Although Shakespeare emphasizes that "the gold of France" (2.2.155) was a partial motive for Cambridge, it is also important to note that he also raises the true dynastic motive for the plot, albeit obliquely. Here are Cambridge's exact words: "For me, the gold of France did not seduce, / Although I did admit it as a motive / The sooner to effect what I intended" (2.2.155–57). Cambridge's "what I intended" clearly refers to his scheme to place Mortimer on the throne.

9. It is important to note that Henry's rhetoric here (which some may regard as stilted and artificial) curiously evokes that of Richard II at those times when the suffering king appears at his most authentic. The litaneutical quality of Henry's string of initial repetitions here is very much in Richard's rhetorical vein. See, for example, the quotations below; the first passage occurs when Richard appears on the walls of Flint Castle, and the second during the deposition scene:

> I'll give my jewels for a set of beads,
> My gorgeous palace for a hermitage,
> My gay apparel for an almsman's gown,
> My figur'd goblets for a dish of wood,
> My sceptre for a palmer's walking staff,
> My subjects for a pair of carved saints....
> (*Richard II*, 3.3.147–52)

> With mine own tears I wash away my balm,
> With mine own hands I give away my crown,

104   *Joseph Candido*

With mine own tongue deny my sacred state,
With mine own breath release all duteous oaths....
(*Richard II*, 4.1.207–10)

10. Also of interest is Guthke who, in his discussion of dying speeches in Shakespeare (35–47), observes that it was a widespread belief during the Renaissance that a dying person's last words were considered always to be true, and demonstrates how Shakespeare works variations on this convention to suit his thematic ends in a variety of plays. He does not mention *Henry V*.

11. Sharpe (160) notes that in moments such as these that "The objective was to produce an active and convinced godliness, even if this was only obtained in the last few days or even the last few hours of the condemned's life. No effort should be spared in bringing the lost sheep back to the flock, even if they were shortly to be transformed into mutton."

12. Hooker's statements on penitence and confession appear in Book Six of *Of The Laws of Ecclesiastical Polity* (III:6–52), ed. P.G. Stanwood (Hill, *Folger Edition*). In attempting to illustrate that there is no biblical, and hence no sacramental, foundation for private, auricular confession as practiced by Roman Catholics, Hooker cites Church Fathers such as St. Cyprian, Salvianus, St. Ambrose, and Gennadius as advocating public confession of sins (23–29). Although he does not dismiss the virtue of private confession entirely, Hooker clearly thinks that the sort of "publick prayers to Almightie God with publick acknowledgment of our sinnes" as practiced in the Anglican Church is sufficient (47).

13. Lancashire's online edition of "An Homilie of Repentance" is not paginated.

14. Wentersdorf points out that the playgoers in Shakespeare's audience at the Globe would have been highly aware of the unspoken but implicit dynastic background to the scene, and cites abundant evidence from Shakespeare's other histories where the text explicitly alludes to the issue (279–85). Such is undoubtedly the case. But this same audience, familiar as they also were with the Homilies and the spectacle of public execution, would no doubt have been equally sensitive to the issues I suggest are just as implicit in the scene.

15. The text of the *Te Deum* is too long to quote in its entirety, but the following excerpts (the first eleven lines of the hymn as translated in the Prayer Book) will give some sense of its tonal and substantive applicability as a song of praise for a great military victory (Booty 53–54).

We praise thee, O God: we acknowledge thee to be the Lord.
All the earth doth worship thee, the Father everlasting.
To thee all angels cry aloud: the heavens and all the powers therein.
To thee Cherubin and Seraphin, continually do cry.
Holy, holy, holy, Lord God of Sabaoth.
Heaven and earth are full of the majesty of thy glory.
The glorious company of the apostles, praise thee.

The Chronicles of Emptiness 105

The goodly fellowship of the prophets, praise thee.
The noble army of martyrs, praise thee.
The holy Church throughout all the world, doth knowledge thee:
The Father of an infinite majesty.

16. See also my "Henry V's *Non Nobis*."

Works Cited

Barton, Anne. "The King Disguised: Shakespeare's *Henry V* and the Comical History." In *The Triple Bond: Plays, Mainly Shakespearean, in Performance*, ed. Joseph G. Price. University Park: Pennsylvania State UP, 1975. 92–117.

Belsey, Catherine. "Making Histories Then and Now: Shakespeare from *Richard II* to *Henry V*." In *Uses of History: Marxism, Postmodernism, and the Renaissance*, ed. Francis Parker, Peter Hulme, and Margaret Iverson. Manchester: Manchester UP, 1991. 32–46.

Berry, Lloyd E., intr. *The Geneva Bible: A Facsimile of the 1560 Edition*. Madison: U of Wisconsin P, 1969.

Black, James. "Henry IV's Pilgrimage." *Shakespeare Quarterly* 34 (1983): 18–26.

Booty, John E., ed. *The Book of Common Prayer 1559: The Elizabethan Prayer Book*. Washington DC: Folger Shakespeare Library, 1976.

Brown, John Russell, ed. *The Duchess of Malfi*. Cambridge, MA: Harvard UP, 1964.

Bullough, Geoffrey, ed. *Narrative and Dramatic Sources of Shakespeare*. 8 vols. London: Routledge and Kegan Paul, 1957–75.

Burckhardt, Sigurd. *Shakespearean Meanings*. Princeton: Princeton UP, 1968.

Candido, Joseph. "Henry V's *Non Nobis*." *Notes and Queries* n.s. 50,1 (March 2003): 42–43.

———. "Blots, Stains, and Adulteries: The Impurities in *King John*." In *"King John": New Perspectives*, ed. Deborah T. Curren-Aquino. Newark: U of Delaware P, 1989.

Cox, John D. *Shakespeare and the Dramaturgy of Power*. Princeton: Princeton UP, 1989.

Dollimore, Jonathan, and Alan Sinfield. "History and Ideology: The Instance of *Henry V*." In *Alternative Shakespeares*, ed. John Drakikis. London: Methuen, 1985.

Evans, G. Blakemore, et al., eds. *The Riverside Shakespeare*. Boston: Houghton Mifflin, 1974.

106   *Joseph Candido*

Goddard, Harold C. *The Meaning of Shakespeare.* Chicago: U of Chicago P, 1951.

Greenblatt, Stephen. *Shakespearean Negotiotions: The Circulation of Social Energy in Renaissance England.* Berkeley: U of California P, 1998.

Guthke, Karl S. *Last Words: Variations on a Theme in Cultural History.* Princeton: Princeton UP, 1992.

Hill, W. Speed, gen. ed. *The Folger Edition of the Works of Richard Hooker.* 3 vols. Cambridge, MA: Belknap P, 1977–81.

Hodgdon, Barbara. *The End Crowns All: Closure and Contradiction in Shakespeare's History.* Princeton: Princeton UP, 1991.

Kantorowicz, Ernst. *The King's Two Bodies: A Study in Mediaeval Theology.* Princeton: Princeton UP, 1957.

Lancashire, Ian, ed. "An Homilie of Repentance." *Renaissance Electronic Texts* 1.1, 1994. http://www.anglicanlibrary.org/homilies/bk2hom 20.htm

Macdonald, Ronald R. "Uneasy Lies: Language and History in Shakespeare's Lancastrian Tetralogy." *Shakespeare Quarterly* 35 (1984): 22–39.

Mallett, Phillip. "Shakespeare's Trickster Kings: Richard II and Henry V." In *The Fool and the Trickster,* ed. Paul V.A. Williams. Cambridge: D.S. Brewer, 1979. 64–82.

Merback, Mitchell B. *The Thief, the Cross, and the Wheel: Pain and the Spectacle of Punishment in Medieval and Renaissance Europe.* London: Reaktion Books, 1999.

Pye, Christopher. *The Regal Phantasm: Shakespeare and the Politics of Spectacle.* London: Routledge, 1992.

Rackin, Phyllis. *Stages of History: Shakespeare's English Chronicles.* Ithaca: Cornell UP, 1990.

Sharpe, J.A. "'Last Dying Speeches': Religion, Ideology and Public Execution in Seventeenth-Century England." *Past and Present* 107 (1985): 144–67.

Spencer, Janet M. "Princes, Pirates, and Pigs: Criminalizing Wars of Conquest in *Henry V.*" *Shakespeare Quarterly* 47 (1996): 160–77.

Traub, Valerie. *Desire and Anxiety: Circulations of Sexuality in Shakespearean Drama.* London: Routledge, 1992.

Wentersdorf, Karl P. "The Conspiracy of Silence in *Henry V.*" *Shakespeare Quarterly* 27 (1976): 264–87.

Winny, James. *The Player King: A Theme of Shakespeare's Histories.* London: Chatto and Windus, 1968.

Spilling Royal Blood:
Denial, Guilt and Expiation in Shakespeare's Second Historical Tetralogy
Charles R. Forker

I

It will come as no surprise to readers of this book to be told that there is a plethora of king-killing in Shakespeare. Examples proliferate: the saintly but inept Henry VI and the boy king Edward V both murdered in the Tower; the crookbacked tyrant Richard III slain at Bosworth; King John poisoned by a monk at Swinstead Abbey; Hamlet's father poisoned in his arbor, and his murderer Claudius correspondingly dispatched in retribution by being forced to drink his own envenomed chalice (not to mention the hacking to death of King Priam in the player's recitation to Hamlet and King Gonzago's poisoning in the "mouse-trap" that the Danish prince stages to expose his uncle); the gracious Duncan of Scotland and his murderer, King Macbeth; Queen Cordelia hanged at Edmund's command; the incestuous King of Antioch shriveled up by a bolt of lightning; and of course the martyr-king Richard II, about whom I shall have more to say at a later point. If we include among the royal victims the close relatives of kings and those who claim or aspire to thrones without ever actually being able to occupy them, the list becomes substantially longer: Henry VI's venerable uncle, Humphrey of Gloucester, strangled in his bed; Richard, Duke of York, massacred savagely on a mole-hill and his son, young Rutland, butchered in combat; Henry VI's son, Prince Edward, triply stabbed by Edward IV and his younger brothers; one of these brothers, the Duke of Clarence, stabbed and then drowned in a malmsey butt; Edward V's brother, the little Duke of York, smothered with his sibling in the Tower; Richard II's troublesome uncle, Duke of Gloucester, mysteriously made away at

108   *Charles R. Forker*

Calais; the Yorkist claimant, Richard, Earl of Cambridge, executed for treason by Henry V; still another Duke of York (the Aumerle of *Richard II* and the older brother of the treasonous Cambridge) a heroic casualty of Agincourt; Prince Arthur, the legitimate heir to the English crown, driven to leap to his death by King John who has ordered his murder; the would-be monarch Julius Caesar assassinated in Rome; and the Trojan Hector, King Priam's valiant son, slain in battle by Achilles' myrmidons. Shakespeare's tragedies and histories are obviously awash in royal blood, and even two of the so-called problem plays contain the motif tangentially.[1]

Judged by the light of the doctrine of the divine right of kings, officially endorsed by Elizabeth I and her Tudor precedessors, and even more strenuously promulgated by her Stuart successor James I, the murder of a reigning sovereign was the most heinous crime that Renaissance Englishmen could conceive. A sacramentally anointed king was uniquely double-natured, deriving his authority not from men but from God. His two bodies consisted of his *body politic* and his *body natural*. The body politic represented the entire state and was thus both ubiquitous and immortal, while his body natural, like that of other men, was subject to ordinary human frailties and limitations. The union of the two bodies, mystical and human, could be sundered only by death. To assassinate a legitimate king was thus to commit a triple crime—to violate not only the sixth commandment but also to be guilty of treason and blasphemy, to attack both the state and the divinely established order of the universe. The consequences of such an act were cataclysmic. When Macbeth contemplates murdering his sovereign, his imagery is apocalyptic: Duncan's virtues

> Will plead like angels, trumpet-tongu'd, against
> The deep damnation of his taking-off;
> And pity, like a naked new-born babe,
> Striding the blast, or heaven's cherubin, hors'd
> Upon the sightless couriers of the air,
> Shall blow the horrid deed in every eye,
> That tears shall drown the wind.
>   (*Macbeth*, 1.7.19–25)

Ordinarily in Shakespeare, the shedding of royal blood is morally unambiguous—treated as either a hideous outrage against established social, political and metaphysical order (as in the case of the innocent child Edward V and the virtuous kings, Hamlet and Duncan) or as the justified removal of a tyrannical criminal (as in the case of Richard III, Claudius and Macbeth, each of whom is

Spilling Royal Blood 109

a usurper). Occasionally in plays where political partisanship becomes a focus of interest, the absolutist opposition between good and evil in the matter of taking royal life is subject to a certain blurring. The death of Clarence in *Richard III*, for instance, is dramatized as a monstrous brutality, made more unnatural because it is also a fratricide; yet the victim in this case is scarcely innocent since the audience is made acutely aware that Clarence has formerly betrayed the White Rose (the political faction to which he had originally belonged) and has then also betrayed the Red Rose by reverting to his earlier allegiance—behavior that earns him the epithet "quicksand of deceit" (*3 Henry VI*, 5.4.26). In recounting his memorable dream to the keeper of his prison, ominously spoken before the hired murderers enter, Clarence himself imagines being accused in hell by the ghost of Warwick as "false, fleeting, perjur'd Clarence, / That stabb'd me in the field by Tewksbury" (*Richard III*, 1.4.55–56). Nevertheless, our sympathies in this scene reside almost wholly with Clarence, not only because he is genuinely repentant for his sins but also because the character responsible for his murder is his dissembling and cold-hearted brother, the satanic Richard of Gloucester. What I propose to argue in this essay is that the two murders in *Richard II*—that of Richard's uncle, Thomas of Woodstock, Duke of Gloucester (which occurs before the play opens but nevertheless dominates the early scenes as an issue) and that of Richard himself (which occurs at the end of the play)—represent special cases in the long roster of royal blood-lettings in Shakespeare; that both murders are handled in such a way as to complicate or problematize the morality and politics of the tragedy in which they figure; and finally that the ambiguities and uncertainties aroused in connection with the murder of King Richard resonate significantly in the later plays of the tetralogy, *1* and *2 Henry IV* and *Henry V*. My thesis is essentially that a certain moral cloudinesss surrounds these acts of violence that sets them apart from the treatment of most other royal murders in Shakespeare and that the dramatist deliberately obfuscates the issues in the interests of dramatic and political complexity.

II

The first third of *Richard II* concentrates on dramatizing Richard's unfitness to rule—his domination by flatterers, his spendthrift self-indulgence, his deafness to wise counsel, his ruinous taxation, his

110   *Charles R. Forker*

farming the realm, his use of blank charters, his unfair meting out of punishments at Coventry, his callous treatment of the dying Gaunt and his self-destructive confiscation of Bolingbroke's patrimony. But perhaps the most shocking of his tyrannies is his treacherous destruction of Gloucester, the uncle he obviously regarded as a threat. This crime is the most damaging element in the multiple charges of treason that Bolingbroke, attacking Richard indirectly through his subordinate, levels at Mowbray in the opening scene:

> Further I say, and further will maintain …
> That he did plot the Duke of Gloucester's death,
> Suggest his soon-believing adversaries,
> And consequently, like a traitor coward,
> Sluiced out his innocent soul through streams of blood—
> Which blood, like sacrificing Abel's, cries
> Even from the tongueless caverns of the earth
> To me for justice and rough chastisement.
>
> (1.1.98–106)

Here Bolingbroke, without fracturing court protocol (he has earlier claimed to be concerned for "the precious safety of [his] prince" [1.1.32]), seems actually to be menacing Richard by appointing himself as the avenger of Gloucester's murder, in effect sanctioning his vow by invoking a parallel to the mother of all slayings in Genesis. But Mowbray with as much passion as his accuser denies the charge as a vicious slander, though, in doing so, he seems partly to be protecting the King as well as defending his own honor:

> For Gloucester's death,
> I slew him not, but to my own disgrace
> Neglected my sworn duty in that case.
> (1.1.132–34)

Just what Mowbray's "neglect" consisted of remains unexplained. The opening episode in fact offers no clarification whatever about the mysterious circumstances of Gloucester's death, leaving us in total darkness about the truth or falsity of the charges and countercharges as well as of the denials and counterdenials. The only thing clear to an audience (unless the performers reveal by their body language more than is contained in their speeches) is that at least one of the two quarrelers, Bolingbroke or Mowbray, must be lying—or distorting facts through bias or willful concealment. Moreover, Richard presides as judge with unruffled demeanor and

Spilling Royal Blood 111

at least a facade of royal impartiality, betraying no hint of personal involvement in the matter of his kinsman's murder.

In the second scene Richard's responsibility for the death comes into clearer focus when Gloucester's widow urges Gaunt to take retribution for her husband's killing. Gaunt acknowledges that the King has "caused" the death but, in blatant contrast to his son (who seems to have cast himself in the role of justicer), he insists that punishment must be left to God since His "substitute, / His deputy anointed in His sight" (1.2.37–39), is himself the murderer; therefore, according to the doctrine propounded by the Tudor homilies on obedience, Gaunt may not bring him to human account. Gaunt, who after all is the murdered man's brother, is no less outraged by the bloodshed than the duchess. But in addition to insisting on the orthodoxy of passive obedience and Christian patience even under a tyrannical monarch, he nevertheless raises the remote possibility that Gloucester's death might somehow have been justified; for in attributing the killing to Richard, he hedges his words with the important and often ignored phrase, "if wrongfully" (1.2.39). As Touchstone says in the context of a more comic quarrel, "Your If is the only peacemaker; much virtue in If" (*As You Like It*, 5.4.102–03). No suggestion of what such a justification might be, however, is ever forthcoming as the play proceeds.

If we are disposed to think that Mowbray has indeed served as Richard's agent in ridding the King of Gloucester and that he has denied the crime to spare his sovereign public embarrassment, the events of the next scene, laid at Coventry, might serve either to confirm or to disconfirm our assumption. Mowbray is ready to die in battle to prove himself a "loyal, just and upright gentleman" (1.3.87), but is rewarded for his services to his King by being banished for life. Is Richard cynically insuring that his agent in villainy will forever be incapable of exposing him? This appears to be a possibile interpretation. Yet, if double-crossed, Mowbray remains mysteriously silent when his adversary urges him to confess his "guilty soul" (1.3.200); and he exits the stage for the last time in the play with another protestation of innocence, buttressed by an echo from the *Book of Revelation*:[2]

> No, Bolingbroke. If ever I were traitor,
> My name be blotted from the book of life,
> And I from heaven banished as from hence!
> But what thou art, God, thou and I do know;
> And all too soon, I fear, the King shall rue.
> (1.3.201–05)

The biblical solemnity of Mowbray's words is striking; and since he has little more to lose at this point by revealing the truth, his permanent exile having been sealed already, his apparent sincerity seems further to obfuscate both his and Richard's morality in the matter of Gloucester's death. Moreover, since his pointed words adumbrate the main action of the play—Bolingbroke's usurpation of the throne and displacement of the King—we may be inclined to credit his veracity in other matters. The Bishop of Carlisle later confirms our positive impressions of Mowbray by reporting his death in Venice where he rendered up "his pure soul unto his captain Christ" (4.1.100) after returning from the Holy Land as a committed veteran of the crusades.

Progressive mystification about just how and why Gloucester was put to death seems to be a deliberate strategy on Shakespeare's part. Holinshed, his principal source, as well as Froissart and the anonymous play *Woodstock*, all have Gloucester smothered or strangled in his prison at Calais,[3] whereas *Richard II* suggests that Woodstock was beheaded as though suffering an extra-legal execution: in his despair, for instance, York exclaims, "I would to God ... The King had cut off my head with my brother's" (2.2.100–02), in addition to which the earlier imagery of sluicing out Gloucester's soul "through streams of blood" (1.1.103) and "tapp[ing] out and drunkenly carous[ing]" his life-blood (2.1.127) supports the idea of a literal blood-letting.[4] To complicate matters further, the dramatist reintroduces "Gloucester's death" in Act IV just before the deposition episode when Bolingbroke (functioning already as Henry IV) inquires, "Who wrought it with the King, and who performed / The bloody office of his timeless end?" (4.1.3–5). He is answered by Bagot, who implicates Aumerle, who in turn vehemently denies the accusation (4.1.27–30). This is the first time that any suggestion of Aumerle's involvement in Gloucester's murder has arisen. Then Fitzwater backs up Bagot's statement, testifying that he had heard Aumerle boast of being the "cause of noble Gloucester's death" (4.1.38) and also that he had heard Mowbray report that Aumerle "did ... send two of [his] men / To execute the noble Duke at Calais (4.1.82–83).[5] The word "execute," even though it is uttered by an enemy of Aumerle, again raises the legal issue of a conceivably justifiable punishment.[6]

We could forgive an Elizabethan audience, let alone a modern one still further removed from the historical events represented, for being totally confused by this collection of unexplained and apparently contradictory statements. Since Gloucester's murder

Spilling Royal Blood 113

had already been staged in the earlier drama, *Woodstock*, some scholars have suspected that Shakespeare was relying on audience familiarity with this play for the circumstances of the crime. But there is some reason to believe that the dramatist's ambiguities about the affair were deliberate. Lily Bess Campbell (196) goes so far as to suggest that Shakespeare may have been drawing a covert and carefully hedged parallel to the execution of Mary, Queen of Scots, which had occurred only seven years before the play was composed and which earned Elizabeth I widespread resentment in many quarters at home and abroad. The precise details of Gloucester's demise and just how it was engineered remain unclear even to modern historians. But we know the basic outlines of what happened. When Richard was still relatively untried in rule, the Lords Appellant (led by Gloucester, and including the earls of Arundel and Warwick as well as Mowbray and Bolingbroke) succeeded in displacing and condemning his favorites and, by their highhanded tactics in Parliament and council, reducing him to a mere figurehead. By 1389 Richard had gained enough maturity to assert his own authority and rid himself of the Lords Appellant. Mowbray, who had formerly been an adversary, now became one of his inner circle, and Bolingbroke also had regained a measure of royal favor. Meanwhile the King continued to resent the senior Appellants' humiliation of him, and in 1397 he settled accounts by arresting Gloucester, Arundel and Warwick and having them tried in Parliament for treason; Warwick was exiled, Arundel beheaded and Gloucester, Mowbray's prisoner at the time, secretly killed at Calais before he had opportuniity to answer the charges against him, probably at Richard's bidding.

Shakespeare would have encountered mixed attitudes to Richard's crime in his sources. Holinshed explains that Gloucester had entered into a treasonable conspiracy to imprison the King together with the dukes of Lancaster and York and to have the other members of his council executed, which, when Richard learned of it, caused him to have Gloucester abducted and assassinated. He also reports that the captious duke, deploring Richard's pacific policy toward France, had insulted his nephew for surrendering the fortified town of Brest to the Duke of Brittany in 1397 in fulfillment of a treaty with Charles VI.[7] Holinshed characterizes Gloucester as "fierce of nature, hastie, wilfull ... and in this greatlie to be discommended, that he was euer repining against the king in all things, whatsoeuer he wished to haue forward" (III, 489); and he attributes Richard's political failures not only to youth and dis-

114   *Charles R. Forker*

soluteness but also to the machinations of Gloucester, the "cheefe instrument" (III, 508), as he phrases it, of Richard's disastrous conflict with his nobles and therefore, by implication, of the deposition which it precipitated. Nearly all the sources treat Gloucester unsympathetically except for *Woodstock*, the play from which Gaunt's characterization of his murdered brother as a "plain wellmeaning soul" (2.1.128) seems to derive.[8] Most writers whom Shakespeare could have consulted moralized the murder as a deed "odious to God" (*The Mirror for Magistrates'* phrase [98]); and Holinshed, although he allows that Gloucester provoked the King by his hectoring opposition and dangerous plotting, nevertheless underlines Richard's depravity in taking his life. Twice, for instance, he alludes to reports that Mowbray undertook his deadly assignment with the greatest reluctance, delaying the murder of Gloucester at Calais as long as possible and acting finally only when Richard exerted pressure by threatening his life.[9] But the *Mirror* (144) also records that attitudes to the death of Gloucester changed, being regarded at first as "Iustice" but later on as "tiranny and wrong."

III

I have dwelt on Gloucester's murder at what may seem disproportionate length because it seems to me that Shakespeare's handling of this incident can serve us as an emblem of the moral and political issues that attend the more important murder of the play—that of the King—as well as illustrate an aspect of Shakespeare's thematic technique in the later histories. *Richard II* begins as though it might, like *Hamlet* or *Macbeth*, turn out to be a play about royal murder and retribution—with the killing of Gloucester as Bolingbroke's chief motive for dispossessing and killing Richard and with perhaps some anticipated depiction of Richard's tortured conscience. Bolingbroke, Gaunt, and York all refer to the murder during the early scenes in a way that may raise such expectations. A tragedy of nemesis would appear possible. But the play we know takes shape along very different lines. After his banishment and return, Bolingbroke never mentions the murder of his uncle again, and by the middle of Act II, the dramatist has dropped the matter as a major element of the plot. By this time we have become more interested in Richard's other misdeeds and follies, with Bolingbroke's burgeoning political power, and, after his return from

Spilling Royal Blood 115

Ireland, with Richard's increasing vulnerability, weakness, suffering and fall—in short with his unique psychology as a man facing the reality of being at once a king and no king. An obvious reason for diminished emphasis on the Gloucester murder as the play unfolds is, of course, the need to draw our sympathies back toward the protagonist in his defeat—a protagonist from whom the early scenes have progressively alienated us—and to develop the theme of royal martyrdom. As Richard contends with the problems of regal identity, with the incoherence and dissolution of dual-natured selfhood, suffering expands his consciousness, brings him to a deepened sense of the humanity he shares with ordinary men, causing him to reflect, however theatrically and self-indulgently, upon his mistakes, his shallowness and, as he himself refers to them, his "sins" (4.1.275). The great "hollow crown" speech (3.2.144–77), the "mirror" episode (4.1.268–302), and the long soliloquy at Pomfret (5.5.1–66) all represent different attempts at honest self-assessment. But never once does Richard express the slightest guilt for the murder of Gloucester. One could say almost that in this case, at least, his reverberant silence conveys a state of what psychologists call denial. And again, to return to the analogy of Mary of Scotland's death, we may recall that Elizabeth, after reluctantly signing her cousin's death warrant, dealt with the guilt she clearly felt by punishing Secretary Davison for going forward with the execution (as Richard punishes Mowbray), even though he had done so with her knowledge and permission.[10]

In an important sense, of course, Shakespeare seems to want us to forget the enigmatic business of Gloucester's murder. By the time Richard loses his crown, he has compared himself several times to Christ, implying that his enemies are latter-day Judases and Pilates delivering him to his own particular Golgotha; and although such self-comparisons are egregiously self-pitying and may even border on blasphemy, we are nonetheless asked to take them in part as markers of the royal christology on which the doctrine of divine right is founded. The play's tragic emphasis on Richard's "Passion" (in the New Testament sense of the term) is so discordant with the notion of a callous murderer that it is no wonder Shakespeare suppresses it. Nevertheless the theme of guilt and denial persists through displacement, for Shakespeare transfers it from Richard, who now functions as tragic victim, to his successor Henry IV, who has just been redefined as the tragic perpetrator of a royal murder. The man who had indirectly accused Richard of

116   Charles R. Forker

shedding a kinsman's blood becomes himself the avatar of the deed he had condemned. And, significantly, Shakespeare invokes the story of Cain and Abel for both murders. By accusing Mowbray, Richard's agent, of Gloucester's death and by arrogating to himself the task of avenging Abel's spilled blood, Bolingbroke identifies Richard by implication with Cain. But when Richard is slain at Pomfret, by Henry's tacit permission if not by his explicit command, the symbolic roles are ironically reversed. The new king repudiates his agent, in this case Exton, just as Richard had repudiated Mowbray, ungratefully condemning him to perpetual exile, again like Mowbray and also like the first murderer of human history:

> With Cain go wander thorough shades of night,
> And never show thy head by day nor light.
> (5.6.43–44)

As in the case of Gloucester's death, Shakespeare surrounds Richard's murder with a similar penumbra of ambiguity. The brief scene (5.4) in which Exton explains what he takes to be King Henry's command to carry out the bloody deed introduces an element of doubt about the precise degree of Henry's culpability because the incriminating words, "Have I no friend will rid me of this living fear?" (5.4.2), are reported rather than heard directly from the King's lips. Like Richard, Henry clings to a stance of deniability by disavowing and exiling the engine of his criminal design. We never know whether King Henry consciously arranged his rival's death or merely encouraged it by innuendo. And when Exton later protests that he had acted in response to words from the King's "own mouth" (5.6.37), he is answered with Machiavellian equivocation: "Though I did wish him dead, / I hate the murderer, love him murdered" (5.6.39–40). These words, of course, can mean either that Henry still loves the cousin who lies before him in the coffin or that he loves him *because* he lies there since he could not otherwise occupy his throne. However we take the lines, it is clear that Henry commences his reign heavily burdened by guilt, guilt which he hopes to assuage by a pilgrimage or crusade to the Holy Land "To wash this blood off from my guilty hand" (5.6.50). That Henry adopts the hand-washing imagery of Pontius Pilate links his statement ironically to Richard's own words at his deposition:

> Though some of you, with Pilate, wash your hands,
> Showing an outward pity, yet you Pilates

Spilling Royal Blood 117

> Have here delivered me to my sour cross,
> And water cannot wash away your sin.
>
> (4.1.239–42)

If Richard represses or evades blame for the murder of Gloucester, he allows another kind of guilt to flower histrionically in the improvised liturgy of his self-renunciation. The figure who had grandly asserted on the coast of Wales that "Not all the water in the rough rude sea / Can wash the balm off from an anointed king" (3.2.54–55) affects at his deposition to wash it away "With [his] own tears" (4.1.207). Forced to "deny [his] sacred state" with his "own tongue" (4.1.209), Richard convicts himself of the treason of shattering his own divinely conferred authority:

> Nay, if I turn mine eyes upon myself,
> I find myself a traitor with the rest;
> For I have given here my soul's consent
> T'undeck the pompous body of a king,
> Made Glory base and Sovereignty a slave,
> Proud Majesty a subject, State a peasant.
>
> (4.1.247–52)

Richard's betrayal of himself, as Shakespeare dramatizes it, involves the paradoxical abnegation of a sacral magistracy that cannot, theologically speaking, be relinquished—a kingship made sacramentally indelible by the holy rite of coronation. And much of the dramatic power of Richard's tragic attempt to come to terms with his fall from majesty to "nothingness" resides in the conflict generated by the simultaneous abandonment and asseveration of his own sacredness. This is the arena in which Richard's guilt expresses itself most eloquently. And it places the *de facto* king, Henry IV, in a peculiarly awkward position, because he cannot deny Richard's sacerdotal royalty without imperiling the doctrine that must undergird his own questionable authority as well as the iconicity of the crown he seeks to wear. In the final scene Northumberland indeed acknowledges Henry's "sacred state" (5.6.6), employing the identical phrase that Richard had used in his speech of self-divestiture at 4.1.209. Holinshed notes that after Bolingbroke had captured Richard and brought him as prisoner to London, he caused a parliament to be called, "vsing the name of king Richard in the writs directed forth to the lords ..." (III, 502). The judicial body that the usurper assembled to convict Richard of unfitness to rule had to be called in the name of the figure it was proposing to unseat. In the play Richard uses every rhetorical evasion he can summon to avoid reading Northumberland's list of

118   Charles R. Forker

"grievous crimes" (4.1.223), the parliamentary grounds for dethronement. Like Charles I, more than a half-century after Shakespeare's play, Richard in effect refuses to acknowledge the legality of his judges, reminding his enemies that "the deposing of a king / And cracking the strong warrant of an oath" is "Marked with a blot, damned in the book of heaven" (4.1.234–36). Richard cleverly transmits to the "silent King" (4.1.290) as much of the guilt of his plight as he can.

IV

Patterns of guilt, denial and displacement reaching back to the deposition and murder of Richard continue to suffuse the later plays of the tetralogy. Shakespeare skillfully prepares for the continuity by having the fallen monarch of the first play predict with uncanny prescience that Northumberland, that "ladder wherewithal / The mounting Bolingbroke ascends my throne" (5.1.55–56), will ultimately prove as disloyal to his new master as to his old. The rebels of the *Henry IV* plays, in fact, become historical revisionists, persistently rewriting their own past out of guilty disappointment at their less-than-hoped-for rewards. In *Richard II* Mortimer's claim to the throne had been passed over in silence, but now Worcester, discontented with the king whose usurpation he had rushed to support, laments the interrupted succession: "was not [Mortimer] proclaim'd / By Richard ... the next of blood?" *1 Henry IV*, 1.3.145–46). In the same scene Northumberland refers guiltily to Richard as "the unhappy king / (Whose wrongs in us God pardon!)" (1.3.148–49); and Hotspur, the Harry Percy of the earlier play, complains that for their part in placing the ungrateful Bolingbroke on the throne, they must now "wear the detested blot / Of murtherous subornation," undergo "a world of curses.... Being the agents or base second means, / The cords, the ladder, or the hangman rather" who had facilitated Richard's death (1.3.162–66). Hotspur's ironic echo of the "ladder" image is potently revelatory—originally used by Richard to portray Northumberland as the contemptible means of Bolingbroke's climb to power but now reinvoked to portray the Percys as reluctant functionaries at Richard's execution. Hotspur instances his father's and uncle's ignominy as an argument for their family's festering resistance to King Henry:

> Shall it for shame be spoken in these days,
> Or fill up chronicles in time to come,

Spilling Royal Blood 119

> That men of your nobility and power
> Did gage them both in an unjust behalf
> (As both of you—God pardon it!—have done)
> To put down Richard, that sweet lovely rose,
> And plant this thorn, this canker, Bullingbrook?
> And shall it in more shame be further spoken,
> That you are fool'd, discarded, and shook off
> By him for whom these shames ye underwent?
>
> (1.3.170–79)

The Percys wish to claim credit for Bolingbroke's usurpation ("My father and my uncle and myself / Did give him that same royalty he wears" [4.3.54–55]), at the same time demeaning him as a liar and ambitious hypocrite, "A poor unminded outlaw sneaking home" (4.3.58), who "Broke oath on oath, committed wrong on wrong," and whose title is now judged to be "Too indirect for long continuance" (4.3.101–05). King Henry becomes the scapegoat for the moral compromise that rankles deep within the souls of men who have now become rebels twice over, and who cannot face up to the contradictions inherent in their own self-aggrandizing tergiversation.

Henry IV sees through their contorted illogic and selective memory with characteristic penetration: they have invented their self-deceiving propaganda, he points out, "To face the garment of rebellion / With some fine color that may please the eye / Of fickle changelings and poor discontents" (5.1.74–76). Yet Henry too is caught up in revisionist historicizing, his motive being the same as that of his rebellious nobles—namely guilt. Compelled to "neglect / [His] holy purpose to Jerusalem" (1.1.101–02), the intended penance for Richard's murder, so that he may deal with the more immediate threat of rebellion at home, Henry conceives of his own son's "riot and dishonor" (1.1.85) as divine punishment for sins:

> I know not whether God will have it so
> For some displeasing service I have done,
> That in his secret doom, out of my blood
> He'll breed revengement and a scourge for me;
> But thou dost in thy passages of life
> Make me believe that thou art only mark'd
> For the hot vengeance, and the rod of heaven,
> To punish my mistreadings.
>
> (3.2.4–11)[11]

120   *Charles R. Forker*

Henry is discreetly vague in these words to Prince Hal about the nature of such "mistreadings" as call for "revengement," but no Elizabethan audience could fail to think instantly of Richard's murder and the political actions that had precipitated it.

A curious aspect of Henry's displacement of guilt entails his identification of his wayward son, whom painfully he calls his "nearest and dearest enemy" (3.2.123), with his dead predecessor. For in rebuking Hal for being unroyally "stale and cheap" to such "vulgar company" (3.2.41) as Falstaff and the other Eastcheap riff-raff, he likens him most unconvincingly to Richard: whereas Bolingbroke had been a model of successful public relations, "dress[ing himself] in such humility / That [he] did pluck allegiance from men's hearts," drawing "Loud shouts and salutations.... Even in the presence of the crowned King" (3.2.51–54), Richard had behaved, like the over-familiar Hal, in such a way as to elicit disgust:

> The skipping King, he ambled up and down,
> With shallow jesters, and rash bavin wits,
> Soon kindled and soon burnt, carded his state,
> Mingled his royalty with cap'ring fools,
> Had his great name profaned with their scorns,
> And gave his countenance, against his name,
> To laugh at gibing boys, and stand the push
> Of every beardless vain comparative,
> Grew a companion to the common streets,
> Enfeoff'd himself to popularity,
> That, being daily swallowed by men's eyes,
> They surfeited with honey and began
> To loathe the taste of sweetness....
>   (3.2.60–72)

Could any spectator who had seen a staging of Shakespeare's *Richard II* recognize without strain this cartoonish re-creation of its generally dignified and complex protagonist? And would any fair-minded theatre-goer, however unsympathetic to the prince's pragmatically tainted shenanigans, dream of associating these with Richard's sentimental weaknesses and follies as Shakespeare depicts them? It seems more reasonable to ascribe Henry's surprisingly skewed characterization of Richard to a combination of emotional blindness toward his son with rationalization of his own political past, at least partly conditioned by guilty feelings for the king he has dethroned and murdered.

Spilling Royal Blood 121

King Henry's guilt about the murder as well as revisionary attitudes toward the preceding reign are further developed in *2 Henry IV*. The play evolves a dense matrix of images and themes that regularly keeps us mindful of the king Henry has displaced. Rumour, the allegorical Chorus who opens the drama, immediately sets a tone of skepticism and uncertainty that serves not only to promote confusion about what happened at the battle of Shrewsbury but also to engender a spirit of malaise concerning the new "anointed head" (Induction, 32), a term that raises the spectre of royal illegitimacy and prepares for the dying King's confession to Hal:

> God knows, my son,
> By what by-paths and indirect crook'd ways
> I met this crown, and I myself know well
> How troublesome it sate upon my head.
> (4.5.183–86)

Later Prince John attempts to sustain Henry's shaky claim to divine right by referring to his father as God's "substitute" (4.2.28), the same term that Gaunt had applied to Richard (*Richard II*, 1.2.37). Informed about Hotspur's death at the hands of Prince Hal, the sour Northumberland erupts in guilty anger, invoking the murderous "spirit of the first-born Cain" (1.1.157) as his incentive for vengeance against the king he had once helped to crown. The biblical image harks back ironically to *Richard II* where, as we have seen, it had been applied to the murders of both Gloucester and Richard. Thomas Mowbray, son of the man charged by Bolingbroke with Gloucester's death in the first play, now denies that his father had been guilty of any wrong, claiming in a statement that seems vaguely also to exculpate Richard that the King was "perforce compell'd to banish him" (4.1.114). Archbishop Scroop, the cousin of Richard's favorite beheaded by Bolingbroke at Bristol and the ringleader of the new rebellion, "Turns insurrection to religion.... And doth enlarge his rising with the blood / Of fair King Richard, scrap'd from Pomfret stones" (1.1.201–05). Working up support for his cause, the prelate expatiates on the old king's martyrdom and the fickleness of public opinion. The rabble who have recently grown sick of Henry, he notes, were once equally sick of his predecessor, having, like a "common dog … disgorge[d] / Its] glutton bosom of the royal Richard" and would now "eat [its] dead vomit up" (1.3.97–99). The repulsive imagery of regurgi-

122   *Charles R. Forker*

tation fused with hunger defines the collective guilt of a society
that now longs to undo what it had once complacently endorsed:

> They that, when Richard liv'd, would have him die,
> Are now become enamor'd on his grave.
> Thou, that threw'st dust upon his goodly head
> When through proud London he came sighing on
> After th' admired heels of Bullingbrooke,
> Cri'st now, "O earth, yield us that king again,
> And take thou this!"
>
> (1.3.101–07)

King Henry too is much obsessed with reconstructing his past,
sadly recalling "Richard, with his eye brimful of tears" (3.1.67) and
ruefully lamenting the mutable loyalties of men engaged in politics—how, for example, "Richard and Northumberland, great
friends, / Did feast together" but were soon afterward "at wars"
(3.1.58–60). Again Henry looks back upon his usurpation through
a prism fashioned by guilt, justifying his actions as taken in response to an historical destiny beyond and removed from personal
volition. He can acknowledge the truth of Richard's prophecy that
Northumberland would be his "ladder" (3.1.70) to the throne, yet
nevertheless disclaim responsibility:

> ... then, God knows, I had no such intent,
> But that necessity so bow'd the state
> That I and greatness were compell'd to kiss.
>
> (3.1.72–74)

But when he is heaping coals of fire on Hal's head for having prematurely assumed the crown at his bedside, Henry sounds more
and more like the pity-invoking, self-dramatizing and guilt-impos-
ing Richard whom he had dethroned:

> Then get thee gone, and dig my grave thyself,
> And bid the merry bells ring to thine ear
> That thou art crowned, not that I am dead.
> Let all the tears that should bedew my hearse
> Be drops of balm to sanctify thy head;
> Only compound me with forgotten dust;
> Give that which gave thee life unto the worms,
> Pluck down my officers, break my degrees,
> For now a time is come to mock at form.
> Henry the Fift is crown'd! Up, vanity!
> Down, royal state!
>
> (4.5.110–20)

Spilling Royal Blood 123

The speech is replete with echoes of Richard's self-pitying rhetoric as if Henry were subconsciously identifying with the man he has murdered[12]—a permutation, perhaps, of the impulse that had led him in the previous play to identify his son with Richard.

For his part, Hal has put on the crown in the recognition that, in doing so, he has relieved his father of the instrument of symbolic regicide:

> Thus, my royal liege,
> Accusing it, I put it on my head,
> To try with it, as with an enemy
> That had before my face murdered my father,
> The quarrel of a true inheritor.
>
> (4.5.164–68)

By conceiving the crown itself as the murderer of kings, the "polish'd perturbation" and "golden care" (4.5.23) of his father's unhappy reign, the future Henry V generalizes the burdens of royal state, thus managing to evade the more specific issue of Lancastrian usurpation with its inherent moral stain. And Henry IV encourages the evasion by assuring his son that the crown, admittedly "an honor snatch'd with boist'rous hand," will descend to him "with better quiet, / Better opinion, better confirmation, / For the soil of the achievement goes / With me into the earth" (4.5.187–91).

Henry V, the final play of the tetralogy, may seem by its concentration on heroic victory abroad and by its conclusion in a symbolic marriage between England and France to offer respite from the guilty burden of past murders. But even here Shakespeare allows the tragic shadow of Richard II to fall briefly across the action. Among the most moving moments in the tense night of anticipation that precedes Agincourt is Henry's prayer for peace of mind and soul:

> Not to-day, O Lord,
> O, not to-day, think not upon the fault
> My father made in compassing the crown!
> I Richard's body have interred new,
> And on it have bestowed more contrite tears,
> Than from it issued forced drops of blood.
> Five hundred poor I have in yearly pay,
> Who twice a day their wither'd hands hold up
> Toward heaven, to pardon blood; and I have built
> Two chauntries, where the sad and solemn priests
> Sing still for Richard's soul. More will I do;

124   *Charles R. Forker*

> Though all that I can do is nothing worth,
> Since that my penitence comes after all,
> Imploring pardon.
>> (*Henry V*, 4.1.292–305)

Clearly King Henry's prayer is answered. English casualties in the ensuing battle are miraculously few, and Aumerle, who has earlier been accused as an accessory in Richard's murder and who has finally succeeded to his father's dukedom, now dies a hero's death. But the play concludes with an epilogue reminding audiences that the burdens of defeat, guilt, bloodshed and disrupted rule have yet to run their course:

> Henry the Sixt, in infant bands crown'd King
> Of France and England, did this king succeed;
> Whose state so many had the managing,
> That they lost France, and made his England bleed....
>> (*Epilogue*, 9–12)

The continued bleeding, as audiences familiar with the first tetralogy might well remember, involved the killing of three different kings—Henry VI, Edward V, and Richard III—as well as several pretenders to the throne.

V

The cumulative web of factual ambiguities, biased memories, evasions or repressions of guilt, and stunted or deflected attempts at atonement associated with the murders of Gloucester and Richard—not only in the first play of the series but also in the dramas that stage the aftermath of these crimes—define a nostalgically tragic view of history. The deposition and murder of Richard II, the last of the Angevin kings, seems to have represented for Shakespeare and his age an almost mythopoeic transition from a politics of transcendental unity and cohesion, in which roles were guaranteed by birth and supernaturally assigned, to one of individual aggression and competition. The shift has sometimes been interpreted as reflecting the crack-up of the high Middle Ages (with its God-centered view of order, hierarchy and subordination) and its replacement by a less harmonious, more power-seeking *Zeitgeist* in which nature has been sundered from eternity and politics from religion. We used to describe this change as the birth of the Renaissance. Latterly, swept along, as it were, by the currents of new historicism, we have been taught to use the more clin-

Spilling Royal Blood 125

ical term for the period—Early Modern. The dramatist himself lends credence to a negative valuation of the succession from Richard to Henry by building into *Richard II* Gaunt's sense of England as "This other Eden," a "demi-paradise" (2.1.42) that Richard has managed through his selfish follies to transform into a mere "tenement or pelting farm" (2.1.60). And Shakespeare further supports the concept of England as a paradise lost through the moralizing commentary of the garden scene and the Queen's allusion to her husband's deposition as "a second fall of cursed man" (3.4.76). Richard himself initiates this fall from grace, in his willful blindness shattering the mirror of all Christian kingship as irrevocably as the physical glass he dashes so theatrically to the ground. His two most fatal violations of the Great Chain of Being, those that recoil to ensure his own catastrophe, are his murder of his uncle and his attack upon the principle of primogeniture on which his own claims to legitimacy rest—the confiscation of his cousin's inheritance. The first of these mistakes provides Bolingbroke with a weighty reason for his indirect attack upon the crown, prompting Richard in turn to banish him. The second mistake fuels, if it does not specifically cause, Bolingbroke's return from exile and the irreversible consolidation of power that follows.[13]

The tragedy of *Richard II*, as Shakespeare structures it, exploits the unresolved ambiguity of whether Bolingbroke seizes the crown, carefully veiling his ambition until ultimate power is within his grasp, or whether Richard in his doom-eagerness and desire to play the martyr, gives it away in a pageant of self-indulgent sacrifice. We are nevertheless made to feel that the corpse both we and King Henry mourn in the final scene stands not only for the failed reign of a particular monarch but also for the loss and desecration of a beautiful, if perhaps no longer viable, idea—the idea of royalty as the glamorous, sanctified, and corporate image of the better angels of our own nature. It is clear, too, that the sordid violence at Pomfret, particularly since Richard heroically resists his assassins and reasserts his identity as a sovereign by divine right, transfers the taint of the old king's guilt to Henry, thereby effecting a sea-change in the political ethos of succeeding reigns. It can be no accident that the *Henry IV* plays, shot through as they are with painful recollections of royal blood-letting, expose us increasingly to the themes of disease, cynicism, and diminished expectations. We come to inhabit a world in which murder is no longer a simple matter of sin and its spiritual consequences but one rather in which a nation, facing complex political problems,

126   Charles R. Forker

may have to accept *Realpolitik* and moral compromise in its leaders as the price of stability and survival. We are led to conclude that the age of "model kings" is gone forever and, with it, "model conceptions of kingship" and "univocal doctrines of social allegiance."[14] The truth of Henry's insomniac suffering is borne in upon us: "Uneasy lies the head that wears a crown" (2 *Henry IV*, 3.1.31). The hope of a penitential pilgrimage or crusade to the Holy Land ends unfulfillingly in Henry's confined death in the Jerusalem Chamber of his Westminster palace. And the royalty that Gaunt had evoked in his great speech on England with its chivalric traditions of Edward III and the Black Prince is seen to have degenerated to the Machiavellian trickery of Prince John's tactics at Gaultree Forest.

Notes

1. Cf. *All's Well That Ends Well*, 2.1.185–86; *Measure for Measure*, 5.1.354–55. Citations of Shakespeare are drawn from *The Riverside Shakespeare*. The exception is *Richard II* from which I quote my own Arden edition.

2. *Revelation* 3:5: "He that overcometh shall be thus clothed in white array, and I will not blot out his name out of the book of life" (Bishop's Bible).

3. Cf. Holinshed: "The earle [i.e., Mowbray] ... called out the duke at midnight ... and there ... caused his seruants to cast featherbeds vpon him, and so smother him to death, or otherwise to strangle him with towels (as some write)" (III, 489). Cf. also Froissart: "whan he [i.e., Gloucester] hadde dyned and was aboute to have wasshen his handes, there came into the chambre foure men, and cast sodaynlye a towel aboute the dukes necke, two at the one ende and two at the other, and drewe so sore that he fell to erthe, and so they strangled hym and closed his eyen" (VI, 298). Cf. also *Woodstock*, which actually stages the strangling with a towel (5.1).

4. Shakespeare could perhaps have derived the beheading from Le Beau's version of the anonymous French chronicle, *Chronicque de la Traïson et Mort de Richart Deux Roy Dengleterre*, which reports that "Le roi envoya son oncle à Calais, et là fut décollé" (10). An anonymous play on Richard II which Simon Forman describes having seen at the Globe on 30 April 1611 also apparently represented Gloucester as beheaded; see Chambers, II, 340. But Shakespeare may have invented the beheading (the customary Elizabethan penalty for noblemen) not only to allow for the motif of sacrificial blood (e.g., at 1.1.103 and 1.2.17) but also to preserve the uncertainty of whether Gloucester had been murdered or unofficially executed.

Spilling Royal Blood 127

5. Aumerle's alleged connection with the murder also comes from Holinshed: "there was no man in the realme to whom king Richard was so much beholden, as to the duke of Aumarle: for he was the man that to fulfill his mind, had set him in hand with all that was doone against the said duke [of Gloucester]" (III, 512).

6. At the time of his official condemnation for treason in Parliament (1397), an abbreviated version of Gloucester's confession was produced in justification (see Saul, 378–79); understandably, the validity of this document has been doubted.

7. See Holinshed, III, 488–89; also III, 487, where Gloucester protests to Richard, "Sir, your grace ought to put your bodie in paine to win a strong hold or towne by feats of war, yer [ere] you take vpon you to sell or deliuer anie towne or strong hold gotten with great aduenture by the manhood of the policie of your noble progenitours." *The Mirror for Magistrates* likewise emphasizes Richard's "fault" (114) in surrendering Brest.

8. In the anonymous play, the frequent epithet "Plain Thomas" (cf. *Woodstock*, 1.1.99) sums up Gloucester's humble dress and outspoken honesty; cf. also "Homely and plain: both free from pride and envy" (1.1.106).

9. Cf. Holinshed (III, 489): "The erle prolonged time for the executing of the kings commandement, though the king would haue had it doone with all expedition, wherby the king conceiued no small displeasure, and sware that it should cost the earle his life if he quickly obeied not his commandment." In a later passage implicating Aumerle in the murder (III, 511), Holinshed says that Mowbray told Bagot he had spared the duke "contrarie to the will of the king … by the space of three weeks, and more; affirming withall, that he was neuer in all his life time more affraid of death, than he was at his comming home againe from Calis … to the kings presence, by reason he had not put the duke to death. And then (said he) the king appointed one of his owne seruants and certein other … to go with him to see the said duke of Gloucester put to death, swearing that as he should answer afore God, it was neuer his mind that he should haue died in the fort, but onelie for feare of the king, and sauing his owne life."

10. See Jenkins, 279–80.

11. Even in *Richard II* the freshly crowned Henry had regarded his "unthrifty son" as a burden: "If any plague hang over us, 'tis he" (5.3.1–3).

12. Cf. *Richard II*: "Cry woe, destruction, ruin and decay. / The worst is death, and Death will have his day" (3.2.102–03); "Let's talk of graves, of worms and epitaphs, / Make dust our paper and with rainy eyes / Write sorrow on the bosom of the earth" (3.2.145–47); "Throw away respect, / Tradition, form and ceremonious duty …" (3.2.172–73); "Long mayst thou live in Richard's seat to sit, / And soon lie Richard in an earthy pit! 'God save King Harry,' unkinged Richard says, / 'And send him many years of sunshine days!'—" (4.1.218–21); "Mine eyes are full of tears; I cannot see. / And yet salt water blinds them not so much / But they can see a sort of traitors here" (4.1.244–46).

128   *Charles R. Forker*

13. The news that Bolingbroke has mounted an invasionary force in Brittany and is already making for England with "eight tall ships" and "three thousand men of war" (2.1.286) is separated from Richard's appropriation of his patrimony, staged in the same scene, by only about seventy lines. Although Bolingbroke later claims, through his agent Northumberland, that his return from exile "hath no further scope / Than for his lineal royalties" (3.3.112–13)—that is, the restoration of his lands and title, the extreme foreshortening of the interval conveys the impression that Bolingbroke has already begun his rebellion against Richard before he could have known about Richard's act of official deprivation.

14. The quoted phrases come from Tomlinson, 58.

Works Cited

Anonymous. *Woodstock, A Moral History*, ed. A.P. Rossiter. London: Chatto & Windus, 1946.

Baldwin, William. *The Mirror for Magistrates*, ed. Lily B. Campbell. Cambridge: Cambridge UP, 1938.

Campbell, Lily B. *Shakespeare's Histories: Mirrors of Elizabethan Policy*. San Marino, CA: Huntington Library, 1958.

Chambers, E.K. *William Shakespeare: A Study of Facts and Problems*. 2 vols. Oxford: Clarendon P, 1930.

Froissart, Jean. *The Chronicle of Froissart Translated out of French by Sir John Bourchier Lord Berners (Annis 1523–25)*, ed. W.P. Ker. 6 vols. London: David Nutt, 1901–03.

Holinshed, Raphael. *The Chronicles of England, Scotland, and Ireland*, 2nd ed. 3 vols. in 2. London, 1587.

Jenkins, Elizabeth. *Elizabeth the Great*. New York: Coward-McCann, 1959.

Le Beau, Jean. *Chronique de Richard II*, ed. J.A. Buchon, in *Collection des Chroniques Nationales Françaises*, 25 (Froissart, vol. 15). Paris, 1826, Deuxième Supplément.

Saul, Nigel. *Richard II*. New Haven: Yale UP, 1997.

Shakespeare, William. *The Tragedy of Richard II*, ed. Charles R. Forker. Arden 3 series. London: Thomson Learning, 2002.

———. *The Riverside Shakespeare*, ed. G. Blakemore Evans *et al.* Boston: Houghton Mifflin, 1974.

Tomlinson, Michael. "Shakespeare and the Chronicles Reassessed." *Literature and History* 10.1 (1984): 46–58.

England as Eden in *Richard II*:
The Implications for the Second Tetralogy
John W. Velz

John of Gaunt's eloquent deathbed speech, characterizing the England that Richard, young and feckless, has desecrated, is justly famous, the best-known of all Shakespeare's patriotic speeches. It is appropriate to quote extensively from it, as it will be seen in this essay as central to the meaning of *Richard II* and—no doubt of it—of the whole *Henriad*. Old Gaunt, King Richard's uncle on his father's side, has been speaking prophetically of the consequences of Richard's selfish exploitation of the land God set him to govern:

> ... This royal throne of kings, this sceptered isle,
> This earth of majesty, this seat of Mars,
> This other Eden, demi-paradise,
> This fortress built by Nature for herself
> Against infection and the hand of war,
> This happy breed of men, this little world,
> This precious stone set in the silver sea,
> Which serves it in the office of a wall
> Or as a moat defensive to a house,
> Against the envy of less happier lands,
> This blessed plot, this earth, this realm, this England,
> This nurse, this teeming womb of royal kings,
> Fear'd by their breed and famous by their birth,
> Renownèd for their deeds as far from home
> For Christian service and true chivalry
> As is the sepulcher in stubborn Jewry
> Of the world's ransom, blessèd Mary's Son,
> This land of such dear souls, this dear dear land,
> Dear for her reputation through the world,
> Is now leased out—I die pronouncing it—
> Like to a tenement or pelting [petty] farm.[1]

130   *John W. Velz*

People who were young during the Second World War know the speech quite well, because in those years the lines about the English Channel: "a moat defensive to a house, / Against the envy of less happier lands" were often quoted, because it was the English Channel that thwarted Hitler's dream of invading England. Many children in both England and the United States memorized these lines in that time to recite in competitions or at assemblies and on patriotic occasions. The whole selection quoted here is germane to the subject of this chapter, but first in importance is the phrase "This other Eden, demi-paradise" which is almost buried in the context, but which has a profound meaning—or rather two profound meanings—both of them in the context of the whole play and in the context of the Second Tetralogy, which in effect the speech introduces.[2]

In the death speech of Old Gaunt we may not at first see more than a hyperbolic praise of England as the best of all earthly places. But we will quickly recognize that the garden image occurs elsewhere in the play to reinforce the fertility imagery Shakespeare chose to hold up as a moral alternative to the barren, the infertile, the dying.[3]

A little later in the play, when Richard is beginning to lose favor with his allies, a Welsh captain sees meaning in an omen of unnatural vegetation, "The bay trees in our country are all withered" (2.4.8). Bushy, Green, Bagot, and other hangers-on at Richard's court are seen by Bolingbroke as "The caterpillars of the commonwealth / Which I have sworn to weed and pluck away" (2.3.166–67). Those fortuitously relevant names, "Bushy" and "Green," must make us pause to wonder whether Shakespeare was provoked to weave fertility and infertility imagery through this play by seeing their names in Holinshed. Each reader must settle that question after this chapter is ended. But at least we may venture to think that Shakespeare took pleasure in making the men with these vegetative names the ones who become "caterpillars." In any case Bushy and Green are the parasitical caterpillars who figuratively feed on the foliage that is the nurture of the nation. Richard himself is associated with barrenness when he despairs in 3.2. He dismisses his followers and tells his officers to "let them go / To ear [plow] the land that hath some hope to grow" (3.2.211–12).

The fertility symbolism extends to human pregnancy. When the Queen hears that the Earl of Worcester "Hath broken his staff,

England as Eden in Richard II   *131*

resigned his stewardship, / And all the household servants fled
with him to Bolingbroke," her response is

> So, Green, thou art the midwife to my woe,
> And Bolingbroke my sorrow's dismal heir,
> Now hath my soul brought forth her prodigy, [a malformed child]
> And I, a gasping new-delivered mother,
> Have woe to woe, sorrow to sorrow joined.
>   (2.2.59–66)

The changing fortunes of the play are reflected in the use of a lap
full of flowers or greenery as a metaphor, first for Richard's England in Act 3.3 and then for Bolingbroke's newly achieved power
in Act 5.2.

The use for moral purposes of vegetable and animal fertility is
not at all unusual in Shakespeare. We may think of the "green
world of comedy" and the "red-and-white world of history" in
Northrop Frye's famous formulation, and if so one has a major beginning to a much broader pattern than one history play. Fertility
is in general in Shakespeare a favored image for good Fortune and
sterility for ill Fortune.[4] Shakespeare might have taken this notion
from the Bible, where again and again we find images of fertility
for those who love God and sterility for those out of His favor.
One might begin with Psalm 1:

> Happy are they who have not walked in the counsel of the wicked,*
>   nor lingered in the way of sinners, nor sat in the seats of the scornful!
> Their delight is in the law of the Lord,*
>   and they meditate on his law day and night.
> They are like trees planted by streams of water,
>   bearing fruit in due season, with leaves that do not wither;*
>   everything they do shall prosper.
> It is not so with the wicked;
>   they are like chaff which the wind blows away.[5]

Perhaps a dozen other Psalms of the 150 have similar imagery—
some of it wonderfully poetic—but here most readers will recall
the green pastures and still waters of Psalm 23. In a semi-arid
country like Israel, it is no wonder that this imagery should appear
in its devotional literature. Shakespeare knew the Psalms by heart
in the Miles Coverdale translation which Cranmer had put into the
Book of Common Prayer, and his characters often quote from the
Psalms. Of all Old Testament books, Shakespeare is fondest of
Psalms, which exceeds the number of allusions to Genesis by a fac-

132   *John W. Velz*

tor of two to one in the frequency with which it is referred to in the Shakespeare canon.[6]

The reference to Genesis' Eden in Gaunt's speech lends this already remarkable imagery of fertility an even more pointed moral meaning, a meaning that becomes more fully recognized as the play unfolds for us. The meaning is complex and profound.

One sees the moral meaning most obviously in Act 3 scene 4 that takes place in a garden complete with a Gardener whom the Queen calls "old Adam's likeness" and the Gardener's two assistants who with the Gardener make an allegorical equation between the care of the garden and the care of the kingdom that a King must take. In Act 3 scene 4, the Gardener instructs his men in such a way as to make very clear that the garden here is metaphorically the commonwealth of England.

> Go bind thou up young dangling apricots
> Which, like unruly children, make their sire
> Stoop with oppression of their prodigal weight.
> Give some supportance to the bending twigs.
> [*To the other*] Go thou, and like an executioner
> Cut off the heads of too-fast-growing sprays
> That look too lofty in our commonwealth.
> All must be even in our government.
> You thus employed, I will go root away
> The noisome weeds which without profit suck
> The soil's fertility from wholesome flowers.
>   (3.4.29–39)

The second assistant suggests the metaphor in case the audience might miss it. Unconsciously he echoes Gaunt's imagery for England with which this chapter began almost two acts earlier.

> Why should we in the compass of a pale
> Keep law and form and due proportion,
> Showing as in a model our firm estate,
> When our sea-wallèd garden, the whole land,
> Is full of weeds, her fairest flowers choked up,
> Her fruit trees all unpruned, her hedges ruined,
> Her knots [decorative flower beds] disordered, and her
>   wholesome herbs
> Swarming with caterpillars?
>   (3.4.40–47)

The Gardener's reply makes the point even more clearly, making Richard's fortunes a matter of vegetation:

England as Eden in Richard II   *133*

> He that hath suffered this disordered spring
> Hath now himself met with the fall of leaf.
> The weeds which his broad-spreading leaves did shelter,
> That seemed in eating him to hold him up,
> Are plucked up root and all by Bolingbroke.
>
> (3.4.48–52)

The Gardener spells out the analogy between the King and a gardener:

> O, what pity is it
> That he ["the wasteful King"] had not so trimmed
>   and dressed his land
> As we this garden! We at time of year
> Do wound the bark, the skin of our fruit trees,
> Lest being overproud in sap and blood
> With too much riches it confound itself;
> Had he done so to great and growing men,
> They might have lived to bear and he to taste
> Their fruits of duty.
>
> (3.4.55–63)

There are classical sources for such an allegorical reading of gardening, among them Aristotle, Ovid, Livy, and Dionysius of Halicarnassus.[7] But it is the Biblical background that must occupy us in this chapter. When the Queen, who has been in the garden all this while listening in with her two waiting women, comes forward to interrupt, we get the Biblical connection that must take center stage in this play.

> Thou, old Adam's likeness,
> Set to dress this garden, how dares
> Thy harsh rude tongue sound this unpleasing news?
> What Eve, what serpent, hath suggested thee
> To make a second fall of cursed man?
> Why dost thou say King Richard is deposed?
>
> (3.4.72–77)

What the Garden scene tells us, if we were in any doubt about it by this point in the play, is that Richard has failed to take his God-imposed responsibility to the Garden of England seriously and that he will be deposed from the throne in the Garden of England as Adam was banished from the Garden of Eden when he failed in obeying *his* God-imposed injunction. The Deposition scene in Act 4 scene 1 follows immediately upon this allegorical scene as if to ratify the prophetic rumors that were voiced in the garden. The Garden scene then is in some sense a mirror scene, a microcosm of

134   John W. Velz

the whole play's macrocosm. Act 3.4 and Act 4.1 "need each other."[8]

This is heavy thematic and structural weight for the Garden scene to carry, as heavy as that of any scene in a history play of Shakespeare's. It is often done badly, this scene, making it too stiff and stylized an allegory. For instance, in the BBC-PBS television film of *Richard II*, the Garden scene was filmed among faux fruit trees, so faux that someone who saw the film said they looked "as if they were bought in the dimestore." That sort of off-hand treatment of the all-important scene is unforgivable. It must, to be effective, be a scene that seems as true to life as any other scene in the play. Directors must not let the allegory run away with the scene. Shakespeare certainly did not intend that treatment. The Queen weeps real tears and flashes into real anger when she hears of her husband's imprisonment and impending deposition.

> O I am pressed to death
> Through want of speaking! ...
> Dar'st thou, thou little better thing than earth,
> Divine his [Richard's] downfall? Say where, when and how
> Cam'st thou by this ill tidings? Speak, thou wretch.
>   (3.4.71–80)

The Queen's anger is real, and her grief for her neglectful husband is overwhelming to her. This is a bit part in the play, but the actress must make the Queen convincing. Her Biblical language in the Garden scene is important to the moral design of the play, but she must seem to the audience to use the imagery incidentally in a real-life situation; she must not be a mere mouthpiece for the ideas of the Edenic reading of the play. Likewise the Gardener's decision to plant "a bank of rue, sour herb of grace" where the Queen let fall a tear has emblematic value as the scene ends, but it must seem to arise not out of its thematic significance but plausibly as a human act to memorialize the real grief of a real Queen.

Surely the allegorical interpretation of the Garden scene means that an Edenic reading of the deposition of Richard is feasible, and it all will go better if the Garden scene is realistic at a human level. Seeing Richard as England's failed gardener enables an interpretation in which the Original Sin of the play is Richard's not having cared for the duties God has assigned him by birth. (This, we will remember, is the interpretation Gaunt intends us to make of his imagery of Eden in Act 2.1.)

Seen another way, as is shown by Act 4.1 and the action that follows, the Deposition of Richard is *Bolingbroke's* Original Sin.

England as Eden in Richard II 135

Both interpretations of the Garden scene are sustainable—the one in which Richard fails in Eden as an Adamic gardener applies very emphatically to *Richard II* as a self-contained story. But *Richard II* is more than a self-contained story; it is the beginning of a longer and even more awesome story in which the deposition becomes the inseminating sin that leads on to the horrible consequences of this Original Sin as the Second Tetralogy unfolds.

This second view of Original Sin, that putting Richard down from his throne is an Original Sin from which all the horrors of the Wars of the Roses are to stem, is an interpretation that is supported by many allusions to crime and punishment throughout the three plays that follow *Richard II* in the *Henriad*. So King Henry IV, newly crowned in *1 Henry IV*, speaks of making a pilgrimage to Palestine to rescue the holy places of Christ's life from the Saracens. He is trying to expiate his crime of seizing Richard's throne and taking his life. *Richard II* ends with this pious intention: "I'll make a voyage to the Holy Land / To wash this blood off from my guilty hand." To be sure that we do not miss this guilt and attempted penitence, Shakespeare repeats it in *1 Henry IV* before twenty lines have been spoken in that play:

> As far as to the sepulcher of Christ—
> Whose soldier now, under whose blessèd cross
> We are impressèd and engaged to fight—
> Forthwith a power of English shall we levy,
> Whose arms were molded in their mother's womb
> To chase these pagans in those holy fields
> Over whose acres walked those blessèd feet
> Which fourteen hundred years ago were nailed
> For our advantage on the bitter cross.
>
> (1.1.19–27)

A prophecy says that Henry will die in Jerusalem, and therefore he expects to expiate his sin against his cousin Richard II in that pilgrimage and to die in the Holy Land afterward. But as we learn in *2 Henry IV*, Henry dies in a room in the palace called "Jerusalem," the stain of Cain-like and Adam-like sin still on his soul. Whenever Henry makes plans to take up his intended Crusade, he is forced by circumstances to set them aside—temporarily, he always thinks. In this first case it is rebellion against his will in the matter of the prisoners taken by Hotspur that must delay the cleansing Crusade: "And for this cause awhile we must neglect / Our holy purpose to Jerusalem" (*1 Henry IV*:1.1.100–101).

136   *John W. Velz*

Henry IV thinks repeatedly that his wayward son Hal's misbehavior is a punishment from God for his crime not only against Richard, but also against God, who placed Richard on the throne that now Henry sits on unjustly. King Henry IV's mind is constantly on his guilt. In 3.2 of *1 Henry IV* in his first confrontation with Prince Hal, he immediately begins with it.

> I know not whether God will have it so
> For some displeasing service I have done,
> That in his secret doom out of my blood
> He'll breed revengement and a scourge for me;
> But thou dost in thy passages of life
> Make me believe that thou art only marked
> For the hot vengeance and the rod of heaven
> To punish my mistreadings.
>
> (3.2.4–11)

Henry is not the first or the last distressed parent to think that God has sent a disobedient child to punish past mistreadings. But few if any have more cause to believe that the mistreadings deserve such punishment. It becomes gradually clear to the audience that Henry himself and others in the seven history plays that follow from the events of *Richard II* see the killing of Richard as an Original Sin, whose stain is not so easily removed. Richard is killed in the fifth act of *Richard II* by an overzealous Piers of Exton in an exact echo of the murder of Thomas à Becket at the behest of a king who finds him a thorn in the guilty flesh and wants him out of the way though he does not want to do the deed directly. It is worth noticing that it is in Henry IV's mind the death of Richard that is his horrid sin. He does not mention deposing him from his throne; that notion is too inflammatory to be spoken.

How does one expiate an Original Sin if it does not work to plan a Crusade against pagans in the Holy Land or to pass blame onto the efficient perpetrators instead of the ultimate perpetrator (to drive Piers of Exton into exile when the sin was Henry's)? As scripture and church doctrine make clear, baptism is the means, a reenactment of the descent of Christ into the grave and then of His resurrection to a new life. As John's Gospel puts it "except that a man be born of water and the Spirit, he cannot enter into the kingdom of God" (3:5). And so, though King Henry IV cannot find redemption from his "Original Sin," his son casts off the sins of his own past and—it is suggested—his inherited curse from his father's sin, when the Archbishop of Canterbury says in the first

England as Eden in Richard II   137

scene of *Henry V* that the new King has undergone a strange baptismal experience.

> The breath no sooner left his father's body
> But that his wildness, mortified in him,
> Seemed to die too; yea, at that very moment
> Consideration like an angel came
> And whipped th' offending Adam out of him,
> Leaving his body as a paradise
> T' envelop and contain celestial spirits.
>
> (1.1.26–32)

As his father dies, the sins of his father against Richard II are carried into the grave with him. The implication is that the Falstaff phase of Hal's life when he suddenly abandoned it at his father's death carried the family guilt with it into oblivion leaving reformation and redemption. When Hal rejects Falstaff, his figurative sinful Father, he rejects by implication the sinful past of his biological Father. The Bishops who are talking about Hal here seem to think a redemption from Falstaffian folly a miracle, but we perhaps know better, because Hal had prophesied this redemption as early as the second scene of *1 Henry IV*:

> So when this loose behavior I throw off
> And pay the debt I never promisèd,
> By how much better than my word I am,
> By so much shall I falsify men's hopes;
> And like bright metal on a sullen ground,
> My reformation, glittering o'er my fault,
> Shall show more goodly and attract more eyes
> Than that which hath no foil to set it off.
> I'll so offend to make offense a skill,
> Redeeming time when men think least I will.
>
> (1.2.202–11)

But Hal still has some doubt in his mind about whether he has escaped the inherited Adam curse of his father. Therefore, when he is preparing himself for battle on the eve of Agincourt he asks God to steel his soldiers' hearts and drive fear from them.

> Not today, O Lord,
> O not today, think not upon the fault
> My father made in compassing the crown!
> I Richard's body have interrèd new,
> And on it have bestowed more contrite tears
> Than from it issued forcèd drops of blood.
> Five hundred poor I have in yearly pay

138   *John W. Velz*

> Who twice a day their withered hands hold up
> Toward heaven, to pardon blood; and I have built
> Two chantries, where the sad and solemn priests
> Sing still for Richard's soul. More will I do;
> Though all that I can do is nothing worth,
> Since that my penitence comes after all,
> Imploring pardon.
>
> (4.1. 290–303)

Henry V here shows astuteness about guilt and expiation. Like Claudius in *Hamlet* who similarly prays that a past sin be extirpated, he is still the beneficiary of the evil done in the past and cannot hope for easy exoneration. This is not only good moral reasoning, but it is historically necessary because the victory at Agincourt and the resulting peace with France is only a hiatus before the figurative Old Testament of English history brings forth the horrible consequences of the Original Sin of deposing and killing Richard.

Much more could be said about the curse of Richard's deposition and death in the three plays that proceed from it, but space will not permit a lingering gaze at those three plays. Perhaps it would be best to go back to *Richard II* to explore more fully the meaning of England as Eden that inculpates not Bolingbroke and his allies, but Richard himself.

As implied earlier, when God installs an anointed king on his throne in Edenic England, He sets him down like Adam in Paradise, as God's surrogate in England, figuratively to till the ground of the garden, to trim it and to manure the earth so that it will bear fruit in time to come. The king is not only an entitled power in the kingdom, he is, as it were, Adam, set to tend God's garden. To the extent that he fails, he may be driven from the garden as Adam and Eve were in Genesis 3. A king does not inherit mere power and license when he ascends a throne; he inherits as well a moral responsibility to the nation. That Richard does not understand this dimension of his kingship is made clear by Gaunt's allusions to leasing out land, farming taxes and other abuses of the land that Richard has committed. These sins against God's garden are conveyed in the context of Gaunt's lines quoted at the beginning of this chapter.

Richard is already a bad gardener. He will become worse as he commits his own Original Sin, regarding the ancestral lands of Gaunt as fit wealth to expropriate. This stealing of Gaunt's land is Richard's forbidden fruit. And it costs him his throne in Eden

England as Eden in Richard II   139

when Gaunt's son Bolingbroke comes back from exile to claim his
rightful inheritance. It is one of the crushing moral ironies of
Richard II that Richard, who has defied the code of primogeniture
in depriving Bolingbroke of his proper inheritance, is punished by
deposition from his throne, which Bolingbroke takes from him il-
legitimately, defying the code of primogeniture.

So Richard is Adam, but he never recognizes that fact, that
part of his contract with God. Another supreme moral irony in the
play is that Richard sees himself as a Christ betrayed by 12,000 Judases (4.1.171–72), when he is not a redeemer at all, but a mere
man, an Adam, who has failed utterly at caring for God's Edenic
land, England. The hybris of Richard's hyperbolic comparison of
himself to martyred Christ is exaggerated when we recognize that
Richard is really a sinful Adam, not a redeeming Christ.[9]

There are, then, two readings of the Eden image for England in
the speech of dying Gaunt in Act 2 scene 1 of *Richard II*. Enor-
mously complicating the moral thrust of the play, Shakespeare
makes Richard both the Original Sin that Bolingbroke commits
against primogeniture and the Adam who fails to tend God's Garden of Eden as God adjured him to care for it when He anointed
him and placed him on the throne. Spelled out as they are in this
essay, the two interpretations of the Edenic England seem mutu-
ally exclusive. How can Richard be both the sinner (Adam) and
another's crime (Bolingbroke's Original Sin)? But Shakespeare persuades the audience to keep both interpretations in their minds as
the play and its successors in the Second Tetralogy unfold.

Instead of stopping here with a conundrum, it is well to go a
little further in thinking of Richard as Bolingbroke's Original Sin.
If we consider that political activity in dynastic plays constitutes
sins against family—and vice versa, sins against family are political activity—it is easy to see that this politico-familial paradox fits
the Bolingbroke/Richard relationship quite well. In this case Bolingbroke returns from exile to get his ancestral lands back—the
ones Richard expropriated from Bolingbroke's father Gaunt
shortly after the dying words with which this essay began. He intends to rectify a wrong done to him and his family, but he cannot
achieve his goal of regaining his lands as long as Richard remains
on the throne. So willy-nilly Henry Bolingbroke becomes a traitor
to his country's anointed king, and when he deposes him, he discovers that there is no safety for him, Henry IV of England, as long
as Richard II of England lives. The tangle of political and personal

140   *John W. Velz*

actions and motives is quite compelling here, as Richard and Henry are first cousins. Shakespeare takes that family relationship a moral step further by bringing in Cain's sin against Abel as if Richard and Henry were siblings instead of the children of siblings.

Shakespeare takes the Cain and Abel relationship all the way through *Richard II* with echoes later in the tetralogy. *Richard II* begins with Bolingbroke's challenge to Thomas Mowbray in the case of the assassination at Calais of Thomas of Woodstock (Gloucester), the uncle of both the young King Richard and of Bolingbroke. Shakespeare's audience—if it had seen *Woodstock* onstage—would know that Mowbray was assigned to hold Gloucester in protective custody in the dangerous town of Calais in hostile France, but that Mowbray, having heard that Richard wanted Woodstock out of the way, as he was a moral thorn in the wayward Richard's flesh, looked the other way and allowed assassins probably sent by Richard to have their way with Woodstock. This is all conveyed allusively in the shouting match between Mowbray and Bolingbroke in Act 1 scene 1 of *Richard II*. Bolingbroke cannot challenge the King directly, and Mowbray cannot defend himself by telling the truth in which Richard was involved. This is ugly palace intrigue. What should interest us here are the terms in which Bolingbroke challenges Mowbray to trial by single combat. He has it that Mowbray

> ... did plot the Duke of Gloucester's death,
> . . . .
> And consequently, like a traitor coward,
> Sluiced out his innocent soul through streams of blood—
> Which blood, like sacrificing Abel's, cries
> Even from the tongueless caverns of the earth
> To me for justice and rough chastisement.
>
> (1.1.100–106)

Though Bolingbroke cannot say it directly, Richard is not only an exploiter of the Garden of England, but also the murderer of his own kin. This complicates the moral implication of the story considerably.

First, to the extent that Richard committed Cain's sin against Abel, no man can avenge it, as in Genesis 4 when God forbade anyone from killing Cain. But murder of a kinsman seems to be competing for position with misgoverning the Edenic kingdom. Shakespeare seems to have had in his mind some fusion between Adam's sin in the Garden and Cain's sin against Abel. In *Hamlet*,

England as Eden in Richard II   141

when Claudius is at prayer, trying what repentance can, he speaks
of his sin against his brother Hamlet Senior:

> O, my offense is rank! It smells to heaven.
> It hath the primal eldest curse upon't.
> A brother's murder.
>
> (3.3.35–37)

The eldest curse was not God's curse against Cain, but God's curse
against Cain's parents, Adam and Eve. But Shakespeare was fasci-
nated with fratricide and included it or the threat of it in more
than a third of the plays in the canon, including such "happy"
comedies as *As You Like It* and *The Tempest* and such tragedies as
King Lear and *Macbeth*. Here in *Richard II* it takes on the nature of
an Original Sin, as the ur-original sin in this play can be said not to
be Bolingbroke's sin against Richard, but Richard's sin against his
Uncle Thomas of Gloucester. Here, as if to complicate the moral
design of the play beyond comprehension, we have yet another
ambiguity in *Richard II*. Richard's Original Sin in the Garden of
England is Adam's sin in the Garden of Eden; but at the same time
his Original Sin is Cain's sin against his brother Abel.[10]

Whatever Richard has to answer to God for, we must observe
that what Richard did to Gloucester, Bolingbroke did to Richard,
and in quite exactly the same indirect way. Each of them gets a
henchman or henchmen to take action against the victim, and in
each case the actual killer is identified with Cain. The lines about
sacrificing Abel's blood crying out for vengeance have already
been quoted. Bolingbroke, who utters these lines as the play begins, has Cain's name on his lips as the play ends. He accuses Piers
of Exton, who played the assassin's role in Richard's death, of being a marked man as Cain was and drives him into exile.

> ... Though I did wish him dead,
> I hate the murderer, love him murderèd.
> The guilt of conscience take thou for thy labor,
> But neither my good word nor princely favor.
> With Cain go wander through the shades of night,
> And never show thy head by day nor light.
>
> (5.6.39–44)

Richard had driven both Mowbray and Bolingbroke into exile in
Act 1 scene 3 of the play. The events of Genesis 4 bracket the play,
from first to last. Bolingbroke even does in Act 5 what Richard had
done in Act 1, that is, require a henchman to take the blame for
what he himself wanted done.

142   *John W. Velz*

The irony is cruel. Not only does history repeat itself, but the change in regimes does not result in eliminating the Cain sin in the successor king's moral makeup. Bolingbroke behaves toward Richard precisely as Richard had behaved toward his Uncle Gloucester. The irony is breathtaking. It is notable that in *Julius Caesar* Shakespeare includes the same historical irony but secularized. Caesar and Brutus are more alike than either would be willing to admit.[11] A change in regime does not result in a change in values in either *Richard II* or *Julius Caesar*. So much for ideology, so much for doctrinaire politics. The Cain and Abel motif in *Richard II* makes it quite clear that a change in governors does not necessarily result in a change in behavior.

Richard II is a complex play. It is easy enough to say it is a two-man play about which man can offer England the better government. But that is only the beginning. Even the Original Sin in the play must be said to be plural—in Richard's case murdering his Uncle Woodstock and treating the Garden (Gaunt's lands especially) as if they were his private property when he was set (i.e., set in place) by God to guard and nourish that Garden. In Bolingbroke's case the plural sin is challenging Richard's right to the throne through primogeniture and murdering Richard afterward. In this sense the Original Sin which both Richard and Henry commit is not Adam's sin, but Cain's. Shakespeare plays fast and loose with scripture in *Richard II*, but in doing so he keeps his tetralogy intimately connected to Christianity.

Notes

1. (2.1.40–60). All quotations from Shakespeare in this chapter are from *The Complete Works of Shakespeare*, 4th edition, ed. Bevington.

2. Bennett makes a secular interpretation of the England-as-Eden motif in *Richard II*. The background in her formulation is Classical, not Christian. An early attempt to identify the Eden motif in the play was Law's. His article is a compilation of Shakespeare's various references to the Fall of Man and its consequences in Genesis. The whole Shakespeare canon is surveyed; only three or four references are taken from *Richard II*, and no coherent analysis of the play is to be found there. The three pages (158–60) that Battenhouse devotes to *Richard II* in *Shakespearean Tragedy* are concerned only with the manner of Richard's death. And Battenhouse's *Shakespeare's Christian Dimension* reprints on *Richard II* only a passage from Coursen, Jr.'s book. Roberts does not point to any interpretation that approaches the Edenic materials in *Richard II* in the way this chapter reads

England as Eden in Richard II 143

them; see her *Richard II: An Annotated Bibliography* and her lengthy "Introduction" to that two-volume work. Of course materials that are peripheral to the present analysis are plentiful there. The work is thorough and comprehensive within its limits, 1940–1982. Candido does not summarize any study that sees the second tetralogy in the terms proposed here. He does not record any study that makes an interpretation of *Richard II* or of the *Henry IV* plays in terms of the England as Eden motif.

3. Wilders senses the nostalgia for a lost and idealized past that inheres in the garden imagery of this as of other Shakespearean history plays. But he does not make a full interpretation of *Richard II* and the *Henriad*.

4. See Northrop Frye.

5. Quoted from *The Book of Common Prayer*.

6. See Noble's Appendix: Index of Biblical Books and Chapters. Shaheen can be compared.

7. See Leon. Ure added Plato to this list in the Fourth *Arden Shakespeare* in 1956. Comito's *The Idea of the Garden* is an excellent background resource for the Garden scene and other allusions to gardens in the play.

8. For other arguments that 3.4 is a moral hinge in the dynamic of the play, see Price; French; and Shalvi.

9. For a more positive view of Richard's comparison of himself to martyred Christ, see Cauthen, Jr. Contrast Roland M. Frye, p. 180, who denies that Richard is a Christ figure, though he sees him as having redeemed himself late in the play. Siegel, p. 50 and passim, sides with Cauthen against the narrower view of Frye. Drawing on Christology, Hapgood makes an interesting negative interpretation of Richard's identification of himself with Christ, but a different one from the one advanced here. Bryant, Jr., comes somewhat closer to the approach taken in the present chapter than others do. He sees the Adam/Christ relationship as a typological one: Richard sins as Adam but takes on Christ's sacrificial role when he is himself immolated.

10. See Robinson, who shows that the expiation of the fratricidal sin in *Richard II* enables Henry V to speak of his soldiers as "we happy few, we band of brothers."

11. See Rabkin.

Works Cited

Battenhouse, Roy W. *Shakespearean Tragedy: Its Art and Its Christian Premises*. Bloomington and London: Indiana UP, 1969.

———. *Shakespeare's Christian Dimension: An Anthology of Commentary*. Bloomington and Indianapolis: Indiana UP, 1994.

Bennett, Josephine Waters. "Britain Among the Fortunate Isles." *Studies in Philology* 53 (1956): 114–40.

144   John W. Velz

Bevington, David, ed. *The Complete Works of Shakespeare*. 4th edition. [New York]: HarperCollins, 1992.

The Book of Common Prayer and Administration of the Sacraments and Other Rites and Ceremonies of the Church Together with the Psalter or Psalms of David. [Episcopal] Church Publishing Company, 1979.

Bryant, J.A., Jr. *Hippolyta's View: Some Christian Aspects of Shakespeare's Plays*. Lexington: U of Kentucky P, 1961.

Candido, Joseph. *Richard II, Henry IV, I and II, & Henry V: An Annotated Bibliography of Shakespeare Studies 1777–1997*. Pegasus Shakespeare Bibliographies. Gen. ed. Richard L. Nochimson. Asheville: Pegasus P of the U of North Carolina, 1998.

Cauthen, Irby B., Jr. "*Richard II* and the Image of the Betrayed Christ." *Renaissance Papers, 1954*, pp. 45–48.

Comito, Terry. *The Idea of the Garden in the Renaissance*. New Brunswick, NJ: Rutgers UP, 1977.

Coursen, Herbert R., Jr. *Christian Ritual and the World of Shakespeare's Tragedies*. Lewisburg, PA: Bucknell UP, 1976.

French, A.L. "Who Deposed Richard the Second?" *Essays in Criticism* 17 (1967): 411–33.

Frye, Northrop. "The Argument of Comedy." In *English Institute Essays, 1948*. New York: Columbia UP, 1949. 58–73.

Frye, Roland M. *Shakespeare and Christian Doctrine*. Princeton: Princeton UP, 1963.

Hapgood, Robert. "Shakespeare's Maimed Rites: The Early Tragedies." *Centennial Review* 9 (1965): 494–508.

Law, Robert Adger. "Shakespeare in the Garden of Eden." *Studies in English* (U of Texas) [26] (1941): 24–38.

Leon, H.J. "Classical Sources for the Garden Scene in 'Richard II.'" *Philological Quarterly* 29 (1950): 65–70.

Noble, Richmond. *Shakespeare's Biblical Knowledge and Use of the Book of Common Prayer as Exemplified in the Plays of the First Folio*. London: SPCK; New York: Macmillan, 1935.

Price, Hereward T. "Mirror-Scenes in Shakespeare." In *Joseph Quincy Adams Memorial Studies*, ed. James G. McManaway, Giles E. Dawson, and Edwin E. Willoughby. Washington, DC: Folger Shakespeare Library, 1948. 101–13.

Rabkin, Norman. "Structure, Convention, and Meaning in *Julius Caesar*." *Journal of English and Germanic Philology* 63 (1964): 240–54.

Roberts, Josephine A. *Richard II: An Annotated Bibliography*. 2 vols. New York and London: Garland, 1988.

England as Eden in Richard II

Robinson, Marsha S. "Mythoi of Brotherhood: Generic Emplotment in *Henry V.*" In *Shakespeare's English Histories: A Quest for Form and Genre*, ed. John W. Velz. Medieval and Renaissance Texts and Studies 133. Binghamton, NY: MRTS, 1996. 143–70.

Shaheen, Naseeb. *Biblical Allusions in Shakespeare's Plays.* Newark: U of Delaware P; London: Associated UP, 1999.

Shalvi, Alice. "Studies in Kingship: *Henry VI, Richard III, Henry IV,* and *Henry V.*" In *The World and Art of Shakespeare,* ed. A.A. Mendilow and Alice Shalvi. New York: Daniel Davey, 1967. 89–118.

Siegel, Paul N. *Shakespeare in His Time and Ours.* Notre Dame: Notre Dame UP, 1968.

Ure, Peter, ed. *Richard II.* The Arden Shakespeare. 4th edition. Cambridge, MA: Harvard UP, 1956.

Wilders, Jonathan. *The Lost Garden: A View of Shakespeare's English and Roman History Plays.* London: Macmillan; Totowa, NJ: Rowman and Littlefield, 1978.

Shakespeare and Religious Polemic: Revisiting *1 Henry IV* and the Oldcastle Controversy[1]

Paul White

I

Few of us would have imagined a decade ago that the subject of religion would command the attention of leading scholars in Shakespeare criticism and Renaissance drama studies as much as it does today. Books within the past decade by Kristen Poole, Huston Diehl, Donna Hamilton, Katherine Maus, and Alan Sinfield testify to the complex, dynamic interchange between religious culture and the theater in early modern England.[2] What accounts for this development is an interesting question. The New Historicism, the dominant critical mode in Renaissance dramatic scholarship in the 1980s and early 1990s, appears to have both delayed and spawned this critical interest. On the one hand, early influential critics like Stephen Greenblatt and Jonathan Dollimore underestimated the significance of popular religion by exploring it too narrowly as an instrument of power by which the Tudor state mystifies and conceals the political structures it wishes to perpetuate.[3] On the other hand, New Historicism's concern with self-fashioning, with questions of personhood and interiority, has led recent scholarship to consider religion, alongside class, race, gender, and sexuality, as a crucial cultural component in the construction of identity.[4]

At the same time, New Historicism's focus on the cultural embeddedness of art, on the material conditions (e.g., patronage relations, economic practice, government censorship, audience composition) under which plays and poems are produced and acquire meaning, on art's function as a vehicle of temporary topical (as opposed to universal) ideas, accounts for the resurgence in topical

148   *Paul White*

or "localized" readings of Elizabethan and Jacobean drama. Among the prominent practitioners of topical readings are those who focus on the drama's engagement with religious and ecclesiastical controversy, an engagement that was hardly acknowledged to have existed twenty years ago. These critics—among them Donna Hamilton, Margot Heinemann, Julia Gaspar, Jerzy Limon, Richard Dutton, and Leah Marcus—share a common interest in exploring the connections between royal, noble, and civic patrons, on the one hand, and playwrights and acting companies, on the other, who either support, or are commissioned to propagate, their religious views and interests.

These connections among patronage, the London playing community, and religion, are what principally concern me in the present discussion. Their interaction is particularly complex when explored within the context of what critics call "the Oldcastle controversy," which extended through the mid-to-late 1590s and directly involved Shakespeare in a dispute with the powerful Cobham family, the patriarch of which was the playwright's Lord Chamberlain in 1596/97. Shakespeare's fellow playwrights Jonson, Drayton and Munday, and various luminaries at court such as the Earls of Essex and Nottingham, also figure in the controversy. In what follows, I hope to show how religion, politics, patronage, and theatrical entertainment all get entangled in this dispute over the Cobham family's most celebrated and controversial religious member, the fifteenth-century Lollard hero, Sir John Oldcastle. Shakespeare's *1 Henry IV* appears to have precipitated the commotion, but we'll also consider how Lord Admiral Nottingham's Men were drawn into the controversy with *The History of Sir John Oldcastle, Lord Cobham*, not to mention several other plays.

II

As is widely known, when Shakespeare's *1 Henry IV* was first performed, probably in mid-to-late 1596, that great comic worldling we know as Sir John Falstaff was named Sir John Oldcastle. Audiences in London and beyond may have known this character from Shakespeare's chief dramatic source, the old Queen's Men's *Famous Victories of Henry V*, yet Oldcastle, the fourth Lord Cobham, was also a widely known historical figure, a Lollard leader who, according to Catholic apologists and sympa-

Shakespeare and Religious Polemic 149

thizers, died a heretic to the true Church and a traitor to the English monarchy. While some Protestants also viewed Oldcastle with disfavor, as a forerunner of puritan separatism, he was more generally hailed by mainstream Protestantism as a godly man who heroically died for his faith.[5] This is how he is perceived in the second edition of Holinshed's *Chronicles*, dedicated to William Brooke, tenth bearer of the Cobham title. Indeed, in direct contrast to the charming figure of vice Shakespeare developed him as, the more strident Protestant chronicles such as Foxe's influential and popular *Acts and Monuments* canonized Oldcastle as a pre-Reformation saint and model of Christian piety, courage, and loyalty to the Crown.

Even though the Elizabethan Lords Cobham were not in the direct line of descent from Oldcastle (Sir John married into the family in 1408 and only became Lord Cobham thereafter), they proudly regarded him as their ancestor. That William Brooke, or his son, the inheritor of his title, were offended by what they perceived to be a smear of their family honor is clear from a letter by one Richard James some twenty years after the fact. James writes:

> In Shakespeare's first show of harry the fifth [*1 Henry IV*] the person with which he undertook to play a buffoon was not Falstaff but Sir John Oldcastle, and ... offence being worthily taken by personages descended from his title (as peradventure by many others also who ought to have him in honorable memory) the poet was put to make an ignorant shift of abusing Sir John Falstaff, a man not inferior of virtue, though not so famous in piety.[6]

It is safe to say, therefore, that under pressure from the Brookes, either the elder Cobham or his son Henry, the inheritor of the family title, Shakespeare dutifully changed the name to Falstaff. Other names were changes as well, those of the old knight's companions, Russell and Harvey (who also had prominent descendants at court), who became Peto and Bardolph.[7] At what point performances of the play started using the name Falstaff is unclear. However, the revision turns up in the first printed quarto of *1 Henry IV* in February 1598, possibly rushed out to press to appease the family, and in the Epilogue to *2 Henry IV* a disclaimer is tacked on after the prayer to the queen which usually concludes it, stating, "Oldcastle died a martyr, and this is not the man." It may have been around this time that Cobham's son, Henry Brooke, demanded that revisions be made to two other plays which allegedly defamed the Cobhams, specifically *Merry Wives of Windsor,*

150   *Paul White*

where "Brooke," the pseudonym taken by Mistress Ford's jealousy-consumed husband, was changed to Broome, and *2 Henry VI*, where a whole section of a scene implicating Eleanor Cobham, wife to the "good duke" Gloucester, in treason, is expunged from the text in the 1623 folio edition.[8] The damage, however, had already been done, with court gossip identifying the younger Cobham, Henry Brooke, with the Oldcastle/Falstaff character. The controversy dragged on through 1599 when, in October or November, the rival Admiral's Men condemned Shakespeare's treatment of Oldcastle as "forged invention" in the Prologue to its own dramatic production of *Sir John Oldcastle*, and when new plays honoring Eleanor Cobham, Duchess of Gloucester, appear to have been in the planning stages.

III

Relevant here is whether Shakespeare and his company deliberately set out to parody the historical Oldcastle, the Lollard martyr and Protestant saint, and in turn, to insult William Brooke, his descendant and holder of his title as the tenth Lord Cobham. We actually have two questions here, one concerning the historical Oldcastle and the other concerning the living Cobhams, and I believe, at least for the moment, it is important to keep them separate and distinct. Both have implications for the study of religion/theater relations and patron/player relations, for in parodying Oldcastle, *1 Henry IV* risked offending puritan-leaning officials at court such as Pembroke and Essex, whom some scholars have identified as Shakespeare's patrons. And in burlesquing William Brooke, the company would, in effect, have been insulting the official who arranged their performances at court.

In tackling divisive religious issues, we think of Jonson or Marlowe before Shakespeare, but Shakespeare was far short of avoiding them altogether, especially in the 1590s. On the one hand, staged prelates such as the "scarlet hypocrite" Cardinal Pandulph in *King Johan* and the reprobate Cardinal Beauford in *1* and *2 Henry VI* illustrate the virulent anti-papalism Shakespeare shared with his playwrighting contemporaries, at least at this time. On the other hand, clearly the "puritan" Malvolio and the "precise" Angelo give voice to some measure of unease with the more extreme tendencies of Elizabethan puritanism. That same unease, it seems to me, is evident in the portrayal of Oldcastle/

Shakespeare and Religious Polemic 151

Falstaff in *1* and *2 Henry IV*. In the play Sir John's old-age debauchery and treasonable offenses both before and after going to war call into question hagiographic treatments of the Lollard leader popularized in Foxe's *Acts and Monuments* and other chronicles. Those more militantly Protestant publications strained credulity to the limit by praising him not merely as a model of Christian piety but a loyal subject of the Crown as well. As Gary Taylor has shown in his analysis of *1 Henry IV*, Shakespeare's contemporaries would have picked up the numerous subtle and not-so-subtle references in the play's dialogue to Oldcastle's treasonable offenses and its punishment. In the play-acting scene of 2.4, for example, Hal describes him as "a roasted manningtree ox" (447), a rather grisly allusion to the Lollard's form of death in which he was suspended by chains around the waist from the gallows and consumed by the fire that even destroyed the scaffold. Catholic accounts of Oldcastle, which Shakespeare generally favors, railed against him as a traitor who fomented revolt and in fact probably instigated the Lollard rebellion in 1414, after which Oldcastle's steward was arrested. This seems closer to the truth than the accounts of Bale and Foxe, which go to some lengths to defend the Lollard reformer's allegiance to Henry V right to the end.

Yet the play's satire goes deeper, for in jesting tones, Sir John repeatedly speaks the language of the conscience-stricken puritan ("Monsieur Remorse" as Poins calls him [1.2.106–07]), who alternately longs for and despairs of repentance (1.2.91–94; 3.3.1–10), mutters about hellfire to Bardolph whom he likens to "the son of utter darkness," fears he is "one of the wicked" and not called to grace (1.2.91; 5.1.128–29), and so on.[9] The religious allusions to Oldcastle/Falstaff continue through *2 Henry IV* and into *Henry V* where the Boar's Head characters debate the dying knight's salvation or damnation, recalling his anxious deathbed outcry "'God, God, God!' three or four times" and other utterances concerning "the Whore of Babylon," and "a black soul burning in hell." It is not surprising, therefore, that while many contemporaries undoubtedly found Sir John endearing and amusing (including the Queen, evidently), some serious-minded Protestants of the period were evidently offended by Shakespeare's characterization. They certainly would have endorsed, if not contributed to, the Cobham family's insistence that Shakespeare make the name-change to Falstaff, resulting in missed puns, irregular meters, and lost topical significance in the surviving text.

152   *Paul White*

Yet Shakespeare was not doing anything particularly new with this kind of anti-puritan satire, and he certainly knew that it would delight his popular patrons at the Theatre and Curtain. Kristen Poole has shown how Oldcastle/Falstaff's mock-puritan cant and burlesque staging derive from the government-sponsored pamphlets and stage propaganda of the anti-Marprelate campaign of the late 1580s.[10] And here we should keep in mind that the *Famous Victories*, from which Shakespeare originally took his Oldcastle character, was a play of the Queen's Men who engaged in anti-puritan satire during the Marprelate controversy. David Bevington has noted the attributes of Falstaff's character taken from Tarleton's comic routine, his "fondness for mock-serious reforming cant, his satiric depiction of psalm-singing Puritans, his use of extemporaneous wit to joke his way out of difficult situations."[11] All of these would have appealed to regular playgoers, many of whom might have remembered the Queen's Men's play.

But does the anti-puritan satire of Oldcastle/Falstaff extend to include William Brooke, Lord Cobham, the Lollard hero's proudly proclaimed descendant? It has been argued that attacking Oldcastle and attacking Cobham essentially amounts to the same thing anyway, since Lord Brooke was himself a puritan zealot, the contemporary manifestation of his Medieval kinsman. Moreover, his preciseness in religion was matched by a puritanical hostility toward the stage (for many critics, religious puritanism and antitheatricality always go together), which provided a further, perhaps even stronger, motive for the players to belittle him. Labeling Cobham a "puritan," however, is very misleading. Indeed, during the early 1570s, Cobham's implication in the Ridolphi plot led to suspicions of him as a closet Catholic, not a puritan extremist, and it is hard to believe that some twenty years later the Privy Council would have assigned him the chief layman's position on the Commission to look into the Martin Marprelate controversy, had he been of immoderate religious persuasion. It now seems likely that he was a moderate Protestant along the lines of his close friend and chief advocate at court, William Cecil. As for his presumed antitheatricality, this is more difficult to assess. It is not irrelevant that early in his career, between 1563 and 1571, he patronized a travelling acting company,[12] and that just before his appointment as Lord Chamberlain in 1596, he served as "ceremonial lieutenant to the sovereign" in the Knights of the Garter festivities.[13] Both these facts tend to challenge the perception of Cobham

Shakespeare and Religious Polemic 153

as an aging puritan courtier, indifferent to or alienated from court festivities, whose appointment to the Chamberlaincy was for life-long service and loyalty to the Crown. It now seems clear that, as Lord Chamberlain, Cobham was an experienced administrator of entertainment at court, coordinating arrangements among the offices of the Revels, the Works, and the Wardrobe in producing the various pageants and plays demanded by the Queen and her circle in the winter season of 1596/97.

Having said that, Cobham does seem to have generated grave doubts among some members of the theater community about his commitment to commercial playing in and around London during his first few months in office. One of those doubters was Thomas Nashe, as evidenced in a letter written in August or September of 1596 to William Cotton, himself a servant of George Carey, Shakespeare's new patron following the death of Carey's Father, Lord Chamberlain Hunsdon, a month or so earlier. Despite the plague which shut down the suburban playhouses, Nashe reports that he stayed in London with the hope of a "harvest ... by writing for the stage and for the presse." No such luck, however. "The players as if they had writt another Christs tears, ar piteously persecuted by the L. Maior & the aldermen." Nashe may have been thinking specifically about Carey's own troupe, the one he hoped to pen plays for, when he adds that "however in their old Lords tyme they thought there state setled, it is now so uncertayne they cannot build upon it."[14] Quite literally, Hunsdon's new company could not build on their investment, since before they had a chance to move into their new public playhouse in Blackfriars, the Privy Council, under Cobham's watch, sided with the precinct's neighborhood petitioners and prohibited it from opening. Much has been made of the fact that Cobham himself, who had previously leased the theater property and at the time occupied another wing of the former friary, did not sign the lease, and thereby indicated either neutrality or opposition to the petition.[15] However, as Andrew Gurr has observed, the Lord Chamberlain did not *need* to sign it. Indeed it may have been inappropriate for him to have done so, since as a member of the Privy Council he was in receipt of the document if not the leading authority on the Council to address the issue at hand.[16]

Another piece of evidence has recently been cited to suggest that Lord Chamberlain Cobham had a falling out with the long-time Master of the Revels, Edmund Tilney, who had enjoyed the privileged and lucrative position of licensing plays and play

154   *Paul White*

venues since 1581. In a letter to William More that has been dated
with some certainty to 1599/1600, Tilney reports a dispute over a
subsidy with one Thomas Vincent, who has sent him the "most
Arroganstist letter that Euer I receuid only for findinge fault
therwith, and yett haue I reciuid diuerss braue letters from the last
Lord Chamberlayne When he and I were att odds."[17] This "last
Lord Chamberlayne" must be Cobham, since his successor
through 1599/1600 was George Carey, the second Lord Hunsdon.
The letter has led Richard Dutton to suspect that Tilney colluded
with Shakespeare's company in an effort to embarrass the new
Lord Chamberlain who interrupted the Hunsdon/Howard line of
controlling theatrical affairs at court from at least the mid-1580s
through to the end of Elizabeth's reign. Dutton suggests that as
Revels Master, Tilney licensed *1 Henry IV* knowing full well of the
Oldcastle/Cobham parallel and how it would play out in public.[18]
Tilney hardly could have failed to see the family connection; he
had just finished writing a book on the genealogy of England's
leading families, including the Falstaffs and the Brookes. And, of
course, he must have also let pass the slight to the Brookes in
Merry Wives in the Spring of 1597 and in *Everyman in His Humour* a
year-and-a-half later, as we shall see shortly.

Dutton is the first to admit that this hypothesis is highly con-
jectural, and one still needs to explain why a company, even if it
could defend itself by arguing that the character in question died
nearly two hundred years earlier and that the Revels Office expressed no objection, would risk insulting a powerful court official
such as the Lord Chamberlain who, as it turns out, gave them the
exclusive privilege among professional companies to perform at
court in 1596/97. In all, Shakespeare's company performed six
times that season; no other troupe, not even the Lord Admiral's
Men, received that honor. For Dutton and others, animosity between Cobham and the playing community—and perhaps specifically Shakespeare's company—developed in the latter half of 1596
and therefore prior to the Christmas season performances at court.
However, there is now good reason to believe that dislike for Cobham developed, or considerably intensified, during that 1596/97
holiday period. For what Shakespearean commentators on the
Cobham/Oldcastle controversy have overlooked is a letter addressed to Lord Chamberlain Cobham involving a court production in December 1596. Interestingly enough, the letter writer, one
Edward Jones, was secretary to Cobham's sworn enemy at court,
the Earl of Essex. He writes to complain of his humiliation at the

Shakespeare and Religious Polemic 155

hands of the Lord Chamberlain at a December Sunday evening play at Whitehall when records show that Shakespeare's company performed. Jones writes:

> Your L. hath done me some disgraces which greive me so much as I must complayne thereof to your L. And that which greiveth me most is the publicke disgrace which your L. gave me at the play on Sonday night not only before many of my frendes that thought your L. did me wronge but in the hearinge of my wife who beinge with childe did take it so ill as she wept and complayned in the place, for I cam to her but to aske her how she did & not to stay there, and your L. liftinge up your staffe at me, called me sirra and bide me gett me lower saucy fellowe besides other wordes of disgrace.[19]

Apparently, Jones had been standing beside his presumably seated wife, who was pregnant, while the play was in progress, inquiring how she was doing, when Cobham approached him with his white staff (in this instance not used merely as a symbol of his office as Lord Chamberlain), calling him" saucy fellowee besides other words of disgrace" and commanding him to "get ... lower," perhaps because Jones was visually as well as audibly distracting the court audience's attention. Presiding over and maintaining order at royal court performances was a routine function of the Lord Chamberlain, and indeed a special "standinge" was constructed by the Office of the Works in the Hall and the Great Chamber at Whitehall from which he kept watch of the audience as well as the play.[20] Contemporary accounts indicate that the he was not above using his white staff to discipline, and usher from the auditorium if necessary, unruly playgoers, the troublemaking Ben Jonson among them a few years later.[21] But in this instance Cobham's intervention created the very disturbance it was designed to prevent. If the indecorous display between the two men was not enough to divert the Whitehall spectators' attention, then the weeping and complaining of Jones's pregnant wife certainly did. This is "the gratest [disgrace] that ever I received in my life and most unworthily," Jones later exclaims in his letter. If the incident distracted the audience, it must have been an enormous disruption to the players themselves who regarded performances the most privileged moments of their careers. It certainly would not have endeared them to the Lord Chamberlain. Unfortunately, we will never know what play Shakespeare's company performed that evening. One is teased with the thought that it was *1 Henry IV*, with William Kempe hamming it up as

156   Paul White

Oldcastle/Falstaff, which may have been enough to put Cobham in a very bad mood during the course of the performance.

What we can say with some confidence is that *after* William Cobham's death in March 1597 Shakespeare's company definitely did target the Brooke family. This is clear in *Merry Wives* where, the jealous Ford, in pursuit of Falstaff whom he is convinced has cuckolded him, assumes the identity of another would-be adulterer named Brooke. Extensive topical references link *Merry Wives* to the Feast of the Garter in April 1597, when the patron of Shakespeare's company, George Carey, was elected a new knight of the Garter. As with the name-change of Oldcastle to Falstaff, the revision of "Brooke" as "Broome" in the folio edition deprives the play of much punning and topical significance. A brook, of course, may be crossed by a ford, and it is brook in this sense that Falstaff puns on when, on his first meeting with the disguised Ford, he says "Call him in./Such Brooks are welcome to me, that o'erflows such liquor."[22] We assume that the specific object of this satire is Henry Brooke, since his father died on 5 March 1597, a month or so before the Feast of the Garter and before George Hunsdon finally secured the highly sought after office of the Lord Chamberlain.

It is not insignificant that a parody of the Cobhams' aggrandizement of the family's lineage, and particularly its ties to Oldcastle, shows up in another Lord Chamberlain's play performed in September 1598: Ben Jonson's *Every Man in His Humour* (with Shakespeare listed as a member of the cast in the first printed edition). There, Cob, the water-bearer, boasts of his lineage drawn from the Herald's Books where his ancestor is shown to be "a mighty great cob," "my great-great-mighty-great-grandfather."[23] In a more explicit reference to Sir John Oldcastle, the fourth Lord Cobham, and the saint's day (first proposed by John Foxe in *Acts and Monuments*) honoring his grisly martyrdom, Cob says: "A fasting day no sooner comes, but my lineage goes to rack; poor cobs, they smoke for it, they are made martyrs o'the gridiron, they melt for passion." This is not overreading the text, as David McKeen, Charles Nicholl and other commentators of Jonson have shown; other plays of the period mock the Elizabethan Cobham barony's complex formula of connecting themselves with Oldcastle by depicting characters who boast that Sir John Oldcastle was my "great Grand-father" and "my great-grandfathers fathers Uncle."[24]

Shakespeare and Religious Polemic

In returning to *1 Henry IV,* whether or not we believe Shakespeare intended the Oldcastle/Cobham identification to be made, what we can say with absolute certainty is that audiences *did,* so much so that the connection between Shakespeare's comic buffoon and Henry Brooke became a familiar joke at court. By February 1598, the Earl of Essex concluded a letter to Robert Cecil saying, "I pray you commend me allso to Alex. Ratcliff and tell him for newes his sister is maryed to Sr Jo. Falstaff." The gossip circulating at court was that Ratcliff's sister, Margaret, was involved with Henry Brooke, whom Essex identifies with Falstaff, formerly known as Oldcastle, and the association was sufficiently widespread that the Earl could count on Cecil, Brooke's brother-in-law, getting the joke. A year later in July 1599 when Southampton was with Essex in Ireland, his wife the Countess wrote to him making the same identification.[25] Ironically, if the Cobhams insisted on the name change, which seems certain, they may have unwittingly validated and perpetuated the topical reading of Shakespeare's plays, one which saw the fictional penniless adventurer and buffoon as representing members of their own family. It now appears that the controversy had taken on a momentum and dynamic of its own, drawn into the factional politics which dominated the latter years of Elizabeth's reign.

It is not merely coincidental that the Essex circle was most active in exploiting the Oldcastle/Brooke identification. The Brookes, especially the younger Lord Cobham, were among the Earl's most hated enemies at court from the mid-90s onward. Henry Brooke had increasingly gravitated toward the rival court faction of his brother-in-law, Robert Cecil, in opposition to Essex, and they were active in securing his estrangement from court.[26] From this vantage point, we see how the Oldcastle controversy may have served to reinforce the acrimony between these rival parties and patronage networks surrounding the monarchy at the end of the Queen's reign.

The Essex connection raises the question of what relationship the Earl and his circle may have had to Shakespeare's company. Influential scholars like Leslie Hotson, Carol Chillington Rutter, and E.A.J. Honigmann follow a long list of scholars linking Shakespeare to the Essex party.[27] Their arguments should not be dismissed. Shakespeare's one-time patron, Southampton, was among Essex's closest advisors from the mid-90s on; Shakespeare himself admired the courtier, as we all know from his famous compliment to Essex near the end of *Henry V,* and Essex's followers appear to

158   Paul White

have repaid the compliment on the eve of the rebellion in February 1601 by giving the Lord Chamberlain's Men an additional 30 shillings to stage *Richard II*. Yet if Shakespeare and his company were so closely allied with Essex, why did they go virtually unpunished for staging *Richard II* at the time of the rebellion and indeed performed back at court within a few weeks' time? Having said that, a playwright and actors who were perceived to denigrate the Cobhams might have become associated with his court faction.

IV

My own reading of events and texts suggests that while Shakespeare and the Lord Chamberlain's Men may have entered the fray of court politics in the late 1590s, the company did not consistently adopt any political or religious allegiance. Shakespeare was too much of a pragmatist, and his company managed to balance a range of demands made by their various patrons at court and in the commercial playhouses. It seems that they did engage in the satire against the Cobhams, but this was always incidental and peripheral to their role as entertainers. This may not have always been the case with the Lord Admiral's Men, by 1599 known as Nottingham's Men to reflect their patron's elevation to the earldom, who with the launching of their own rival *Oldcastle Play* at the Rose in November of 1599 reaffirmed an identity with London's puritan-leaning audiences. This play, and almost certainly its non-extant sequel, were as close as one could get to Protestant propaganda in the theater, as a comparison with Shakespeare's "Oldcastle" plays will demonstrate. That the play was explicitly answering the false depiction of the Lollard hero in Shakespeare's drama is proclaimed by the Prologue: "It is no pampered glutton we present, / Nor aged counsellor to youthful sin."[28] The Admiral's men play championed the Foxian representation of Oldcastle as a godly, brave, and loyal servant of the Crown. The timing of the play is interesting. Shakespeare's Globe had recently been built on Bankside a few streets away from the Rose, perhaps opening with *Henry V*, which had so optimistically anticipated Essex's triumphal return from Ireland. Now in November, with Essex back home in disgrace and facing charges of treason and cowardice, the Lord Admiral's Men seized the opportunity to stage a play honoring as a valiant warrior and godly Christian the ancestor of Essex's

Shakespeare and Religious Polemic 159

hated enemy at court, the man Essex repeatedly stated was out to destroy his reputation and even murder him.

If Henslowe was simply exhibiting sharp business acumen in taking some attention away from his competitors down the street at the newly opened Globe, he may also have received backing from a higher authority, namely Charles Howard, Lord Admiral and by this time the Earl of Nottingham. Howard became a political ally of Henry Brooke, the younger Cobham, when the latter became engaged to his daughter, the widowed Countess of Kildare.[29] Moreover, by 1599, the Lord Admiral had become estranged from Essex, who vehemently objected to Howard's being granted the Earldom of Nottingham for achievements Essex claimed for himself, namely the sacking of Cadiz in the summer of 1596. It stands to reason, then, that Howard and Cobham would have supported a play rehabilitating the memory of Cobham's martyred ancestor and in turn enhancing his own reputation, after an extended period of public ridicule, partially at the hands of the Essex faction. Indeed, they may have financially contributed to its production. For the script of *Sir John Oldcastle* and its planned sequel, Henslowe paid its authors, Munday, Drayton, Hathaway, and Wilson, a bonus of ten shillings recorded "as a gift."[30] There is reason to believe that this gift came from an outside party, not unlike the 30-shilling gift paid by the followers of Essex to the Lord Chamberlain's Men to stage *Richard II* in 1601.

Whatever the case, Lord Admiral Nottingham's Men further advanced the Cobham cause by idealizing the portrait of Eleanor Cobham in John Day and Henry Chettles' *The First Part of the Blind Beggar of Bednall Green*, a historical folk drama set in the same time period as Shakespeare's *2 Henry VI*, and to which it served as an answer of sorts. Following Foxe, who predictably broke with the pre-Reformation tradition which treated Lady Eleanor as a witch and a traitor (the model for Shakespeare's Eleanor), Chettle and Day portray her as an innocent pursued by the wicked Cardinal Winchester, and it is only through the goodness of Duke Humphrey of Gloucester, whom she marries, that the Duchess escapes the clutches of the devious prelate. Henslowe paid the playwrights £5 10s for the play in May 1600, and like *Oldcastle* its success sparked a sequel, indeed two sequels, neither of which survives. In following the Foxian narrative, no doubt, these plays traced her career to martyrdom at the hands of a corrupt church.[31] The Admiral's troupe, along with the other companies Henslowe managed at the Rose and later at the Fortune, established an iden-

160   Paul White

tity with the more advanced Protestant party by staging a series of plays based on Protestant heroes, many also modeled directly on the biographical narratives in Foxe's *Acts and Monuments*. These "elect nation" plays, as they have been called, included *Sir Thomas Wyatt*, *Robert Earl of Huntington*, *When You See Me You Know Me*, and *The Whore of Babylon*.

V

The Oldcastle controversy illustrates ways in which the nature and dynamics of theatrical patronage changed from the middle years of the sixteenth century. Back then, playing companies, closely tied to their patron's households, performed only intermittently during the year and advanced their patron's interests and reputation. Following the advent of commercialism in theaters of London during the 1570s, companies gained some measure of autonomy and self-identity apart from their patrons yet managed to combine economic self-interest and artistic integrity with an ideological commitment to their patrons, as Scott McMillin and Sally-Beth MacLean have convincingly shown in their study *The Queen's Men and Their Plays*. This political alignment, it seems to me, extended into the next century with the Henslowe companies, especially around the close of the century with the Lord Admiral's or Nottingham's Men. Yet in the 1590s, we see the Lord Chamberlain's Men emerging as a company that managed, with Shakespeare as their leader, some degree of autonomy, at least to the extent that they could possibly resist or subvert the views of court patrons. Ironically, however, the rich signifying potential of Shakespeare's plays, particularly his history plays, makes them perhaps more vulnerable to topical controversy than those of his rivals. The theatrical controversy involving the Elizabethan Lords Cobham offers more sophisticated insights into the relationship between patronage and professional theater. If Shakespeare and his fellows *did* intend to satirize the Elizabethan Cobhams, then we have a case of where an acting company was sufficiently independent to criticize, perhaps subvert, the reputations of their own governing class patrons. But even if no satire was intended, then we have an instance of where a company's play content is subject to the whims of topical interpretation by certain playgoers, in this instance the Essex faction, who used the Oldcastle/Falstaff character to attack their enemies. The final insight that the Oldcastle

Shakespeare and Religious Polemic 161

controversy provides is that Shakespeare's text has been used as a means of reinforcing antagonism and political opposition between factions at the royal court.

Notes

1. I would like to thank Cambridge University Press for permission to draw extensively from my book chapter, "Shakespeare, the Cobhams, and the Dynamics of Theatrical Patronage," published in my *Shakespeare and Theatrical Patronage in Early Modern England*.

2. See "Works Cited" for bibliographical details.

3. See "Works Cited" for bibliographical details.

4. Katherine Maus makes this observation: "Tudor and Jacobean religious dissidents face self-definitional challenges similar to what Eve Sedgwick describes as the challenges of modern homosexual identity— the expediency, even at times the apparent necessity, of concealment; the physical perils and psychic relief attendant upon open declaration; the uncertainty about who and what might betray half-secret allegiances; the context-dependent fluidity of what 'counts' as a heretical orientation" (Maus, 18). See also Cartelli, 213–23.

5. On the Lollards' associations with radical puritanism in late Elizabethan England, see Kastan, 100–01. Kastan is mistaken, I think, in arguing that late Elizabethans came to identify Oldcastle primarily with puritan radicals. Both the Drayton-Munday-Hathaway-Wilson *Oldcastle* play, as well as John Weever's poetic tribute *A Mirror of Martyrs*, carefully distinguish Oldcastle from the separatists and other extremists, placing him in the mainstream of serious Protestantism. See Honigmann, *John Weever*, 34.

6. Cited in Corbin and Sedge, 10.

7. See Bevington, "Introduction," 5.

8. See Craik; and Cairncross, Appendix 4.

9. See Taylor. References are to Bevington, *The First Part of Henry IV*, in *The Complete Works of Shakespeare*, 768–69.

10. See Poole, "Saints Alive!"

11. Bevington, "Introduction."

12. Dawson, 14 and 138; Murray, II, 82.

13. McKeen, 629–31.

14. Nashe's letter to Cotton is reproduced in Nicholl, Document 10, between pp. 274 and 275; see also 236–37.

15. See particularly McKeen, 650–51.

16. Gurr, 282–83.

17. See Fehrenbach.

18. See Dutton, 101–07.

162   *Paul White*

19. The full text of the letter is reproduced in Chambers, "Elizabethan Stage Gleanings," 75–77; 76–77. To my knowledge, except for McKeen, 652–54, students of the Cobhams and of the Oldcastle affair have failed to examine this document.

20. See Astington, 91 and 110, and references cited there.

21. See Chambers, *Elizabethan Stage*, I, 39; Astington, 176–77.

22. Craik, 2.2.141–42.

23. Ben Jonson, *Every Man in His Humor*, ed. Gabriele Bernhard Jackson (New Haven, Yale UP, 1969), 1.4.14–18. See also Nicholl, 247–48; and Scoufos, 246–62.

24. McKeen, 24.

25. See Dutton, 103.

26. Honigmann, "Sir John Oldcastle," 118–32.

27. See "Works Cited" for bibliographic details.

28. References are to the edition in *The Oldcastle Controversy*, 40.

29. Hotson, 157–60.

30. Gurr, 245.

31. See Day. Also see Scoufos, 154–65, who discusses this and other Elizabethan accounts of Eleanor Cobham.

Works Cited

Astington, John. *English Court Theater*. Cambridge: Cambridge UP, 1999.

Bevington, David, ed. "Introduction," *1 Henry IV*. Oxford: Clarendon P, 1987.

———. "Introduction," *1 Henry IV*. Oxford: Clarendon P, 1987.

———. *1 Henry IV* in *The Complete Works of Shakespeare*. New York: Longmans, 1997.

Cairncross, Andrew S. *2 Henry VI. Arden Shakespeare*. 1957, rpt. London: Routledge, 1988.

Cartelli, Thomas. "Queen Edward II: Postmodern Sexualities and the Early Modern Subject." In *Marlowe, History and Sexuality: New Critical Essays on Christopher Marlowe*, ed. Paul Whitefield Smith. New York: AMS P, 1998.

Chambers, E.K. "Elizabethan Stage Gleanings." *Review of English Studies, Old Series 1* (1925) 75–77.

———. *Elizabethan Stage*, 4 vols. Oxford: Clarendon P, 1923, I.

Corbin, Peter, and Douglas Sedge. *The Oldcastle Controversy, Part One and the Famous Victories of Henry V*. Manchester: Manchester UP, 1991.

Craik, T.W. (ed.) *Merry Wives of Windsor*. New York: Oxford UP, 1989.

Dawson, Giles, ed. *Records of Plays and Players in Kent 1450–1642, Malone Society Collection VII*. Oxford: Oxford UP, 1965.

Shakespeare and Religious Polemic 163

Day, John. *The Blind Beggar of Bednall Green*. London: Pollard and Dring, 1659.

Diehl, Huston. *Staging Reform, Reforming the Stage: Protestantism and Popular Theater in Early Modern England*. Ithaca and London: Cornell UP, 1977.

Dollimore, Jonathan. *Radical Tragedy: Religion, Ideology, and Power in the Dramas of Shakespeare and His Contemporaries*, 2nd Edition. (1988, Durham: Duke UP, 1993).

Dutton, Richard. *Mastering the Revels: The Regulation and Censorship of English Renaissance Drama*. Iowa: U of Iowa P, 1991.

Fehrenbach, Robert. "When Lord Cobham and Edmund Tilney 'were att odds': Oldcastle, Falstaff, and the date of 1 Henry IV," *Shakespeare Studies 18* (1986), 87–101.

Greenblatt, Stephen. *Renaissance Self-Fashioning, From More to Shakespeare*. Chicago: U of Chicago P, 1980.

Gurr, Andrew. *Shakespearean Playing Companies*. Oxford: Clarendon P, 1996.

Hamilton, Donna. *Shakespeare and the Politics of Protestant England*. Lexington: U of Kentucky P, 1992.

Honigmann, E.A.J., Jr. *John Weever: A Biography of a Literary Associate of Shakespeare and Jonson*. New York: St. Martin's P, 1987.

———. "Sir John Oldcastle: Shakespeare's Martyr." In *Fanned and Winnowed Opinions*, ed. by Mahon, John W. and Thomas Pendelton. London: Methuen, 1980.

Hotson, Leslie. *Shakespeare's Sonnets Dated and Other Essays*. London: Macmillan, 1948.

Kastan, David. *Shakespeare After Theory*. New York: Routledge, 1999.

Maus, Katherine. *Inwardness and Theater in the English Renaissance*. Chicago: U of Chicago P, 1992.

McKeen, David. *A Memory of Honor: The Life of William Brooke, Lord Cobham*. Salzburg: U of Salzburg, 1986.

Murray, J.T. *English Dramatic Companies 1558–1642*. 1912; reprint New York: Russell, 1963.

Nicholl, Charles. *A Cup of Newes: The Life of Thomas Nashe*. London: Routledge and Kegan Paul, 1984.

———. 24

Poole, Kristen. "Saints Alive! Falstaff, Martin Marprelate, and the Staging of Puritanism," *Shakespeare Quarterly 46* (1995): 47–75.

———. *Radical Religion from Shakespeare to Milton: Figures of Nonconformity in Early Modern England*. Cambridge: Cambridge UP, 2000.

164 Paul White

Rutter, Carol Chillington. *Documents of the Rose Playhouse*. Manchester: Manchester UP, 1984.

Scoufos, Alice–Lyle. *Shakespeare's Typical Satire: A Study of the Falstaff-Oldcastle Problem*. Athens: Ohio UP, 1979.

Sinfield, Alan. *Faultlines: Cultural Materialism and the Politics of Dissident Reading*. Berkley: U of California P, 1992.

Taylor, Gary. "The Fortunes of Falstaff," *Shakespeare Survey 38* (1985): 85–100.

White, Paul Whitfield, and Suzanne R. Westfall, eds. *Shakespeare and Theatrical Patronage in Early Modern England*. Cambridge: Cambridge UP, 2002.

"Judge, My Masters":
Playing Hal's Audience

Ellen Summers

In *The First Part of King Henry IV*, Prince Hal's soliloquy at the end of I.2 is a focal point for contention over the play. This is his statement of his plan to use his image as wastrel to leverage his political future as heir-apparent: "I'll so offend to make offense a skill, / Redeeming time when men think least I will." Specifically, critics and audiences during the history of the play's performance have argued over the acceptability of Hal's apparently Machiavellian manipulations of his image as a political figure. There are problems on both sides of the fictive line to be addressed here: Hal's difficulty in gaining support as the playboy son of a usurping king, and the audience's reluctance to embrace as hero of the play such a cold-blooded young man, and to enjoy his pleasures in the tavern without paying the penalty in terms of his subjects' assessment of his character.

The language of Hal's speech to the audience opens yet another problem, the solution to which may take us in an entirely different direction of analysis, one reflecting the instability in the aesthetic, political, and religious arenas of Elizabethan experience. In my brief argument here, I want to link this moment of contact between an image of authority and an audience to a transformational process well underway by the 1590s in the relation between hearer and word, subject and authority, soul and conscience. Shakespeare's history plays participate in this process of change, in fact are predicated upon it. As Robert Weimann points out, it is a mistake to view Shakespeare's language in a way abstracted from its dynamic contemporary context: "dramatic speech must be considered both as a process between actors and audiences and as a vision of society, as an integral part of the history of the nation

166   *Ellen Summers*

that Shakespeare's theater both reflected and helped to create" (Weimann, xii).

"I know you all," Prince Hal begins, immediately after the exit of Poins; they have just made a plan to foil Falstaff's robbery at Gadshill. The obvious referent of the pronoun "you" in Hal's line is Falstaff and Poins, because, having just left his company (and our presence), they are the natural target of Hal's next words: "and will awhile uphold / The unyoked humor of your idleness." Who is the image of idleness, if not Falstaff? Who has just condescended so far as to join him on that moral level, if not Hal? Besides, if Hal indeed refers to the tavern crew in explaining in their absence a plan to turn the tables on their view of him as their wholehearted crony, this moment alone with the audience becomes the third movement in one of Shakespeare's beloved sequences of three. *1 Henry IV* is full of them: first we hear the plan for the Gadshill robbery (I.ii), then we see it played out (II.ii), and then we listen to the participants discuss it in detail (II.iv). The result is an amazing degree of humor. In the present case, Poins enlists Falstaff and Hal in agreeing to the robbery; then, after Falstaff exits, Poins enlists Hal in agreeing to a contrary plan intended to foil the robbery; lastly, in his soliloquy, Hal enlists us, the audience, in his plan to overturn his apparently settled pattern of behavior as a time-waster. We are to Hal as Hal was to Poins: our collusion through silent consent to the plan is a key to its success. And indeed, Hal lives up to his promise to "redeem time" in his heroic behavior as king's man at the battle of Shrewsbury.

The audience, therefore, given no clear signal to the contrary, may assume that Hal's "you" is aimed at characters offstage. If one follows the reading of this moment according to suggestions in the new Cambridge edition of *1 Henry IV*, however, "The position and stance of the Prince will determine whether he includes the audience in the theatre as part of 'you all'" (Weil and Weil, eds., 11). As Herbert Weil's and Judith Weil's inclusion of an illustration demonstrating an actor playing Prince Hal in the Globe theater shows, this suggestion opens up a number of different possibilities for readers of the play: the sense of "I know you all," according to the Weils, "may even extend to all the people in the audience and in the realm" (Weil and Weil, 81n). Such an interpretation of this moment opens up not only a reading of the entire play, but of Shakespeare's theater as an undertaking of public consequences beyond the realm of aesthetic and even the political.

"Judge, My Masters": Playing Hal's Audience   *167*

When one situates Hal face to face with an audience in the theater, "you" is aimed at us, standing in the yard of the Globe, seated in the galleries, or almost invisible in the darkened house of today. With this new referent in mind, "I know you all, and will awhile uphold / The unyok'd humour of your idleness" may be taken to mean "I know you all, audience members, and temporarily I will tolerate your idle behavior in coming to see a play rather than getting serious work done elsewhere." To spend an entire afternoon at the play might indeed be seen to resemble the habitual pleasure-seeking and escaping from responsibility on the part of Falstaff and company. The observed of all observers, Prince Hal looks at the crowd looking at him, and in saying "I know you all" he conflates us into Falstaff's crew. We care for nothing but our own entertainment, as our trifling choice in coming to the play reveals. We may even see ourselves mirrored in the playacting scene in the tavern in II.iv. Taken so, this speech confirms us in the role of irresponsible revelers, rebels against order and authority, bound for hell in a handbasket. As in the other history plays, moreover, the play structures the audience into its event in performance. Audiences become participants in the drama (in the largest sense; the theatrical event as a whole) rather than passive onlookers. In this case, Hal's speech casts us not only in the part of Falstaff's henchmen, but also in a second role: we become aware of ourselves as the subjects of the king of England at the start of the fifteenth century. In order for Hal's soliloquy to make sense, the audience must consent to play the rhetorical object of Hal's attempt at persuasion. From now on, Hal knows us as typical English citizens, whose political and moral bearings have been shaken by Richard II's deposition and his father's irregular enthronement, and are shortly to be challenged to take sides in yet another rebellion against the crown.

Prince Hal's condemnation of the audience, and his implied expectation of their reformation as viewers of a dignified spectacle well worth the seeing, resonates within the English controversy over the morality of playgoing. The view of the theater as a breeding ground for idleness, common in Shakespeare's day, may seem today to raise only the faintest of moral objections. But on the contrary, as Paul Jorgensen points out, "idleness was undoubtedly 'grievous sin' to Shakespeare's audience" (62). He cites the existence of an official sermon on the subject, "An Homily against Idleness," to be heard by conforming churchgoers once annually on pain of a fine (levied against any absence from Sunday services

168 *Ellen Summers*

in the Anglican church). Jonas Barish delves into the Puritans' motives more deeply: in his view,

> serious economic motives underlay the Puritan hatred for the theater. The theater symbolized, or was taken to symbolize, a whole complex of attitudes anathema to the sober burgesses from whose ranks the London magistrates were elected, and whose views weighed heavily on the pulpits of the town. The theater stood for pleasure, for idleness, for the rejection of hard work and thrift as the roads to salvation. Its siren song held prentices from work and fickle parishioners from the church pew. (114)

In Shakespeare's day, Puritan polemics seemed to identify the devil's workshop with the "wooden O" itself. These purveyors of antitheatrical prejudice, suspicious of the fleshliness of theatrical events and of the illusions and deceptions by which they operate, articulated for the society of Shakespeare's audience the dubious moral consequences of frequenting the theater. At the same time, the vigor of their attacks witnesses the popularity of these spectacles and probably constituted an important source of free advertising. Still, expectations of audiences were shaped by their pronouncements; one knew that, unless a countering case could be made, that one was a guilty creature to go to a play at all.

Ben Jonson's view of those populating theater audiences seems to draw upon and to corroborate such low moral estimation of plays themselves. Barish summarizes this:

> Playgoers [to Ben Jonson] ... came clamoring for more of the same empty, noisy amusements that had always diverted them in the past: plays filled with shrieks and battles, plays with ghosts and devils, emperors and clowns. Whatever strained their attention or swerved from stereotype they would "censure" in boorish ways, turning aside with rude remarks, rising noisily from their places to create a disturbance, or even addressing disruptive remarks to the players. To entertain such audiences was to have to cope with them, to devise stratagems to combat their apathy and circumvent their prejudices. (134)

Although Jonson ultimately gave up trying to reform playgoers, it seems arguable that Shakespeare did not. But if he were to succeed, he would have to change not only the way in which players interacted with audience members, but also the way in which playgoers understood the significance of their action in attending a play as an active participant. Jonson, in the end, chose to address not playgoers but readers; whereas Shakespeare never in his career

"Judge, My Masters": Playing Hal's Audience 169

turned away from the project of redefining his audience and the theatrical event itself. In his plays, his hearers are deferred to as "gentles," "masters," and "friends"; at various points they are bidden to "judge" the action and to "piece out" the players' imperfections with their "thoughts." Unlike Hamlet, whose scorn for the groundlings has sometimes unfortunately been confused with Shakespeare's own view of them, even the basest born member of his audience is expected to accept the play's recognition of his serious intellect, innate gentility, and moral earnestness. Far from providing entertainment which is based on contempt for its audience, Shakespeare's theater called upon a thinking, discerning audience, and by assuming it to be present in the theatrical event, helped to create it.

Ultimately, the case against the theater as based on an assumption that it worked moral harm in its audience proved hollow, especially when one keeps plays like *1 Henry IV* in mind. A pivotal point occurs in the controversy over the nature of the "recreation" offered by plays. In Barish's analysis of a fourteenth-century Lollard treatise against miracle plays, he discerns the weakness of the reasoning underpinning a key section:

> To the claim that some men can more readily be converted to God by play than by seriousness, the homilist answers scathingly that those who are not converted by the sacraments will never be converted by plays, since a man who was truly penitent would abhor to behold such vanities. To the suggestion that plays offer innocent recreation he answers that they offer false and worldly recreation, "feigned" recreation; the only true recreation would consist of the doing of deeds of mercy for one's unfortunate neighbors. It is true enough that the action of plays is "feigned," and that pious offices, almsdeeds, and the practical duties of devotion might be regarded as having priority for the zealous Christian, but that plays therefore provide merely feigned *recreation* comes as a stunning non sequitur. (69)

Although often reiterated by later opponents of the English theater, the case against plays on the ground that they do not promote "innocent recreation" is never conclusive. For Shakespeare's project, as I imagine it, it was not only necessary to assume that playgoing was harmless and even beneficial, but it was crucial that the playgoers themselves helped to promote the benefits of recreation in themselves by becoming aware of and collusive in such an effect upon themselves.

170   *Ellen Summers*

Plays were defended as "honest recreations" by several sixteenth-century writers, as John Redford puts it in his interlude *Wit and Science* (Whitney, 44). In the late sixteenth century, however, the word "recreation" had two distinct meanings, only one of which was "the action of refreshing oneself or others by some pleasant amusement," the sense most often used in references to the effects of playgoing. Shakespeare uses the word in this first sense in *Twelfth Night*, when Maria promises to make "a common recreation" out of Malvolio (II.3.). The second sense of "recreation" was "the action of creating anew." For the Puritans, it was vital to one's chances of salvation to take seriously the way in which one passed the time, for only by cooperating in God's transformation of the self's sinful man (as descended from Adam) could one look forward with confidence to the Day of Judgment. The term "recreation" had a spiritual dimension not only for Puritans but for all Christians in Shakespeare's day. As Charles Whitney notes, "The focus of recreation remains much more on the life-world of audience members than the focus of many versions of aesthetic experience" (42). It was taken for granted by Shakespeare's contemporaries that the theater could work powerfully to intervene in the life-world of audience members. The question was, did it work to their spiritual and moral advantage?

In *1 Henry IV*, Shakespeare may have undertaken the project of reclaiming the second sense of "recreation" for his theater, designing the play so as to enmesh audience members in something resembling Prince Hal's reformation. The emphasis in Hal's soliloquy upon the idea of "redeeming time" provides an analogous concept which organizes the trajectory of the narrative as parallel with the restorative, re-creational effects upon an attentive audience. Jorgensen points out that "to the Elizabethan audience, to redeem (or 'rescue') time would be clearly understood as meaning to take full advantage of the time that man is given here on earth for salvation" (59). As he notes, members of early audiences of *1 Henry IV* would have annually been reminded of the appropriate passage in the New Testament in The Third Part of the Homily for Rogation Week in the prescribed book of Homilies. By statute, each year, from every pulpit in England, this quotation was read: "St. Paul willeth us to redeem the time, because the days are evil. It is not the counsel of St. Paul only, but of all other that ever gave precepts of wisdom" (*Certain Sermons* (1574; ed. G.E. Corrie, Cambridge, 1850), 492; cited in Jorgensen, 58). Jorgensen puts the link between fictional prince and real listeners in this way: although

"Judge, My Masters": Playing Hal's Audience   171

"Hal's method of redeeming time is disturbingly unorthodox," "he is taking full advantage of the time he has on earth for salvation" (64–65). "Early audiences would have recognized *Henry IV* … as an essay on the subject of redeeming time…. They would have accepted gratefully … the realization that time could be redeemed sociably, actively, and interestingly. Their favorite prince had done so" (69).

Prince Hal ends his soliloquy with a promise: "I'll so offend, to make offence a skill, / Redeeming time when men think least I will." Hal promises to redeem the time by making amends for wasted time, time frittered away in the tavern, in the theater, in the red-light district of London, Bankside, by turning serious when "men think least I will": on the field at Shrewsbury. He expects a reciprocity of amendment in his audience, holding the mirror up to us who have been dawdling at the play rather than fighting the good fight in our respective theaters of responsibility. Hal therefore promises that the stage spectacle itself will be redeemed, made valuable and in earnest, by showing the audience how to turn from idleness to faithfulness. On our part, his promise enfolds us into a completion of that turning: we need to expect to be surprised at the worth of what awaits us in the action; we paid our penny to buy an afternoon's oblivion, and Hal warns us that this is no time for such frivolity, for "the days are evil." We are to be serious in our playing his audience.

Therefore, we in Hal's original audiences become part of an operation to raise the perceived cultural value of theatergoing. In Shakespeare's time, the London theater industry had been established for only twenty years. The Globe, Rose, and other public stages were located in the red-light district of Bankside, where after the play one could go to brothel or tavern to complete the day's entertainment. Players (as actors were termed) were so low in status as to be just this side of criminal: under one Elizabethan statute, players were liable to be arrested on the public roads for vagrancy or highway robbery if they could not produce the name of a patron to legitimize their alleged professional identity. When Ben Jonson published his collected plays under the title of "Works," people scoffed: how could a play be considered literature? In short, at the turn of the seventeenth century, the English theater was not considered a serious arena of endeavor for poet, player, or playgoer.

That Shakespeare was conscious of the low status of his chosen profession is shown by many tokens: to take one instance, his

172   *Ellen Summers*

arranging for his father to be granted a coat of arms, so that he (William) could be considered as the son of a gentleman. His colleagues followed Jonson's example by producing another "Works" after the poet's death; this time, little scorn was articulated. After his accession, King James took over as patron of the troupe, and by 1604 the King's Men were not an inconsiderable cultural force in London, being the premiere tragedians of the city, and of Europe as a whole.

But this rise in significance for the theater could not take place without a change in the expectations of its audience. Was an afternoon at the Globe only slumming, a purchase of pleasure with no consequences to speak of? Or was it a dynamic encounter with powerful language and ideas, marking the engaged auditor forever? I think we can see some evidence in *1 Henry IV* that the latter was to become the paradigm for Shakespeare's theater. As Herbert Weil and Judith Weil argue, "The Morality pattern of spiritual reform that underlies the Prince's soliloquy may be one method of inviting an audience into the play" (10). John Marshall goes even further when he points out that in morality plays "there is a deliberate dramaturgical attempt to satisfy doctrinal purpose by collapsing the boundaries of the stage and real world.... the accurate identification of the audience by the playwright may have been an essential requirement for the empathetic reception of the play" (191). Prince Hal must indeed "know" his audience in order for this new interaction to work. What he helps to promote is self-knowledge in those he points to at the start of his soliloquy.

In order to improve the status of the theater, Shakespeare and his fellow players took advantage of the dynamic between audience and player that was an inheritance of the medieval stage. In fact, this dynamic preceded in importance and credibility any purely literary merit a playwright could claim for a script, which was regarded as mere ephemera. As Charles Whitney puts it,

> Audience response rather than the plays themselves was the central element in the early modern theater. And to a greater extent than has been recognized, response was ante-aesthetic, that is, productive, purposeful, and perfomative, linking the world of the play to the world beyond and to the lives of playgoers, rather than referable primarily to an aesthetic dimension. (42)

Performing in the Globe afforded a public intimacy with the audience that allowed, indeed enforced, a much more genuine interaction between listener and actor than is typical (or indeed practical) in today's theaters. Hanna Scolnicov argues that the architectural

"Judge, My Masters": Playing Hal's Audience 173

space of a theater helps to influence a performance's "theatrical space," within which the performed event happens. Further, she suggests that "Far from being accidental or arbitrary, the articulation of the theatrical space is, at its best, an expression of the playwright's philosophical stance. As such, it becomes of thematic and structural importance to the play" (15). The intimate collusion between player and listener in *1 Henry IV* that I have been describing is a natural complement and outgrowth of what I take to be Shakespeare's "philosophical stance": that the theater should speak directly to its audience members' intellectual, moral and spiritual development, not instead of, but rather *as a means of,* entertaining them. This would be recreation with a difference.

It seems relevant at this point to note the relevance of the play's manipulations of history, and in raising this topic, it becomes important to take up Phyllis Rackin's book on the history plays, *Stages of History*. Many of her lines of argument anticipate those present in this paper: for instance, Rackin builds a wonderful case to support the claim that Shakespeare's theater works to "encourage their audiences to meditate ... rather than attempting to beguile them into an uncritical acceptance of the stage spectacle" (139); she analyzes several ways in which the plays become "increasingly self-reflexive," including metadramatic devices that "direct the audience's attention to the present reality of actors and audience in the theater" (29); and she investigates the functions of "upper" and "lower" plot in both of the Henry IV plays in regard to reception, and concludes that the audience is drawn into that fifteenth-century world by means of the scenes in Eastcheap (142). Her emphasis throughout her essay, however, is on how the second tetralogy problematizes historical representation rather than upon any transformation of its audience's moral assessment of itself and of playgoing. Although her writing enfolds and stimulates recognition of the primary role of the audience in *1 Henry IV*'s production of meaning, her framework of analysis is primarily political rather than moral or spiritual. This is not to imply that the realms of politics and morality are discrete, but rather to point out that her book helps to open the door upon the sort of transformations in audiences that has not yet been explored in detail.

Rackin's comments on the detachability of the Eastcheap scenes from the other scenes' historicized representation of Henry IV's times draw one's attention to the spiritually dynamic nature of an audience's experience of time in the Henry IV plays. As she puts it, "the world of Eastcheap is set outside of time.... Falstaff

174   Ellen Summers

and his disorderly world ... constitute the most vivid dramatic presence on Shakespeare's stage.... The comic scenes provide the only bridge between the modern world of the audience and the historical world of Henry IV" (139). Obviously, an audience could see an image of itself in such scenes as not divided from those devoting a stretch of time solely to pleasure: historical location of the action becomes irrelevant to reception. In another way, however, viewers of 1 Henry IV, and of the history plays in general, might undergo a challenge to their ordinary unself-conscious mode of using time merely by becoming engaged in the play's layers of applicability to Elizabethan life.

A familiar Christian tradition from the middle ages provides an analogy for such a challenge. One of the appeals to persuade sinners to achieve self-reflection was the image of death-in-life, the *memento mori*. Ubiquitous in fifteenth-century art and letters, the *memento mori*'s purpose was to emphasize the potential crisis latent in every moment of human life, especially of an individual's personal existence. Seeing skulls and other symbols of mortality in unexpected contexts was meant to stimulate the conscience's realization that any day might be one's last. Hence, a manipulation of a sinner's sense of time resulted: every minute was now charged with potential significance demanding a state of preparedness in anyone experiencing it. One could not walk through life oblivious to one's position in time, in cosmic history. One had to keep in readiness for the Day of Judgment, since no one knew when it would fall.

In a similar way, attending a history play in the late sixteenth century could have a reorienting effect upon contemplative members of the audience in regard to their sense of personal time. Instead of being passive consumers of the period of physical life, or passive receivers of a mere entertainment, audiences of 1 Henry IV would be confronted in the Eastcheap scenes with unflattering images of their damnable slackness in being in the theater seeking pleasure only and in consenting to the immoral waste of time on the part of fictional people like Falstaff. Participating as a listener of this play meant being challenged to take control of one's time, to put every minute to a good purpose. James Calderwood notes one way in which Hal functions in this connection:

> as a future king Hal knows very well that his business is to shape history, not to be shaped by it.... To Hal ... history is a series of roles and staged events. He creates for himself the role of princely roisterer as a means of dramatizing to good

"*Judge, My Masters*": *Playing Hal's Audience* 175

advantage his conversion to the regal role of Henry the Fifth."
(139)

Hence those who admire and follow Hal may reflect upon their
own deliberate plan for life with a renewed sense of urgency: one
must accept the part of self-reforming penitent in addition to one's
other roles in order to "shape" one's spiritual "history."

The structure of the action in the history plays of the second
tetralogy enjoins the audience in a special kind of obedience. We
are not automatically to accept, as if by imposition by authority,
any protagonist proferred us; rather, we must judge such a figure
worthy of our support. Thus, in *Richard II*, we cannot unreflec-
tively accept Richard as our hero: the logic of events forces us to
weigh and measure him in comparison with his rival, Henry Bolingbroke, as both strive for followers. Although Richard is the image of the lawful king of England, the play will not allow us to
suspend judgment of him as a man or as a king. Hence our playing
subjects before the stage action of *Richard II* involves us in the serious, history-determining process of evaluating Richard's kingship, and in discerning which of two contenders for the throne
should claim our loyalty, and why.

In a more complex way, *1 Henry IV* presents three rivals for
our affection, respect, and acceptance as hero: Hotspur, Falstaff,
and Prince Hal. Discerning who best deserves our loyalty is no
easy matter, and what little authority the Prince of Wales can claim
makes a simple answer troubled. We cannot simply assume that
the attractive qualities of Hotspur—energy, loyalty to clan, bold-
ness—should claim for him the position of ownership of England
(and this is indeed what he seeks, along with his partners in the
rebellion). We cannot follow Falstaff wherever he would take us,
down the flowery way to the great bonfire, despite our pleasure in
his company. Nor can we accept Prince Hal at face value, because
of his wildness and willfulness: he may prove in the end a worthless candidate for king.

The history plays enjoin an active mode of reception appropriate to a sunlit theater house in which all audience members can see
each other, as well as the players, throughout the action. They
provide exercises in perception, and they force the use of one's
judgment. Instead of bonding automatically to the figure of authority, regardless of who plays it in any given scene, both *Richard
II* and *1 Henry IV* force the audience to choose, and the stakes
could not be higher. In other words, to be an obedient audience,
compliant with the role prepared for us to complete the theatrical

176   *Ellen Summers*

event, we cannot be passively obedient. We must instead act as judges, and choose which person to follow as subjects.

The view that the purpose of playing was to "hold the mirror up to nature" was not new in Shakespeare's day. Aristotle defined plays in terms of this effect on the audience: that spectators would see a figure on stage like themselves, recognize their own possible fate as human beings, and feel both compassion for a fellow sufferer and terror of one's own death to come. But Shakespeare's histories, although they may not evoke catharsis, surely deepened the extent to which mimesis functioned in English dramaturgy: he constructed fictional actions which implicated the audience, which could not be complete without them, in part by framing plots and characters in which spectators could see themselves revealed. One might call this a play's resemblance to the literary form of the parable, for in parabolic discourse, the point of an utterance is to reveal the hearer's true state, which has been disguised to the self by ignorance, lack of reflection, or other inhibiting states of consciousness.

Further, in *1 Henry IV* at least, this revelation was not a simple occurrence with no appreciable result, but a process of change: for once one perceived one's own spiritual or moral condition somehow presented, one could not proceed as spectator in the same state of mind as when one entered the theater—that is, probably oblivious of one's need for reformation. What is the image of the audience held up for us to see? I think we see ourselves most clearly in the tavern after the Gadshill robbery, when these harlotry players, Falstaff and Hal, perform for their cronies, and for us. When Hostess Quickly laughs drunkenly, and her customers applaud or boo or egg on the extempore entertainment, we see and hear ourselves in the process of the same reactions. The tavern, the brothel, the theater, the thieves' den—all merge in the recognition of ourselves lowered, dishonored, abrogators of duty.

But reformation is abruptly promised by Hal, who surprises Falstaff and us by stating his present and future renunciation of leaving plump Jack and all the world: "I do, I will." Hal's action from that point forward in the play is to make good on that renunciation, in order to "redeem" the time wasted in Eastcheap. Hal also redeems our time spent playing his worthless partners in frivolity by engaging us as the witnesses of his reformation: a worthy spectacle that redeems everything touching it—audience, players, poet. Suddenly, at the battle of Shrewsbury, we are taken from low jests and practical jokes to the space where "blood is

"Judge, My Masters": Playing Hal's Audience 177

their argument"; as Hotspur protests to his wife, "This is no world / To play with mammets and tilt with lips." Triflers may exit to the rear: we must have bloody noses and crack'd crowns if the play is to be played out. And so our purpose as the audience is in earnest: we witness the upshot of the play's contest between Hotspur and Hal, order and rebellion, triflers and king's men. Have we chosen the right side?

For the play enjoins us to choose between the two, and to declare the style of our state as subjects: either as those, like Hotspur, who blindly follow tribal loyalties and promptings of blood to throw all away on a harebrained scheme; or as those, like Hal, who play the part given by the moment to serve the larger order, and who discern whom to trust, when to act, and how to transform the self when the script of history requires it. Perhaps, as Annabel Patterson argues of the readers of Holinshed's *Chronicle*, the audience members of *1 Henry IV* must become each one "his own historian" in order to complete the action prescribed by the literary frame (189). For the second half of the sixteenth century in England, one's political, spiritual and physical survival could depend upon the capacity to discern; and woe betide those who cling to old loyalties of religion without reflecting upon consequences. As Thomas More phrased similar advice to his contemporaries, "What part soever you have taken upon you, playe that aswel as you can and make the best of it.... But you must with a crafty wile and subtell trayne studye and endevoure youre self, asmuche as in you lyeth, to handle the matter wyttelye and handsomelye for the purpose" (41–42).

So, in the tavern skit in II.4, when Falstaff calls upon his companions to decide between his own and Hal's portrayal of the king, he is enjoining us, his "masters," to "judge": to choose who is to be our best king, the fat lord of misrule, or Prince Hal, who will become Henry V and the "mirror of all Christian kings." To discern among these pretenders, with Hotspur and the Percies too, is not the task of a passive, thoughtless pack of revelers, slumming for an afternoon, evading earnest endeavor, but is a test and formative exercise in developing a discerning, well-judging citizenry. By 1590, little stability could be taken for granted in any sphere of English religious or political life: hence the need to "search, examine, trie and seeke," not to grant authority lightly to others, but to develop one's own authority to choose the best option possible as a necessary part of attaining salvation, both in the world to come and in the present one. In the world of post-Reformation England, the authority of Rome was no longer the established source of spiritual wisdom: as Protestants, English souls had to develop discernment, the capacity to judge, interpret, and choose, in order to work out salvation gravely, with fear and trembling.

Works Cited

Barish, Jonas. *The Antitheatrical Prejudice*. Berkeley: U of California P, 1981.

Calderwood, James L. "*1 Henry IV*: Art's Gilded Lie." *ELR* 3 (1973): 131–44.

Jorgensen, Paul A. *Redeeming Shakespeare's Words*. Berkeley: U of California P, 1962.

Marshall, John. "Addressing the Audience of *Mankind*." In *European Medieval Drama 1 (1997)*. Ed. Sydney Higgins. Brepols: Turnhout, 1997. Pp. 189–202.

More, Thomas. *Utopia*. London: Everyman Library, 1910.

Nassar, Eugene Paul. *The Rape of Cinderella: Essays in Literary Continuity*. Bloomington: Indiana UP, 1970.

Patterson, Annabel. "Rethinking Tudor Historiography." *SAQ* 92 (Spring 1993): 185–208.

Rackin, Phyllis. *Stages of History: Shakespeare's English Chronicles*. Ithaca, NY: Cornell UP, 1990.

Scolnicov, Hanna. "Theatre Space, Theatrical Space, and the Theatrical Space Without." In *The Theatrical Space*, ed. James Redmond. Themes in Drama IX. Cambridge: Cambridge UP, 1987. Pp. 11–26.

Shakespeare, William. *The First Part of King Henry IV*. Ed. Herbert Weil and Judith Weil. Cambridge: Cambridge UP, 1997.

Weimann, Robert. *Shakespeare and the Popular Tradition in the Theater: Studies in the Social Dimension of Dramatic Form and Function*, ed. Robert Schwartz. Baltimore: Johns Hopkins UP, 1978.

Whitney, Charles. "Ante-Aesthetics: Towards a Theory of Early Modern Audience Response." In *Shakespeare and Modernity: Early Modern to Millennium*, ed. Hugh Grady. London: Routledge, 2000. Pp. 40–60.

Index

Abel, 30, 116, 140, 141, 142

Abraham's bosom, 149

Achilles, 74, 108

Acts and Monuments, 6, 149, 151, 160

Adam, 86, 133, 135, 137, 138, 139, 140, 141, 170

Admiral's Men, 150, 154, 158, 160

Aeneas, 74

Against Disobedience and Wilful Rebellion, 10, 18

Agincourt, 13, 16, 27, 35, 40, 46, 48, 50, 52, 83, 87, 98, 100, 103, 108, 123, 137, 138

Alexander, Michael, xiii

Allegory and Mysticism, x

Angelo, 102, 150

Annals of England, The, 38

Antony, 74

Aquinas, 12

Archbishop of Canterbury, 47, 48, 136

Archbishop of York, 10

Aristotle, xii, 133, 176

Ars Moriendi, 93

Arthur, Prince, 108

Arundel, Earl of, 29, 113

Asimov, Isaac, 35

As You Like It, 141

Auden, W.H. 38, 70

Augustine, xii

Aumerle (Edmund Langley), 34, 35

Aumerle, of Richard II, 108, 112, 124

Bagot, 84, 112, 130

Bankside (London), 158, 171

Bardolf, 14

Bardolph, 16, 45, 49, 50, 66, 67, 83, 84, 149, 151

Barish, Jonas, 168

Barton, Anne, 98, 99

Bastard (King John), 102

Bates, 50, 98

Battenhouse, Roy, x, x–xii

Beauford, Cardinal, 150

Beauregard, David, xiii

Becket, Thomas à, 10, 136

Bellerophon, 74

Bennett, Josephine Waters, 142 (n 2)

Berger, Harry, 57

Bethell, S.R., xi

Bevington, David, 65, 152

Bible, The/Biblical background, 84, 110, 131, 133, 134

Black, James, 84, 85

Book of Common Prayer, 47, 48

Book of Homilies, 10

Book of Revelation, 111

180

Boot/bootless, 66, 67, 69
Borders, 59, 60, 61, 62, 63
Bosola, 84
Bowden, Henry S., x
Bradley, A.C., ix
Brooke, Henry, 149, 150, 156, 157, 159
Brooke, William, Tenth Lord Cobham, 149, 150, 152, 156, 157
Bryant, J.A., xi
Bullingbrook/Bolingbroke, 29, 30, 31, 32, 33, 34, 35, 37, 44, 46, 57, 58, 61, 62, 65, 83, 84, 102, 110, 112, 113, 114, 118, 121, 128, 130, 131, 134, 138, 139, 140, 141, 142, 175
Burgess, William, x

Cain, 30, 43, 116, 121, 135, 140, 141, 142
Calais, 50, 108, 112, 113, 114, 140
Calderwood, James, 174
Calypso, 74
Cambridge, 86, 90, 92, 96
Cambyses, 15
Campbell, Lily B., 113
Cappers' Harrowing of Hell and Resurrection play, The, 6, 8–9
Careles, John, 6
Carey, George A. (the second Lord Hunsdon), 154
Carlisle, Bishop of, 33, 58, 59, 64, 66, 112
Cecil, Robert, 157
Cecil, William, 152
Chain of Being, 125
Charles IV, 48
Charles VI, 48, 49, 113
Charles of Orleans, 49, 50, 51
Chester Whitsun play, 13, 14

Christian fulfillment, 70, 71, 74, 83, 84, 85, 86, 88, 102, 111, 142, 158
Christian Neoplatonism, 57, 63
Christian tradition, Christianity, 84, 85, 86
Christianity and Christian Paradox, 85, 86
Christians, 63, 65, 70, 102
Christological, 87
Chronicles of England, The, 38
Clarence, 109
Claudius, 57, 59, 99, 139, 141
Cleopatra, 74
Clitheroe, Margaret, 10
Cobham, Eleanor, 150, 159
Cobham, Lord Chamberlain, 153, 154, 155, 156
Cobham family, the, 148, 149, 150, 151, 152, 153, 154, 156, 158, 159
Colossians, 63, 65
Comedy of Forgiveness, xi
Cordelia, Queen, 107
Corpus Christi, 3, 4
Corpus Christi Plays, 4, 5, 6, 17, 18, 86
Corrie, G.E., 170
Cotton, William, 153
Court, 50, 98
Coventry, 1, 3, 4, 6, 10, 14, 110, 111
Coventry Last Judgment play, 13
Coventry Mystery Plays, 3, 6, 8, 19
Coventry plays, 5, 6, 7, 17
Coventry Smiths' play, 12
Coverdale, Miles, 131
Crispin, St., 13, 51
Crispinian, Saint, 51

Index

181

Croo, Robert (a Capper), 6, 8
Curtain, 152

Dance of Death iconography, 13
Daniell, David, xiii
Daniel's *Civil Wars*, 35, 47
Dauphin, The, 50, 52
Davison, Secretary, 115
Day, John and Henry Chettles, 159
de Beauvoir, Simone, 73
de Groot, John Henry, xi
Denial, 115, 116, 118, 121
Deposition, 92, 116, 117, 124, 133, 134, 138, 139
de Voragine, Jacobus, 6
Dido, 74
Diehl, Huston, 147
Dionysius, 133
Disappointment, 83, 86, 98, 99, 100, 102, 118
Displacement, 112, 115, 118, 129, 121
Dissertation on the Pageants or Dramatic Mysteries Anciently Performed at Coventry, 3
Divine Right of Kings, 108, 121
Doll, 72, 83, 84
Dollimore, Jonathan, 147
Dowden, Edward, 36
Drapers, The, 6, 9, 14, 15
Duchess of Malfi, 84
Duncan, 107, 108
Dutton, Richard, 148, 154

Earth, the, 32, 58, 59
Eastcheap, 38, 39, 43, 46, 49, 120, 173, 174, 176
Eden, 125, 130, 132, 133, 134, 138, 139, 141
Edmund, 107
Edward II, 48

Edward III, 48, 126
Edward IV, 107
Edward V, 107, 108, 124
Edward, Prince, 107
Edwards, Michael, xiii
Elizabeth, Queen, 100, 108, 113, 115, 157
Elizabethan World Picture, xi
Empson, William, 71, 73
Ephesians, 63
Equestrian Imagery, 59
Erpingham, Sir Thomas, 99
Essex, Earl of, 93, 150, 154, 157, 158, 159
Eve, 86, 138, 141
Everyman in His Humour, 154, 156
Expedient/Expedience, 63, 65, 67
Expiation, 85, 135
Exton, 36, 116, 136, 141

Faith and Folly, xii
Falconbridge(s), 102
Fall, 84, 92, 125
Falstaff, 14, 15, 16, 27, 38, 39, 41, 43, 44, 45, 46, 50, 64, 66, 67, 71, 72, 73, 75, 83, 89, 120, 137, 148, 149, 151, 156, 160, 166, 174, 175, 176, 177
Famous Victories of Henry the Fifth, 38, 152
Farnham, Willard, x
Fatherhood, 31, 34, 39, 41, 45, 68, 69, 70
Fathers and Sons, 36, 39, 40, 42, 44, 45, 46, 50, 88, 90, 137
Feet: hitting the ground, 57; subject's feet, 58; feet of the body, 59; "treacherous feet," 65; blessed feet, 65; "nail'd feet," 65, 66, 68, 74; un-nailing

182   *Index*

Christ's feet, 65; Christ's feet, 68; Mercury-like feet, 74
Ferdinand, 84
First Part of the Blind Beggar of Bednall Green, The, 159
Fitzwater, 112
Flint Castle, 33
Foxe, John, 6, 16, 149, 151, 160
France, 61
Frecerro, John, 59, 68
Froissart, Jean, 112

Garden/Garden imagery, 125, 132, 133, 134, 135, 138, 140, 141, 142
Gaspar, Julia, 148
Gaultree Forest, 42–43, 44, 126
Glendower, Owen, 32, 38, 40, 61, 66, 67
Globe Theater, 158, 159, 166, 167, 171, 172
Gloucester, Duke of, 110, 111, 112, 113, 114, 115, 116, 121, 124, 142
Gloucester, Duke of (Richard II's uncle), 107, 111
Gloucester, Earl of, 30, 31
Goddard, Harold, 85
Golden Legend, 6
Golgotha, 58, 115
Gollancz, Sir Israel, x
Green, 63, 84, 130
Greenblatt, Stephen, 73, 147
Greenery or Vegetable metaphor, 131
Grey, Lady Jane, 93
Grey, Sir Thomas, 49
Guilt, 99, 115, 116, 117, 118, 119, 120, 121, 122, 124, 125, 135, 136
Gurr, Andrew, 153

Hal, 68, 70, 71, 73, 74, 75, 87, 88, 89, 90, 120, 121, 122, 123, 136, 137, 151, 165, 166, 167, 170, 171, 172, 174, 175, 176, 177
Hamilton, Donna, 147, 148
Hamlet, 169
Hamlet, 51, 99, 107, 114, 138, 140
Hamlet (old), 108, 141
Hand-washing imagery, 116, 117
Harfleur, 50
Hassel, Chris, xii, xiii
Hector, 74, 108
Heinemann, Margot, 148
Henry IV Plays, 118, 173
Henry IV, 5, 9, 13, 36, 38, 39, 40, 41, 43, 45, 46, 49, 51, 53, 58, 61, 62, 64, 65, 69, 70, 72, 84, 85, 87, 88, 89, 91, 98, 112, 115, 116, 117, 118, 119, 120, 121, 122, 123, 125, 126, 135, 136, 173, 174
1 Henry IV, 9, 13, 15, 34, 37, 42, 43, 46, 53, 60, 62, 63, 64, 66, 67, 83, 88, 109, 135, 136, 148, 149, 150, 151, 154, 155, 157, 165, 166, 167, 170, 173, 174, 175, 177
2 Henry IV, 68, 69, 71, 84, 86, 89, 90, 109, 121, 149, 151
Henry V, 5, 10, 16, 35, 46, 48, 52, 53, 57
Henry V, 13, 15, 16, 28, 35, 37, 46, 47, 48, 49, 50, 51, 52, 57, 66, 84, 86, 87, 90, 91, 92, 93, 94, 109, 123, 137, 151, 157, 158
Henry VI, 52, 107, 124
1 Henry VI, 150
2 Henry VI, 150, 159
Henry VIII, 18
Hexter, J.H., 61

Index

Hippolyta's View: Some Christian Aspects of Shakespeare's Plays, xi
Holinshed, 149, 176
Holy Land, 59, 65, 66, 84, 112, 116, 126, 135
Honigman, E.A., Jr., 157
Hooker, Richard, 95
Hotson, Leslie, 157
Hotspur, 83, 89, 118, 121, 135, 172, 173, 175, 177
Howard, Charles, 158
Humphrey of Gloucester, 107
Humphries, H.R., 42
Hunsdon, Lord Chamberlain, 153
Hunt, Maurice, xiii
Hunt, Simon, 8
Hunter, R.S., xii

Incarnation, 86
Isabella, Queen, 34

Jacques, 102
James, Richard, 149
Jenkins, Harold, 42
Jerusalem, 65, 69, 85, 89, 98, 135
Jerusalem Chamber, 45, 47, 84, 85, 89
John of Gaunt, 28, 30, 31, 32, 36, 44, 61, 110, 111, 114, 121, 126, 129, 130, 132, 134, 138, 139
John of Lancaster, 10, 18, 46, 53, 121, 126
Jones, Edward, 154, 155
Jonson, Ben, 148, 150, 155, 156, 168, 171, 172
Jorgensen, Paul, 167, 170
Judas, 115, 139
Julius Caesar, 108
Julius Caesar, 142

Kastan, David, 161
Katharine (daughter of Charles VI), 52, 98
Kempe, William, 155
King Gonzago, 107
King James, 172
King Johan, 150
King John, 107, 108
King-killing, 107, 108, 124, 125
King Lear, 141
King Priam, 107, 108
King's Men, The, 17, 172
King's Two Bodies, The, 87, 92, 98, 108
Knight, G. Wilson, x

Ladder imagery, 118, 122
Lady Percy, 68, 83
Lancaster, Duke of, 113
Langley, Richard, Earl of Cambridge, 49
Limon, Jerzy, 148
Literary Criticism and the English Tradition, xi
Little Duke of York (Edmund V's brother), 107
Livy, 133
Lollard, 148, 151, 158, 169
Lopez, Judith, xiii
Lord Admiral Nottingham's Men, 148
Lord Chamberlain's Men, 158, 159, 160
Lord Chief Justice, 38, 42, 45, 46, 63
Loss/Failure, 83, 86, 87, 88, 92, 98
Louis the Dauphin, 48

Macbeth, 107, 108
Macbeth, 19, 114, 141

184   *Index*

Machiavelli/Machiavellian, 83, 84, 85, 89, 116, 126, 165
Malvolio, 16, 102, 150, 170
Marcus, Leah, 148
Maria, 170
Marlowe, Christopher, 83, 150
Marprelate Controversy, 152
Marshall, John, 172
Mary, Queen of Scots, 113, 115
Maus, Katherine, 147
McKeen, David, 156
McMillin, Scott and Sally-Beth MacLean, 160
Medieval Heritage of Elizabethan Tragedy, The, x
memento mori, 174
Merback, Mitchell B., 93, 94
Mercers, 6
Mercury, 74, 75
Merry Wives of Windsor, 149, 154
Milward, Peter, 10, 11
Mirror, The, 114
Morality of Playgoing, 167, 168, 169, 170, 172, 176
More, Sir Thomas, 93, 177
More, William, 154
Mortimer, Edmund, 40, 90, 118
Mowbray, Thomas, 29, 30, 34, 44, 46, 110, 111, 112, 113, 114, 115, 116, 121, 140, 141
Mutschmann, H. and K. Wentersdorf, xi

Nashe, Thomas, 153
Nedelsky, Jennifer, 76 (n 17)
Neville, Ralph, Earl of Westmoreland, 44
New Historicism, 124, 147
New Testament, 6, 115, 170
Nicholl, Charles, 156
Noble, Richard, x
Non nobis, Domine, 52, 100, 101

Northumberland, Duke of, 31, 41, 44, 59, 68, 69, 83, 117, 118, 122
N-Town and Towneley collections, 6, 8, 12
Nym, 16, 49, 50

Odysseus, 74
Of the Laws of Ecclesiastical Polity, 95
Oldcastle, Sir John, 16, 27, 38, 72, 148
Oldcastle family, 148, 149, 150, 151, 152, 156, 157, 160, 161
Oldcastle Play, 158, 159
"Old Faith" and Old Religion, 10, 11, 13
Old Testament, 130, 138
Original Sin, 86, 134, 135, 136, 138, 139, 141, 142
Orleans, Duke of, 50
Ovid, 133

Palmer, D.J., 75 (n 2)
Pandulph, Cardinal, 150
Paradise Lost, 86
Parker, M.D.H., xi
Patterson, Annabel, 177
Paul (the Apostle), 170
Pembroke, 150
Perseus, 74
Peter, 49, 149
Pilate, 65, 115, 116
Pistol, 46, 49, 50, 72, 84
Plato, 59
Poins, 14, 49, 66, 151, 166
Pomfret Castle, 35, 115, 116, 125
Poole, Kristen, xiii, 147, 152
Prospero(s), 102
Proteus, 73
Psalms, 131

Index

185

Puritanism/Puritans, 16, 17, 150, 151, 168, 170

Queen's Men, 152
Queen's Men and Their Plays, The, 160
Quickly, Hostess, 43, 83, 176

Rackin, Phyllis, 173
Raleigh, Sir Walter, 93
Ravenspurgh, 31
Reconciliation, 88, 89, 90
Redemption, 84, 92, 102
Redford, John, 170
Red Rose, 109
Regnans in excelsis, 10
Regurgitation imagery, 121
Religion of Shakespeare, The, x
Repentance, 92, 93, 95, 96, 97, 98, 109
Richard II, 3, 4, 9, 12, 28, 29, 30, 33, 34, 35, 36, 37, 41, 42, 44, 46, 51, 53, 58, 59, 61, 62, 63, 65, 66, 69, 70, 71, 72, 84, 87, 88, 91, 92, 107, 109, 110, 111, 112, 113, 114, 115, 116, 117, 118, 119, 120, 121, 122, 123, 124, 129, 130, 132, 133, 134, 135, 136, 137, 138, 139, 140, 141, 142, 167, 175
Richard II, 11, 12, 28, 30, 36, 37, 44, 46, 53, 57, 64, 65, 87, 89, 109, 114, 118, 120, 121, 125, 129, 134, 135, 136, 138, 140, 141, 175,
Richard III, 107, 108, 109, 124
Richard III, 9, 12, 97, 109
Richard, Duke of York, 107
Richard, Earl of Cambridge, 108
Richard's Queen, 125, 130, 132, 133
Rogationtide, 59, 63, 170

Rose (theater), 158, 159, 171, 173
Rutland, 107
Rutter, Carol Chillington, 157

Salic Law, 52
Scolnicov, Alan, 147
Scroop, Henry Lord, 49, 87, 90, 91, 92, 96, 100, 121
Scrope, Richard, 10, 18, 44, 45
Second Book of Homilies, The, 95
Shakespeare and Catholicism, xi
Shakespeare and the Popular Dramatic Tradition, xi
Shakespearean Tragedy, Its Art and Christian Premises, xii
Shakespeares and the 'Old Faith,' The, xi
Shakespeare's Biblical Knowledge and the Use of the Book of Common Prayer, x
Shakespeare's Christian Dimensions, an Anthology of Commentary, xii
Shakespeare's Dramatic Art, x
Shakespeare's Knowledge and Use of the Bible, x
Shakespeare's Religious Background, xii
Shakespeare's Tragic Heroes, x
Shallow (Justice), 73, 83, 84
Sharp, Thomas, 3
Shearmen and Taylors and The Weavers, 9
Shearmen and Taylors' Pageant, 5, 7
Shedding Royal blood, 108, 116, 124, 125
Shrewsbury, 40, 41, 42, 44, 59, 69, 74, 166, 171, 176
Silence, 83, 84
Smiths' Passion play, 8, 9

186 *Index*

Sound and Conscious, 165
Spenser, Edmund, 17
Stages of History, 173
Stow, John, 38
Stratford Grammar School, 8
Subject and Authority, 165

Tamburlaine, 83
Taylor, Gary, 151
Te Deum, 52, 100, 101
Tempest, The, 84, 141
Theatre, 152
Thomas of Clarence, 70
Thomas of Woodstock, 28, 29, 91, 109, 112
Tiffany, Grace, xiii
Tillyard, E.M.W., x
Tilney, Edmund, 153, 154
Traitors, 49, 139
Tudor Apologists, 84, 111, 147
Twelfth Night, 161, 170

Ulrici, Hermann, x
Urc, Peter, 32
Usurper/Usurpation, 88, 109, 119, 122, 123, 165

Vincent, Thomas, 154

Walking Imagery, 57, 58, 62, 68
Walter, J.H., 47
Wars of the Roses, The, 18, 135
Warwick, 29, 113
Watson, Robert, xiii
Weaver's Pageant, 6
Weil, Herbert and Judith Weil, 166, 172
Weimann, Robert, 165
Wentersdorf, Karl P., 90, 93, 97
Wheel of Fire, The, x
White, Rose, 109
Whitney, Charles, 170, 172
Williams, 50, 98
Winter's Tale, The: A Study, xi
Wit and Science, 170
Woodstock, 28, 113, 114, 140
Worcester, 118, 130
Wordsworth, Charles, x

Yeats, William Butler, 53
York, Duchess of, 3, 4, 35
York, Duke of, 31, 32, 35, 112, 113, 114

The Locust Hill Literary Studies Series

1. *Blake and His Bibles*. Edited by David V. Erdman. ISBN 0-933951-29-9. LC 89-14052.

*2. *Faulkner, Sut, and Other Southerners*. M. Thomas Inge. ISBN 0-933951-31-0. LC 91-40016.

3. *Essays of a Book Collector: Reminiscences on Some Old Books and Their Authors*. Claude A. Prance. ISBN 0-933951-30-2. LC 89-12734.

4. *Vision and Revisions: Essays on Faulkner*. John E. Bassett. ISBN 0-933951-32-9. LC 89-14046.

5. *A Rose by Another Name: A Survey of Literary Flora from Shakespeare to Eco*. Robert F. Fleissner. ISBN 0-933951-33-7. LC 89-12804.

*7. *Blake's Milton Designs: The Dynamics of Meaning*. J.M.Q. Davies. ISBN 0-933951-40-X. LC 92–32678.

8. *The Slaughter-House of Mammon: An Anthology of Victorian Social Protest Literature*. Edited by Sharon A. Winn and Lynn M. Alexander. ISBN 0-933951-41-8. LC 92-7269.

9. *"A Heart of Ideality in My Realism" and Other Essays on Howells and Twain*. John E. Bassett. ISBN 0-933951-36-1. LC 90-46908.

*10. *Imagining Romanticism: Essays on English and Australian Romanticisms*. Edited by Deirdre Coleman and Peter Otto. ISBN 0-933951-42-6. LC 91-36509.

*11. *Learning the Trade: Essays on W.B. Yeats and Contemporary Poetry*. Edited by Deborah Fleming. ISBN 0-933951-43-4. LC 92–39290.

*12. *"All Nature is but Art": The Coincidence of Opposites in English Romantic Literature*. Mark Trevor Smith. ISBN 0-933951-44-2. LC 93–27166.

13. *Essays on Henry David Thoreau: Rhetoric, Style, and Audience*. Richard Dillman. ISBN 0-933951-50-7. LC 92–39960.

*14. *Author-ity and Textuality: Current Views of Collaborative Writing*. Edited by James S. Leonard. ISBN 0-933951-57-4. LC 94-15111.

15. *Women's Work: Essays in Cultural Studies*. Shelley Armitage. ISBN 0-933951-58-2. LC 95-6180.

16. *Perspectives on American Culture: Essays on Humor, Literature, and the Popular Arts*. M. Thomas Inge. ISBN 0-933951-59-0. LC 94-14908.

188 *The Locust Hill Literary Studies Series*

*17. *Bridging the Gap: Literary Theory in the Classroom.* Edited by J.M.Q. Davies. ISBN 0-933951-60-4. LC 94–17926.

18. *Juan Benet: A Critical Reappraisal of His Fiction.* Edited by John B. Margenot III. ISBN 0-933951-61-2. LC 96–51479.

19. *The American Trilogy, 1900–1937: Norris, Dreiser, Dos Passos and the History of Mammon.* John C. Waldmeir. ISBN 0-933951-64-7. LC 94-48837.

20. *"The Muses Females Are": Martha Moulsworth and Other Women Writers of the English Renaissance.* Ed. by Robert C. Evans and Anne C. Little. ISBN 0-933951-63-9. LC 95-22413.

21. *Henry James in the Periodicals.* Arthur Sherbo. ISBN 0-933951-74-4. LC 97-11720.

22. *"Miss Tina Did It" and Other Fresh Looks at Modern Fiction.* Joseph J. Waldmeir. ISBN 0-933951-76-0. LC 97-28923.

*23. *Frank O'Connor: New Perspectives.* Ed. by Robert C. Evans and Richard Harp. ISBN 0-933951-79-5. LC 97-32626.

24. *Aldous Huxley & W.H. Auden: On Language.* David Garrett Izzo. ISBN 0-933951-80-9. LC 98-11922.

25. *Studies in the Johnson Circle.* Arthur Sherbo. ISBN 0-933951-81-7. LC 98-35292.

26. *Thornton Wilder: New Essays.* Ed. by Martin Blank, Dalma Hunyadi Brunauer, and David Garrett Izzo. ISBN 0-933951-83-3. LC 98-48986.

27. *Tragedy's Insights: Identity, Polity, Theodicy.* Ed. by Luis R. Gámez. ISBN 0-933951-85-X.

28. *Denise Levertov: New Perspectives.* Edited by Anne Colclough Little and Susie Paul. ISBN 0-933951-87-6. LC 00-035705.

29. *W.B. Yeats and Postcolonialism.* Edited by Deborah Fleming. ISBN 0-933951-88-4. LC 00-059801.

30. *John Quinn: Selected Irish Writers from His Library.* Ed. by Janis and Richard Londraville. ISBN 0-933951-93-0. LC 2001029303.

31. *W.H. Auden: A Legacy.* Ed. by David Garrett Izzo. ISBN 0-933951-94-9. LC 2001050308.

32. *A Companion to Brian Friel.* Ed. by Richard Harp and Robert C. Evans. ISBN 0-933951-95-7. LC 2002069372.

33. *Prophetic Character: Essays on William Blake in Honor of John E. Grant.* Ed. by Alexander S. Gourlay. ISBN 0-933951-96-5. LC 2002075208.

34. *Prodigal Father Revisited: Artists and Writers in the World of John Butler Yeats.* Ed. by Janis Londraville. ISBN 0-9722289-3-4. LC 2002043385.

35. *Shakespeare's Second Historical Tetralogy: Some Christian Features.* Ed. by Beatrice Batson. ISBN 0-9722289-4-2. LC 2003066045.

*Denotes out-of-print title